75 Practical Tips for Technical Trainers (in Virtual Classrooms)

Proven methods based on the latest theories
in the neuroscience of learning and
cognitive psychology*

*including what I have learned after
 25+ years of technical training

75 Practical Tips for Technical Trainers

by Kevin Ruse

ISBN: 979-8-9860998-0-4

Published by Kevin Ruse + Associates Inc.

Copy editor: Elisabeth Beller

Front cover photo:
54164193 / Rock Climbing © Galyna Andrushko | Dreamstime.com

Praise for 75 Practical Tips for Technical Trainers

"75 Practical Tips for Technical Trainers is the perfect and concise overview of training that can help every trainer stay at the top of their game. Highly recommended!"

—Barbara Oakley, instructor of Learning How to Learn,
one of the world's largest massive open online courses.

"I started my career in professional technical training over 25 years ago. At the time, the "train the trainer" programs were more knowledge checks than helping an instructor become an expert at their craft. Not until Kevin shared his book with me, did I realize "this is what I've been looking for all along". Kevin has compiled an amazing set of tips, tricks, and insights that only come from being in the field. Whether you are new to the technical instructor path or a seasoned expert, this IS THE book you should read and study to help you elevate your craft. Your learners will be grateful for the tips you bring into the classroom. Amazing work Kevin - thanks for your dedication to our profession and your willingness to share to help our profession to continue to grow and mature."

— Kelby Zorgdrager, Founder of DevelopIntelligence"

"Anyone who has taken a class with Kevin Ruse knows he is one of the best technical trainers in the industry. Training center owners and executives consider him to be a model of what they are looking for when they hire a trainer. After reviewing the pre-release copy he sent, I now consider this book to be one of Kevin's true masterpieces. It could very well be the best book on the specifics of master level technical training that I have personally ever read. This book will help even long-term experts in the field greatly improve their performance, both online and in person. It does so while remaining accessible to beginners and newer trainers as well. It is filled with not only personal anecdotes and experience, but also tons of resources, tools, and techniques. From this point on, I would recommend any one managing or hiring technical trainers to consider it required reading for all technical trainers."

— Sterling Ledet, Founder of Ledet Training

"Kevin has taught for my firm (Accelebrate) for more than 16 years and is one of the highest-rated instructors with whom we work. In addition to teaching for more than 1,000 of our learners, Kevin is a true student of the craft of teaching and has led successful, impactful train-the-trainer sessions for our instructors. In this easy-to-read and thoughtful book, Kevin draws from his more than 25 years of technical teaching experience to guide instructors through everything they need to be successful, including class preparation, technical gear, teaching techniques, and strategies for keeping learners engaged. Whether you are a new instructor or an experienced one, Kevin's advice will help you up your game."

— Steve Heckler, President of Accelebrate

"I've been working with Kevin Ruse for about 15 years. He is a consistently outstanding trainer. When he asked me to review this book, I expected it to be filled with high quality tips based on his years of experience in the classroom. It is that and much more. Readers of the book will quickly learn that Kevin has clearly spent years studying his trade and he draws not only on his own experience, but on the experience and wisdom of other trainers and of scientists and philosophers who have researched how adults learn. Kevin's tips are accessible and actionable. This is a great book for both new and experienced trainers who want to become better at effectively teaching students in a way that helps them retain their knowledge long after the class is over."

— Nat Dunn, Founder of Webucator

Table of Contents

Note from the Author

I did not formally study the art of presenting, nor did I set out after college to become a technical trainer. I don't have a degree in education or a K–12 teaching certificate. My career as a technical trainer grew quite accidentally. My trade was in the printing industry, and I had a career as a typesetter.

As the printing industry evolved, traditional desktop publishing replaced typesetting. Software available to anyone with a personal computer eliminated the need for commercial typesetting and the expensive equipment associated with it. I learned desktop publishing quickly and soon found myself teaching at printshops. What started as consulting and mentoring evolved into training individuals and small groups of three or fewer. I sensed some enjoyment and satisfaction in the process, but it wasn't until my first of-ficial teaching gig at a vocational school in the mid-1990s that I embraced my passion for teaching. Since then, it has been a long, slow learning curve that has never ended, and I still enjoy every minute of it. This book is a collection of the tips I learned, sometimes the hard way, which have greatly enhanced my students' experience and my sense of joy and satisfaction after a well-taught class!

You may agree or disagree with some of these tips, and I'd love to hear from you either way. Perhaps you even tried some of them, and they failed. I gleaned many of these tips from watching colleagues, reading books, and talking with full-time college professors. My first attempts sometimes failed miserably. If you have a coach to discuss your issues with, that's great. Absent that, careful and honest retrospection can often reveal why you failed. Don't give up on the technique altogether. Try refining it and making it your own.

This book is not a one-size-fits-all book of solutions, and I'm sure there are numerous ways to expand on my ideas or even scratch them entirely in favor of some other technique. My only rule is that the learner comes first and that every method you use is done with the learner in mind, first and foremost.

Contact the Author

I'd love to hear about your experiences with tips that work (or don't work) for you. I'm also available for train-the-trainers sessions and individual mentoring. Feel free to contact me at:

email: kevin@kevinruse.com

LinkedIn: https://www.linkedin.com/in/kevinruse/

Website: 75-tips.com

            kevinruse.com

About the Tips

Many of the tips include personal anecdotes. They are the results of many big and small failures— mistakes I made that I was determined not to repeat. Some tips come from reading numerous books about the art of training. Sometimes they worked, and sometimes they didn't. Even when they failed, I've continued to implement them until I've gotten it right. You will see numerous quotes from successful trainers that I've met, well-respected educators, or simply trainers whose constructive video blogs have inspired me. Some of the most helpful tips come from my students. You will identify these tips by their casual voice and storytelling quality.

I've developed the remaining tips after much research on the neuroscience of learning and cognitive psychology. After decades of teaching, I've found that reading about the science of how we learn presents me with instantly actionable techniques. Just one study can yield countless implementations. I've tried to explain these methods in an accessible, usable format for you to implement. You'll recognize these tips by the scientific approach and the numerous references and scientific studies.

Terminology: Technical trainers will be referred to throughout the book as instructors or trainers interchangeably. Learners will be referred to as students, attendees, and workers interchangeably.

I sincerely hope that these tips resonate with you, and you find them to be as worthy a practice as I did.

A Note about the Front Cover

I chose an image of a rock climber for the front cover because, as you'll read in the "How to Do it" section in chapter 2, successful rock climbing is the result of hundreds of micro-movements. Alex Honnold is a renowned climber whose free-solo ascent of the 3,000-foot El Capitan in Yosemite National Park was the subject of a 2018 Oscar-winning documentary. Honnold's climbing philosophy is exemplary of continuous improvement. "Yes, that philosophy of marginal gains is central to climbing. When I have a big goal—like free-soloing El Cap—I look at everything I do. I'm training; I'm watching my diet, I'm making sure I sleep enough. I'm outrageously focused on constant improvement." In addition to the training topics mentioned above, rock climbers are continually trying new holds, learning new finger grips, mastering the art of smearing your climbing shoe against the rock while moving up to use friction, and monitoring body weight. At the same time, your other foot supports your body on a foothold the size of a peppercorn. All the while focusing on your next move and much, much more. I encourage you to think of the training tips presented here as micro-movements. The culmination of these micro-movements will get you to the summit!

A Brief Overview of What Happens to Your Learners While You Teach

1

"Any fool can know.
The point is to understand."

— Albert Einstein

Understanding how our learners absorb the information we disburse in our lessons is crucial to understanding the tips. This section provides the scientific background for many of the tips in this book. You'll see that many of my recommendations refer to this introduction as you learn how to take advantage of what we know about how the brain works.

Let's assume you've begun the teaching portion of your training session. You might be lecturing, writing code, presenting complex concepts via diagrams and charts in your slide deck, and your students are presumably learning. As your learners focus on the information, their brains work hard to "record" what we instructors are teaching. The neurons in a learner's brain are doing the heavy lifting.

A neuron, more commonly known as a nerve cell has three parts: multiple dendrites, a single axon and the body of the nerve cell known as the soma. While we teach, our learner's neurons connect thoughts in unique pathways in the brain. This pathway is part of the synaptic function (more about that below). The neuron uses its multiple appendages to send and receive messages via chemical and electrical signals in our brains. The neuron is like a telephone operator, receiving and sending signals that create these unique pathways. One type of appendage is the dendrites, each with additional appendages called dendritic spines. Dendrites are the receivers of messages, and they receive synaptic inputs from another type of appendage called an axon. Neurons have a single axon that contains smaller branches. The terminal end of an axon contains a small swelling called a synaptic bouton, and it's here where synapses with other neurons are found. New pathways are created when the axon of a neuron reaches out to other neurons through their synaptic boutons.

Each learner's brain is thought to have 100 billion neurons! Pathways are formed as chemical signals pass from the synaptic bouton of an axon to the dendritic spine of a dendrite, resulting in the creation of a synapse:

> Synaptic function is to transmit nerve impulses between two nerve cells (neurons) or between a neuron and muscle cell. Synapses connect one neuron to another and are thus responsible for the transmission of messages from the nerves to the brain and vice versa. The synapse, rather, is a small pocket of space between two cells where they can pass messages to communicate. A single neuron may contain thousands of synapses. Synapses are also important within the brain and play a vital role in the process of memory formation.[1]

---

1   K. Kumar, "What is Synaptic Function?," March 12, 2021, https://www.medicinenet.com/what_is_synaptic_function/article.htm.

For a two-minute explanation of synaptic function, visit https://tinyurl.com/24bkmrc7, part of the two-minute neuroscience series.

These chemical signals are the foundation of our thoughts and are shown in Figure 1 on page 14 as 4 circles within the larger circle. Think of these circles as one small concept you're teaching or a single idea you would like your learners to remember when they return to their jobs. Eventually, these thoughts are stored in your learner's long-term memories. As we will soon see, however, this is not always true.

When the learner's pathways are not stored in long-term memory, the result is a student who appears to do well in class, a student who provides positive feedback on the end-of-course evaluations but who has stored little of the course material in long-term memory. Thus, they return to work with little to no increased productivity! The training is considered a failure, and at best, poor use of the company's resources.

Fortunately, science has uncovered how we can improve the learning process by implementing simple techniques that help solidify the connections made in the brain. The tips in this book are based on learning that sticks beyond the duration of a training session.

The type of learning described above is called *Hebbian learning*. It's based on the theory that "when our brains learn something new, neurons are activated and connected with other neurons, forming a *neural network*. These connections start weak, but each time the stimulus is repeated, the connections grow stronger and stronger and the action becomes more intuitive."[2] That's why each tip in this book is designed to make these connections stronger.

In *A Mind for Numbers,* Barbara Oakley describes one of the pathways with a graphic similar to the one below. I have added the descriptions.

2 "Hebbian Learning," The Decision Lab, https://thedecisionlab.com/reference-guide/neuroscience/hebbian-learning/

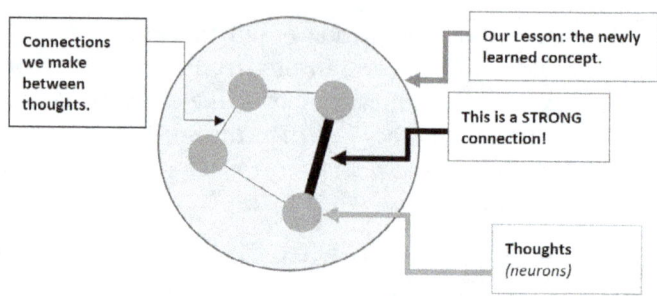

Figure 1: A diagram of thoughts, neurons, and connections.

What goes wrong and how we fix it

Now let's look at what can go wrong. Why does the transfer of knowledge in our training session disappear after the training ends, and most importantly, what can we do about it?

Let's go back to the beginning of our description, where our learners are focused on the current topic. First, connections between neurons can be made more robust with active focus on the learning topic. That, by the way, is the essential tip in the book: keep learners engaged! The learner's brain converts what we're saying into meaningful thoughts, and their neurons are firing.

This process, called *encoding*, is strengthened by the learner when they make mental pictures of what we're teaching. Helping the learner at this stage is powerful. We can ask them to describe this mental representation, show them a picture, and encourage them to generate a mental model by asking them to paraphrase what we've said. The brain encodes these thoughts into what neuroscientists call *brain traces*. The brain traces are stored in our learner's short-term or working memory.

Our working memory is much like the piece of paper on which you jot down a phone number which you quickly lose or the paperless experience of repeating the phone number ten times only to be unable to retrieve the number ten minutes later. If we fail to make these connections stronger, the thought is soon lost and irretrievable.

To be effective as technical trainers, we must do everything we can to make learning stick by moving these brain traces from working memory to long-term memory. We can help optimize learning if we know what has been shown to help and what has been proven to weaken this process.

Consolidation

That takes us to our next step, called *consolidation,* when the brain organizes the brain traces into clear and stable pathways. Imagine the proteins within neurons synthesizing like glue that stitches all the memories together. Consolidation is a time-dependent process, thus without time for consolidation short-term memories will not become long-term memories. The process has two parts: synaptic consolidation and system consolidation. The synaptic process happens within hours of learning and encoding. System consolidation is where the hippocampus guides the information stored in the neocortex (long-term memory) so that it is completely independent of the hippocampus. It is believed that consolidation takes place during sleep. Perhaps we should give our students a nap after lunch, like we used to have in kindergarten! Scientists believe that this stage takes place over several hours or longer, during which the brain rehearses and replays what is has learned. Consolidation is a vital part of maximizing the teaching process. Throughout the book we will revisit this process with the main themes being that rehearsal/practice and linking new information to prior knowledge are critical methods for trainers to utilize.

Chunking

One of the fundamental skills used to store massive quantities of information is a process called *chunking:* "Chunking takes seemingly meaningless information and reinterprets it in light of the information that's already stored somewhere in our long-term memory."[3] In tip 22, trainers are encouraged to ask students to introduce themselves and answer precise questions. One of the questions involves a learner's background knowledge, which provides that learner with information that's stored in their long-term memory. Why is this so powerful? Because "Prior knowledge is a prerequisite for making sense of new learning, and forming those connections is an important task of consolidation."[4]

---

3   J. Foer, *Moonwalking with Einstein,* (New York: Penguin Books), p.62.
4   P. Brown, H.L. Roediger III, M.A. McDaniel, *make it stick,* (Cambridge: The Belknap Press of Harvard University Press), p. 74.

The study of memorization can be helpful here. Believe it or not, there's a USA Memory Championship where memory athletes compete in memory competitions. Memory athletes have shown that it's possible to improve working memory capacity which they do to win memory competitions. Using ancient techniques like a memory palace, the number of items remembered can and does exceed the typical magical number of seven. Our goal as technical trainers is to enhance worker productivity so a larger working memory capacity may be helpful despite the fact that it is not memory exactly, that we are trying to improve, but understanding.

This is arguably the most compelling part of training workers. In this phase, imagine the worker, now on the job and in need of the information provided during the training. The worker has already consolidated information in the brain: new information with the prior knowledge they mentioned when they introduced themselves. Fortunately, throughout the training session, the trainer has "tied" the existing information to the new material presented in class, creating a hook, if you will. At work, the worker routinely thinks of what they already know, but now it comes attached to new information in the brain. On the flip side, if we fail, the learner has retained little to no new information.

This step is critical for getting information that the learner is forming in their short-term memory into long-term memory, which will persist beyond class.

Short-term vs. Long-term Memory

Where are short-term and long-term memory in the brain, and why might information be stored in short-term rather than long-term memory?

Long-term memory is in the *neocortex*, which is the gray matter or outer layer of the brain. The location of the working memory is a bit more complex. Working memory involves the *prefrontal cortex* and the *hippocampus*.

The hippocampus is a brain structure thought to play a critical role in memory. Although suspected to be involved with memory for some time, the importance of the hippocampus in this respect was solidified in the twentieth century by the case of a patient named Henry Molaison. Molaison, known simply as H.M. until he died in 2008 (to preserve his anonymity while he was alive), underwent surgery to treat severe epilepsy in his late twenties. In that surgery, much of his hippocampi was either removed or damaged. The surgery relieved Molaison of his seizures, but he paid a price for that relief. Molaison developed a type of amnesia called anterograde amnesia that typically occurs after a significant head injury. This type of amnesia results in the inability to form new memories that involve conscious recollection of facts or experiences. Molaison's experience was unique because his memory for nonconscious procedures like using utensils or riding a bike was intact. Imagine trying to retain what you learn when forced to live entirely in the present. Any material known on Monday was gone by Tuesday. The scientific conclusion formed around Molaison's case is that the hippocampus is a crucial structure in memory consolidation or the formation of new memories. Thus, as trainers, we must understand and implement the techniques that work on long-term memory and utilize the hippocampus's role in the learning process. [5]

Molaison's story confirms that the hippocampus is the part of the brain engaged when we first learn something new. Current information is stored here and can be retrieved as long as we focus on it. Again, keeping learners engaged is imperative at this stage. Without the learner's undivided attention, information won't make its way from brain traces to working memory, which is its first stop along the journey to becoming workable, on-the-job knowledge.

Trainers have a lot to bear in mind at this stage, starting with the limited capacity of working memory (more on that in a bit). For now, consider working memory to be a large parking garage where many cars are stored. Think of this garage as similar to the neocortex or long-term memory. Now picture a valet parking stand. The hippocampus is like the busy attendant; he can only manage about four cars at a time. He must juggle greeting the car owner, handing over half of the parking ticket, and filing the other half, all while monitoring other incoming cars. The hippocampus can juggle a lot of information and quickly hand someone the "vehicle" that's in working memory, knowing right where the car is, the status of the ticket, and so forth, because that information is in working memory. The hippocampus can also provide a hook to the long-term memory. The point is to be able to retrieve your car whenever you need it. The hippocampus encodes the memories we make in short-term memory so that, at some point, they can be put in long-term memory and retrieved at will by way of the initial encoding. To make this work, the attendant must make a connection between the arrival of the car in short-term storage and its location in long-term storage.

In short, the hippocampus (think, working or short-term memory) can pick up information quickly (as we see from learners in class) but that isn't learning. The short-term memory makes new connections to the neocortex (think, long-term memory). Our goal as trainers is to get knowledge into long-term memory where a great deal of information can be held for a long time. This is very different from teaching to working memory, which may result in positive feedback during class but often leads to less-than-desirable results several weeks later.

Teaching Methodologies

When you focus your attention on a topic in working memory, it's functioning properly. But, like a juggler spinning objects in the air, the working memory can hold only a certain amount of information while the learner is focusing. When the juggler loses focus, he drops the prop. Most adults can keep four pieces of information in working memory at one time. Of course, this isn't true for all people. Some can hold more information in their working memory, and some believe working-memory capacity can be increased. You will find several tips throughout the book designed to increase working-memory capacity.

When links are first formed, they're developed in the working memory. Knowing that the average individual can hold only four pieces of information at once, our first thought should be to avoid information overload by not exceeding four information units until solidifying the new connections using retrieval practice. Also keep in mind that retrieval practice differs from memorization, and it improves understanding. The tips in the book will cover many ways to implement effective retrieval practice, including using compare and contrast and implementing "no stakes testing." Regardless of the methods you use, your goal should be to feed information gradually into working memory, followed by reinforcing practices that I'll describe later.

See https://tinyurl.com/2kwr96mp for an excellent explanation of no-stakes testing. Other techniques include using example problems and partially completed problems.

Another important finding is the significance of paying attention. The hippocampus can better encode current information if the learner is entirely focused. A good trainer must ensure they have the attention of each learner. Without it, the lesson is essentially useless, even if it's successful in the short term.

Beyond the initial learning, teachers must also reinforce what has been learned during class so learners can retain it. Bear in mind that while you're introducing a new concept, your learners are only beginning to make these connections in the brain. Our learners greatly benefit if we know how to strengthen these connections. It helps to understand that these connections are made throughout the class—when we're lecturing and when learners are doing lab exercises, speaking to one another, taking a quiz, or asking questions. That's why the tips in this book address all of these circumstances and more. These events help us facilitate the learning process so that newly gained knowledge lasts long after class ends.

Eventually, students must complete tasks independently without any guidance from us. It's during independent practice times that neural connections strengthen. Providing opportunities to recall knowledge is why we use lab exercises, and it's also why the ratio of lectures to hands-on practice is so important. The lecture is the weakest way to transfer knowledge—it's passive learning—and it simply doesn't stick!

If you must lecture, and sometimes you must, limit your lecture time to no more than fifteen minutes because student attention during lectures tends to wane after approximately ten to fifteen minutes. While this notion has been debated and even proven incorrect in subsequent studies[6], I think it's a wise guideline in the area of technical training. That's not to say that lengthy lectures are always wrong. Combined with other techniques, they can prove to be the most efficient method of knowledge transfer. What remains is the retention of that knowledge, and for that, we can look to the science-based tips presented here.

The neuroscience of learning combined with cognitive psychology tells us that the three most effective training methods involve *spaced repetition*, *practiced retrieval*, and *interleaving*. The vast majority of the tips in this book were developed from these three methods, with many of the recommendations directly gleaned from scientific studies. These tips are tried-and-true techniques based on scientifically proven formulas and real-world experiences.

There is a direct relationship between the time spent in class preparation and the deep understanding of new information (including training materials, lectures, and labs). If it were fast and easy to create your course and learning materials, your learners probably wouldn't be effective in placing this new knowledge into their long-term memory. Unfortunately, most end-of-course evaluations (also known as "smile sheets") don't confirm or deny this theory. This is because learners are poor judges of when they've learned our material in a way that ensures greater on-the-job success. They have instead put our

---

6   N.A. Bradbury, "Attention span during lectures: 8 seconds, 10 minutes, or more?," Advances in Physiology Education, Nov. 8, 2016, https://journals.physiology.org/doi/full/10.1152/advan.00109.2016

class content into their working memory, where it's proven to be lost to the proverbial "forgetting curve." Learn more about this in tip 41.

By practicing the tips in this book, you'll be laying the groundwork that helps ensure that your learning sticks.

Introduction **2**

*"Every man, if he is so determined, can
become the sculptor of his own brain."*

— *Santiago Ramon Y Cajal*

Question: What was Joe Philbin (60-year-old offensive line coach for the Dallas Cowboys and former head coach for the Miami Dolphins) referring to when he said: "This was the best hour I spent in the NFL in my entire career"? Philbin's career spans four decades of coaching.

Answer: Virtual training (done right!).

Is that how your students feel after your virtual training sessions?

Virtual training is impactful regardless of the arena: sports, business, science, or technology. It's a modern communication tool that lowers costs, increases accessibility, and is environmentally friendly. Those are just a few reasons virtual training has become an established and proven form of learning. The primary reason remains that, done right, virtual training works. It's the "doing it right" part that's challenging!

There are many reasons virtual training fails, from insufficient technology to poor instructional design. Technical flaws and limitations are often solved with additional funding. Larger training budgets mean companies can invest in everything from modern hardware (like virtual reality devices) to increased internet bandwidth to virtual worlds like the metaverse.. Poor instructional design can be overcome by hiring professionals in adult learning and curriculum development proven to help workers on the job. These professionals excel at ensuring that the training is aligned with the company's business objectives.

Poor technology and weak instructional design are only two of the reasons, albeit significant ones, that virtual training fails. I've spent most of my COVID-19 shutdown time exploring why virtual training fails—from pre-kindergarten to university and, in many instances, in corporate training. The one area that ultimately lead to Joe Philbin's enormous satisfaction is the subject of this book.

After the 2020 NFL season, the Dallas Cowboys coach hired two experts to help his coaches improve their coaching. The two experts he hired had zero football experience—absolutely no background in football. They were experts in virtual training and had been responsible for thousands of courses taken by tens of thousands of students. They had, in one week, converted 7,700 university classes to online remote learning.

They were tasked with teaching coaches how to engage players via virtual meetings and video calls. Think about what they were being asked to do: coaches had to be taught how to engage players during training that consisted of watching snippets of the game film, asking questions between clips, and teaching—in short, simple sessions.[7] Sound familiar? Sure, we corporate technical trainers do it all the time, but it's not a skill that should be taken for granted, and it isn't something that you master without constant attempts to improve. "Successful on-ground instruction doesn't always translate to successful online instruction. If facilitators are not properly trained in online delivery and methodologies, the success of the online program will be compromised."[8]

How to do it

A *crux* in rock climbing is the toughest move or sequence of moves on a climb's route. A route is a path by which a climber reaches the top of a mountain, rock, or ice wall. Rock climbers routinely work on routes after they and their fellow climbers have determined the route has one best solution, and it's not uncommon for several climbers to attempt the route where only one climber succeeds. In his book, *How to Climb 5.12,* Eric J. Horst suggests the reason for climber failure: "Ultimately, it's the aggregate of minor inefficiencies and slight flaws in technique that brings a climber down short of reaching the summit. The key to nixing these problems is self-awareness—never-ending checks and rechecks of the goings-on in your mind and body, followed by tiny adjustments. Elite climbers probably do this hundreds of times during a single ascent (often unknowingly). Beginners, on the other hand, may never do it because they're overwhelmed by fearful thoughts or the inability to solve the next move. Make a conscious effort to foster high self-awareness early on in your climbing career. It will empower you to identify and eliminate many bad habits of moving, making way for steady long-term improvement."[9]

Think of this book as a way to resolve minor inefficiencies and slight flaws once and for all. You will undoubtedly recognize some of these seemingly minor tips and believe they don't apply to you because you feel you've fixed that problem long ago. I encourage you to hire a coach or, at the very least, review some of your recorded classes and see where you might improve. It is, indeed, only through the flaws you reveal that you can improve. In other words, reaching the summit or teaching the perfect class requires imperfection. It's similar to writing code and put very elegantly by Reshma Saujani, founder of Girls Who Code (a nonprofit organization dedicated to supporting

7   A. Beaton, "What a Science Teacher Taught the Dallas Cowboys About Coaching," *Wall Street Journal,* (Dec. 30, 2021), https://www.wsj.com/articles/dallas-cowboys-covid-omicron-nfl-11640825981

8   "Strentgths and Weaknesses of Online Learning," University of Illinois, Springfield, https://www.uis.edu/ion/resources/tutorials/online-education-overview/strengths-and-weaknesses/

9   E.J. Horst, *How to Climb 5.12,* (Guilford, CT: FalconGuides, an imprint of Globe Pequot Press), p. 27-28.

and increasing the number of women in computer science). Ms. Saujani said, "Code breaks and it falls apart, and it often takes many, many tries until that magical moment when what you're trying to build comes to life. It requires perseverance. It requires imperfection."

Even leaders in their fields can find flaws in their technique. Stephen Curry holds the NBA Finals record for most three-pointers made in a game, most consecutive regular-season games with made three-pointers, regular-season record for made three-pointers, most points scored in an overtime period, most career three-pointers of all-time, and these are just a few of his amazing accomplishments. He's arguably the best shooter ever to play basketball. Yet, Curry is often quoted as saying, "I feel like I can get better at putting the ball in the basket." He says this because he's proven it to himself time and again. In his 2016 season, he had the highest true-shooting percentage of all time ("true-shooting" is an advanced statistics that measures a player's efficiency at shooting the ball). That was until 2017, when he shattered his own record.

Serena Williams is another athlete not content to let her career peak while she still has room for improvement. Williams has won a record thirteen Grand Slam singles titles. Other records include the Open Era record for most women's singles titles at the Australian Open, most women's singles matches won at majors, and most singles majors won since turning 30 years old, and she's the only tennis player, male or female, to win three of the four Grand Slams at least six times. Like Stephen Curry, Serena Williams concentrates on making small, incremental improvements in key areas that result in a new phase of excellence. If the likes of Stephen Curry and Serena Williams can consistently find ways to improve, surely you and I can.

What it takes

Successful classes and positive end-of-course evaluations don't help improve training. "Success is a moment, but what we're always celebrating is creativity and mastery."[10] To make improvements to your training, all it takes is a willingness to put your ego aside and honestly evaluate your performance. "Mistakes make your brain grow."[11] Asking your learners how you can improve is a positive start. Another technique is to hire a coach or collaborate with your fellow trainers.

I hope that the tips in this book resonate with you. I've been teaching for over 25 years, and I have yet to teach the "perfect class" but, together with my fellow trainers and learners, I continue to hone my craft.

---

10   S. Lewis, *Beautifully Said*, (New York: Rock Point)
11   J. Boaler, *Beautifully Said*, (New York: Rock Point)

The Neuroscience of Learning: Main concepts

"Exciting discoveries in neuroscience are allowing us to fit educational methods to new understandings of how the brain develops."

— *John Katzman*

Despite positive end-of-course evaluations, students may not have the ability to recall material when they return to work.

"Education that appears successful from immediate posttests and learner evaluations can result in knowledge that is mostly lost to recall over the ensuing days and weeks…[O]ne-time educational activities can provide a misleading sense of permanent learning even when, as in the present study, the evaluation of the activity is very positive and the initial gains in learning very substantial. Educators, too, need to be aware that activities producing rapid learning and high learner satisfaction may nonetheless result in poor retention."[12]

The forgetting curve can be reduced if the trainer knows what brings it about and what diminishes it. The following tips will help learners reduce the impact of the forgetting curve.

Make sure you have your learner's attention before you begin

Introducing new material before you've ascertained that you have everyone's undivided attention is an exercise in futility. If a distracting event has just transpired (an off-putting question, a technical issue with audio or video, and so on), make sure everyone has dealt with the issue and that all learners are ready to resume learning.

Avoid distractions during training

Any actions that cause the learner to lose focus (going off on tangents, answering an unrelated question, and so on) results in less effective encoding in the hippocampus, making the new information more difficult to recall later. Ask your learners on day one if they'll be distracted during class, have meetings to attend, or expect to be multitasking during class. If so, let them know the dangers of multitasking.

Avoid multitasking

Research on the hippocampus suggests that we have limited resources available when encoding new information for later retrieval. Dividing those re-

12   Bell, Douglas S et al. "Knowledge retention after an online tutorial: a randomized educational experiment among resident physicians." Journal of general internal medicine vol. 23,8 (2008): 1164-71. doi:10.1007/s11606-008-0604-2.

sources between simultaneous competing tasks puts a burden on the system that is realized later when the learner attempts to recall the new information.

Encourage learners to find answers by themselves

First, we present new material for the learner to process. The actual learning part that takes place is most effective if it's the result of the learner making their own connections. For example, we can introduce a coding algorithm but leave it to the learner to understand when that algorithm makes sense within a greater context. Ideally, we want workers to be on the job, solving problems on their own by recalling information from our training sessions. It's more effective for us to allow in-class time for the learner to make their own connections, even if they're wrong. The key is to provide additional time for the learner to spend understanding the correct answer. This is, of course, more time-consuming than if we simply cut the time in half by providing the correct answer, but that's not going to help the learner weeks later when they're on the job. Minor tweaks like this can mitigate the forgetting curve.

Other tweaks include introducing planned difficulties during learning. These are known as *desirable difficulties, spaced reinforcement, interleaving, practiced retrieval,* and *spaced practice.*

Introduce desirable difficulties

After initially teaching the material, provide exercises that present the material in a different setting or context. Force the learner to mentally rearrange the information before they can apply it. Don't fall into the trap of making learning easy. Yes, your learners might be frustrated at times. Remind them that the difficulties they're encountering are helpful; their capacity to learn is not hardwired at birth and they can control their brain's capacity to a larger degree than they might think. "Understanding that this is so enables you to see failure as a badge of effort and a source of useful information."[13] The desirable difficulties you add to your course need not be a secret. Tell your learners you know the exercises are challenging—you designed them that way for their benefit.

Space your reinforcement

Rather than conclude a long learning session with a single review or summary session, space the summary throughout the remainder of the learning session. Begin each new exercise with a short task that incorporates some

---

13 P. Brown, H.L. Roediger III, M.A. McDaniel, *make it stick*, (Cambridge: The Belknap Press of Harvard University Press), p. 7.

prior material. Allow time for reviewing information more than once. Use flash cards. Make students answer questions that require them to recall previous topics, not just the current subject. Remind students that forgetting material is expected and that recalling previous exercises helps make current lessons more challenging, which has proven effective for retention.

Interleave prior topics

For new material to stick, it must be related to existing knowledge. Always relate new information to what the learner has already committed to long-term memory. Throughout the class, repeatedly return to prior topics.

There is a fine line between repetition and appearing to jump from topic to topic randomly. This is because, if done correctly, it will be challenging for your learners, and they may express some frustration. The payoff is that they'll retain the information much longer as a result of switching between ideas during class.

The key is to ensure there is initial understanding before you start switching and be sure to verbally make the links between ideas for your learners. More than one student has responded to my request for feedback with a comment like, "I'd prefer to stay on a subject until I master it before we move on." This sentiment is also implicit when students indicate the pace is too quick. Numerous studies suggest we serve our learners well by distributing practice sessions across different skills before mastery of any one skill.

Implement practiced retrieval

The correct implementation of practiced retrieval happens when learners are forced—with no help from you to retrieve and/or apply the information from a prior lesson. It can be as simple as a round-robin question-and-answer period where you ask one student to tell you one or two things about a topic and then move on to the next learner with the same question until you've exhausted the topic. It's important that they not simply recall words or definitions, but also are able to recall concepts and how and when to apply those concepts.

Consider ending class early enough for one final exercise: announce to learners one of the most important topics of the day and ask them to write everything they can remember from class about that topic. Alternatively, you can supply a simple but thought-provoking question that requires reflection. It won't simply be a fact-based question that tests the learner's memory. It should be a question that simulates an on-the-job problem. This is an example of learning from the bottom up.

Space their practice

Spaced practice can be challenging during short 1- to 3-day classes, but it can be done. You can space practice by starting each day with material from the previous day. Implement as many quizzes as time permits and remind your learners that you expect them to forget. The quiz doesn't test their memory but reinforces the learning by forcing the recall process. Make sure your reviews and quizzes are cumulative and also include previously covered material each day. Don't let yourself fall into the trap that correctly answered questions equal mastery. Just because learners answer questions correctly doesn't mean we should stop asking them. Remember, we're not asking them to test them; we're asking them because the practice is backed by scientific evidence that it can help them become more productive workers.

Tips for Class Preparation

*"Give me six hours to chop down a tree
and I will spend the first four
sharpening the axe."*

— Abraham Lincoln

Make a preflight checklist to be used at the start of class and check off each item after you complete it.

Background

The best webinars I've attended always had one thing in common: a well-prepared trainer. From the moment they "hit the stage," most trainers want to excel, and I'm sure you're no different. Like most of you, I used to carry a backpack full of preparation items to my engagements. It wasn't easy to forget to prop the door open when I had a doorstop with me (yes, I was locked out of my own classroom once). Likewise, I wouldn't forget my class roster because I carried both the attendee roster sheet and tent cards with each student's name printed on them. Without our handy backpacks, it has become easy to forget these essential steps in today's virtual classroom.

How to do it

An excellent preflight checklist ensures that you're completely prepared for class. I prefer to print my preflight checklist so I can check off each task as I complete it. My checklist is broken down into two sections. The first is for hardware. I need a hardware checklist because my training environment is complex with many moving parts, including a teleprompter, a camera switcher, two microphones, a DSLR camera, four monitors, a big-screen TV, and two computers. As a result, I have to boot up my desktop computer, laptop computer, and applications in a specific order to ensure all my hardware works as expected. The second section is for tasks that I have to do before class starts for anything non-hardware-related. Tasks here include signing in as a student on a separate device, ensuring I have water and mints nearby, and so on. Figures 2, 3, 4 and 5 show sample pages of my hardware and software setup checklist for teaching in a Zoom classroom.

Teaching Setup

ZOOM

Order of operations

- ☐ Turn on ATEM Mini Pro .... ☐
- ☐ Boot up Lenovo computer .... ☐
- ☐ Pull down green screen .... ☐
- ☐ Confirm monitor setup .... ☐

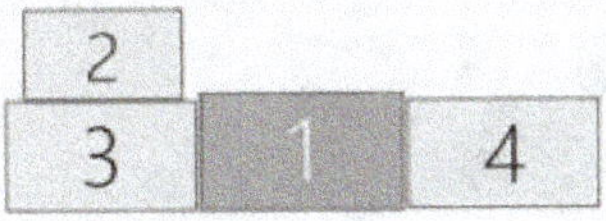

- ☐ Turn on M-Audio speakers .... ☐
- ☐ Turn on Yeti microphone .... ☐
- ☐ Turn on Shure microphone .... ☐
- ☐ Remove lens cap and turn on Sony camera .... ☐
- ☐ Confirm Logitech C920 backup camera works .... ☐
- ☐ Turn on Stream Deck with "KR Start Profile" .... ☐

- ☐ Launch software .... ☐
  - ☐ Chrome
  - ☐ Acrobat
  - ☐ IDE (WebStorm/VSCode)
  - ☐ PowerPoint
  - ☐ HotKey Script
  - ☐ Launch Presentation
  - ☐ Set PowerPoint to display on the correct screen

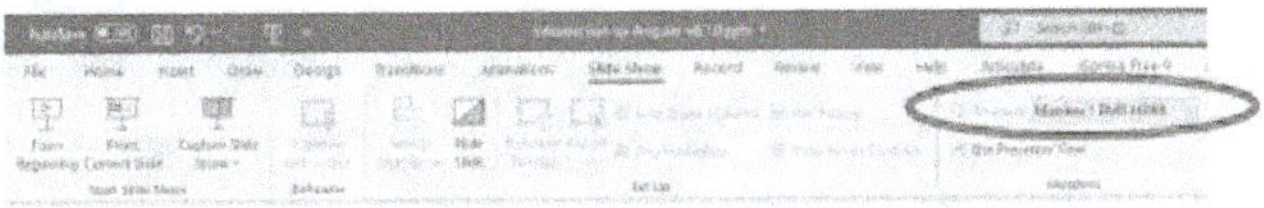

1

Figure 2: Teaching setup checklist for a class taught in Zoom (page 1). You can download copy at
https://75-tips.com/

☐ Zoom
☐ Companion
☐ OBS
　　☐ Start Virtual Camera or stream deck button

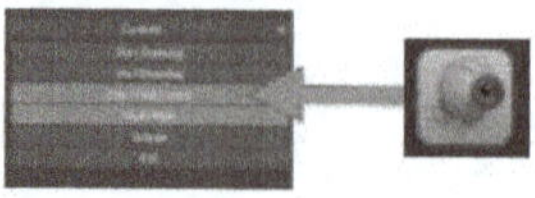

☐ H2R Graphics
☐ Krisp
☐ Set Stream Deck Profile to "KR IN PROGRESS"................................☐

☐ Launch Zoom meeting...☐
　　☐ Screen Share → Advanced → Content from Second Camera
　　☐ ZOOM SETTINGS:
　　　　☐ No background
　　　　☐ No green screen
　　　　☐ Click "Switch Camera" from top left of screen
　　　　☐ Uncheck "Optimize for video clip"

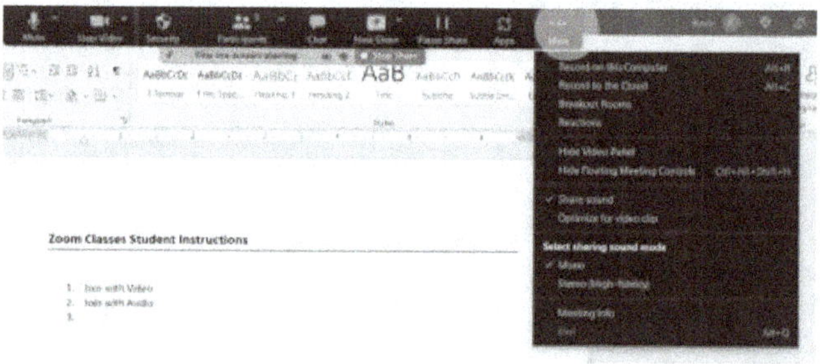

☐ Setup Microphone..☐
　　☐ Via ATEM

2

Figure 3: Teaching setup checlis for a class taught in Zoom (page 2). You can download copy at https://75-tips.com/

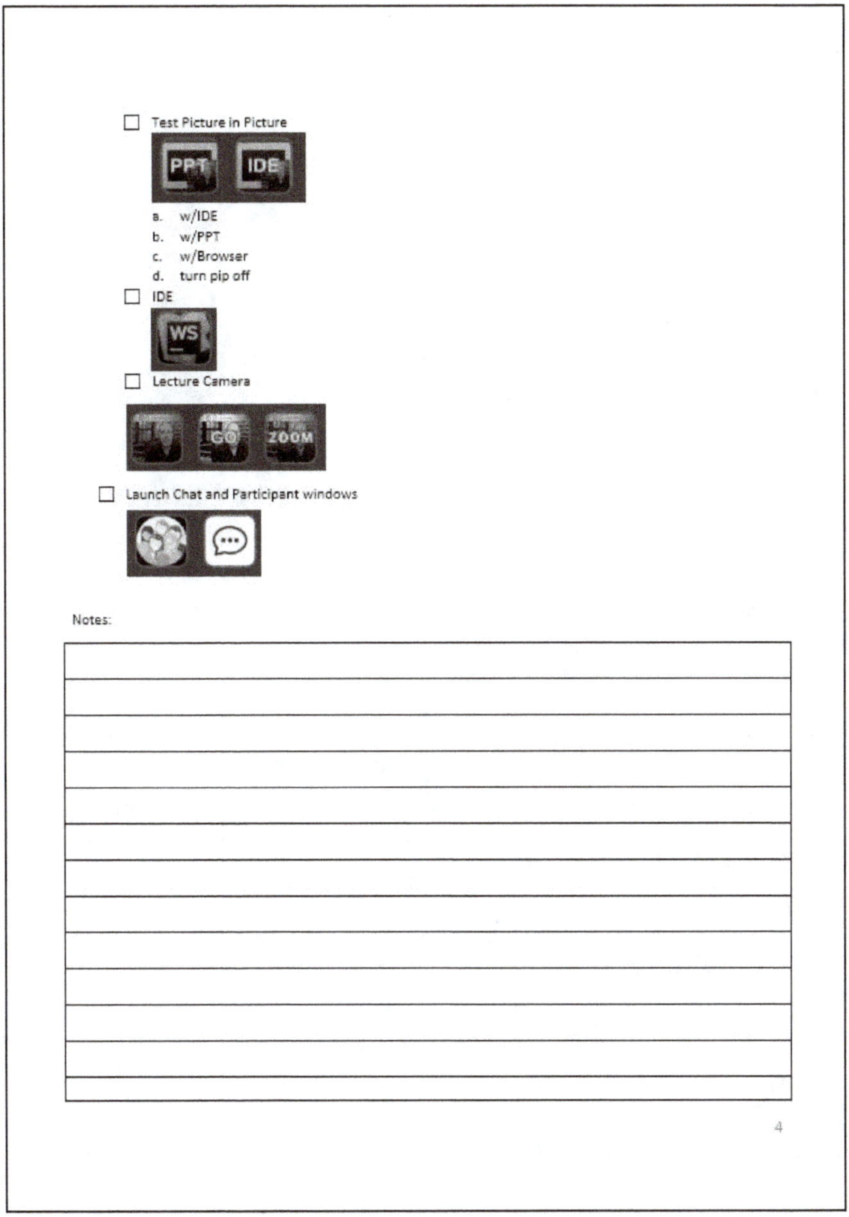

☐ Test Picture in Picture

a.   w/IDE
b.   w/PPT
c.   w/Browser
d.   turn pip off

☐ IDE

☐ Lecture Camera

☐ Launch Chat and Participant windows

Notes:

4

Figure 4: Teaching setup checklist for a class taught with Zoom (page 4). You can download copy at https://75-tips.com/

Figure 5 below is an example of my class startup checklist. You can download copy at https://75-tips.com/

❑ I've logged into the class on my laptop as a student.

❑ I've reread all class logistical information.

❑ I've reread needs assessment notes, student backgrounds, and related information.

❑ I've checked my ethernet for internet access.

❑ I've checked my wi-fi for internet access.

❑ I have a backup internet connection available (wi-fi hot spot).

❑ I have a second internet connection available (cell phone).

❑ I have a backup audio connection ready to go (mobile phone, VOIP).

❑ I have a backup mic and speaker via a hands-free headset (wired and wireless).

❑ I have a backup computer that is booted up and ready to go.

❑ I have all courseware, workbooks, handouts, job aids on my desk and ready to go.

❑ I have electronic versions of all courseware, workbooks, handouts, job aids, and they're accessible on my primary and backup machines.

❑ I have all relevant links to start class as host, presenter, and student, and they're available as a text document (ready to cut and paste as needed), including username and passwords as needed.

❑ I have a printed participant list with relevant notes next to each attendee.

❑ I have bottled water nearby.

❑ I have mints and gum nearby.

❑ I've turned off all desktop notifications (or moved them to a screen that I don't share), distracting noises, and email chimes on all computers.

Figure 5: Class startup checklist.

The first use of a preflight checklist was inspired by an event that took place on October 20, 1935, at Wright Air Field in Dayton, Ohio. On that day, there was a flight competition for airplane manufacturers. At stake was a contract with the U.S. military to produce a long-range bomber.

Figure 6: The B-17 prototype crashed in Dayton, Ohio. (Courtesy of the Boeing Company Archives).

Boeing Corporations Model 299, dubbed "the flying fortress" was a shoo-in to win the competition (historians have said that the Army had already planned to order 65 Model 299s). Sadly, the plane exploded after turning on one wing during its run down the tarmac. The pilot, Major Ployer P. Hill, and two crew members died in the crash. Because the crash was deemed the result of "pilot error," the conclusion was that the Boeing Model 299 was "too much airplane for one man to fly."[14]

But the error was simply that the crew had neglected to release the flight control gust locks intended to prevent damage to the control surfaces while on the ground. Ultimately the Army Air Corps chose the B-18 Bolo built by the Douglas Aircraft Company. The Army subsequently purchased a few aircraft from Boeing Corporation as test planes. As a direct result of the pilot error, Boeing decided to forgo more extended training by its pilots. What? Go without additional training? Instead, the pilot's checklist was created. Such was Boeing's confidence in using a checklist as opposed to relying on the pilot and crew's memory that the checklist has been used by pilots ever since.

Your class may not be as complex as flying a modern aircraft, but it's just as important to your students.

---

14   A. Gawande, *The Checklist Manifesto*, (New York: Picador). pgs. 32-33.

There are many examples of the compelling use case for checklists in the medical field. Peter Pronovost began studying hospital-acquired infections in 2001. His study determined that doctors should take these steps:

- Wash their hands with soap.

- Clean the patient's skin with chlorhexidine antiseptic.

- Put sterile drapes over the entire patient.

- Wear a sterile mask, hat, gown, and gloves.

- Put a sterile dressing over the catheter site.

His ultimate conclusion was that the "use of this simple five-item checklist would greatly reduce infections when inserting a central venous catheter.[15]

In 2003, another study called the Keystone Initiative[16] was conducted by a collection of Michigan hospitals and health organizations. The results of this study were astounding: "In December 2006, the Keystone Initiative published its findings in a landmark article in the *New England Journal of Medicine.* Within the first 3 months of the project, the central line infection rate in Michigan's ICUs decreased by 66 percent. Most ICUs—including the ones at Sinai-Grace Hospital—cut their quarterly infection rate to zero. Michigan's infection rates fell so low that its average ICU outperformed 90 percent of ICUs nationwide. In the Keystone Initiative's first 18 months, the hospitals saved an estimated $175 million in costs and more than fifteen hundred lives. The successes have been sustained for several years now—all because of a stupid little checklist."[17]

Resources

You can create your checklist with any word processor like Microsoft Word and back it up as a PDF for portability and printing. Alternatively, the following websites offer checklists suitable for printing:

- You can create a nice-looking checklist at http://printablechecklist. org/, but it can't be saved.

---

15 J. E. Brody, (2008-01-22). "A Basic Hospital To-Do List Saves Lives." The New York Times. Retrieved 2009-01-08.
16 P. Pronovost et al., "An Intervention to Decrease Catheter-Related Bloodstream Infections in the ICU", The New England Journal of Medicine, Vol. 355, No. 26, (Dec. 28, 2002), https://jamesclear.com/wp-content/uploads/2015/03/keystone-initiative-checklist-central-lines-nejm.pdf
17 A. Gawande, *The Checklist Manifesto,* (New York: Picador). p. 44

- Checkvist offers a free version for their app to create private or share-able checklists at https://checkvist.com/, and it can be saved.

- Visit http://www.75-tips.com to download the checklists described in this tip.

Challenges

- What do you typically forget to do just before class starts?

- What about during the class? And at the end of class?

- What do you do to remind yourself?

2 Prepare a template to write the students' names, gender, and notes.

Background

According to Dale Carnegie, we should remember "that a person's name is to that person the sweetest and most important sound in any language." Some students have names that are difficult to pronounce. Don't be shy about asking them if you're pronouncing it correctly. They'll welcome and appreciate this simple effort.

How to do it

Have a sheet of paper with each student's first and last name printed on it. After introducing themselves, you can write out their names phonetically next to their printed names. If gender is not clear from their name, you can confirm pronouns with the learner; be sure to write it down as well. Leave room on the template after each learner's name for notes regarding the student's background and goals for the class. See tip 22 for more information about learning each student's background and goals. Figure 8 shows a sample template.

Resources

- Visit http://75-tips.com to download the form in Figure 7.

Class _____

Attendees _____

Name	Pronunciation	Gender	Background	Goals

Figure 7: A sample class roster for taking notes. You can download this form at https://75-tips.com.

Challenges

- Have you ever had someone repeatedly mispronounce your name? How did it feel?

- Did you correct them or just let it go?

Have one monitor devoted to logging in as a student.

Background

This tip serves both a practical and an andragogical purpose. The practical objective is related to the technology involved in virtual training, namely, the bandwidth of the internet connection of your learners. As stated in *Virtual Training* by Jeb Blount, "No internet connection, no virtual training. Poor internet connection, poor virtual training session." He goes on to state, "Spend the money to upgrade to the fastest upload speed your broadband provider offers. Most providers tout their download speeds. That's great for streaming movies but doesn't help a bit with delivering a video training livestream. For this, you need to max out your upload speeds."[18] Mr. Blount advises that trainers avoid connecting to the internet via wi-fi during their training sessions as it's often unreliable and unstable. They should instead connect via an ethernet cable connected directly to a router. While I believe this to be true for the trainer role, it may be helpful to log on to the training session a second time via wi-fi to see and feel the training experience as your learners do.

Logging in as a student can be helpful for several reasons. You'll experience the lag time that many of your students will encounter and can therefore adjust your rate of speed when teaching live materials. In other words, it will help keep you from speaking to a slide on your slide deck that your students haven't seen yet. It also lets you immediately notice when you are sharing the wrong screen. For example, you've been teaching from your slide deck and then you move on to some code examples, but your students still see the slide deck. You have failed to switch screens (see tip 29 and 80 for information about switching screens and camera switchers).

The andragogical purpose behind this tip is simply the idea of putting yourself in your learner's shoes. The psychological impact is more substantial than you might suspect. Try simply watching your second screen while you teach for a bit of time. Watching two screens is challenging when performing exercises, but it's undoubtedly doable while lecturing alongside displayed graphics.

How to do it

I prefer a second machine with a separate internet connection for logging in as a student. It's still okay if you have only one internet connection available

---

18   J. Blount, *Virtual Training*, (Hoboken, NJ: John Wiley & Sons), p. 79.

to you, and it doesn't have to be a computer. Any device will work, and I sometimes use a tablet or iPad to log in as a student.

When logging in as a student, I prefer the user name "Kevin as student" so my learners know not to use that name when directing chat messages to me. When logging in as the trainer, I use the user name "Kevin (the instructor)."

Be sure the device you're logged–into as a student is within your peripheral vision. It's useless if you can't glance at it quickly while teaching.

Technology

You can check both your upload and download internet speeds at https://www.speedtest.net/.

Challenges

- What techniques do you use to put yourself in your learner's shoes?
- How do you see the class from your learner's perspective?

Remove any content on the screen that you don't want to share with learners.

Background

Do we really need to discuss why you don't want to share your latest internet search to remove warts or your most recent bank statement? Probably not! I think we've all been there, though.

The problem with creating a clean machine with no residue of personal or unrelated information is that information tracking follows you everywhere on the internet, most significantly, the web browsers.

How to do it

First and foremost, be sure you have no screens open on any of your monitors that are not related to the class. In the hardware-related tips, you'll see the use of utility apps: applications and websites that help us teach. If you choose to use these apps, place them all on a separate monitor and never share that monitor's contents.

Here are some tips for working in a browser that holds personal information:

- Just don't do it (see the virtual machine hint below this list).
- If you must, then try the following:
  - Make a training profile (Google's Chrome browser allows you to set up profiles that store bookmarks, viewing options, reading lists, and more on an individual basis).
  - The training profile will contain only those bookmarks you require for class and no user names or passwords. You can set up most browsers with as little or as much information as you need.
  - See https://tinyurl.com/3tuwd99e for more information about setting up profiles.

The easiest solution is to use a clean virtual machine. Virtual machines are beyond the scope of this book, but you can learn more about them at https://www.vmware.com/topics/glossary/content/virtual-machine.html.

If you'd like to create a virtual machine for training, see the resource below.

Resource

For free open-source software for creating virtual machines, see https://
www.virtualbox.org/.

Challenges

- How do you prepare your computer for class?
- Do you have a separate computer used only for training?

Have a backup computer ready to go.

Background

Computers crash. It's a fact of life. Without a backup computer, a system crash can end the class. What if it's a class that took more than a year to come to fruition? What if it took six months to coordinate all of the attendees, and on top of that, it would be at least six months to a year before you could gather the same group again? And do you know what else happens? Two computers can crash! Have a backup for your backup!

The idea of having a backup computer can be an overwhelming and time-consuming thought for most trainers. After all, you may have carefully put your system together to deliver a stellar virtual class. You've got multiple cameras, a whiteboard, and lots and lots of additional utility software to make sure the course runs as expected for a seamless learner experience.

Read on for multiple tips to make having a backup system less complicated.

How to do it

Self-employed trainers typically don't have the luxury of a corporate setup with redundant systems and the ability to roll out software quickly and easily. Having a separate piece of hardware would be as far as you could hope for from a computer crash. It is, after all, a completely different system, including hardware. I like to maintain two computers (or more) with the same software setup. Warning: Testing your environment independently may not be sufficient. You must also ensure that any setup instructions your students follow conform to their corporate environment such as firewalls or black-listed websites.

It can help to make a list of everything you would need to set up a new machine to keep the class rolling after a severe system crash. Saving as much as possible in the cloud can help you upload the contents to a backup system more quickly. Those who teach programming languages keep their materials in the cloud on sites such as Bitbucket and GitHub. (See "Resources" at the end of this tip for additional helpful tools.)

What else can you put in the cloud for easier retrieval?

- Courseware
- Handouts
- Job aids

- Slide presentation
- Demo files

Also have a printed and digital copy of each training file associated with the session on your training computer. Keep another electronic copy of each training file associated with the session on a different computer. Be sure you can access one of your backups without internet access.

Be sure all software, drivers, plug-ins, extensions, and so on are installed on both your primary and your backup computer. By the way, a backup computer for the backup computer isn't a ridiculous idea; it has saved me more than once.

Ensure all your devices, including backup machines, are powered on and ready to go at least an hour before class starts. Make sure your backup devices are fully charged and run from battery power if necessary.

You must test your backup system to confirm that you can run a successful class with it. Does the mic work? Does the camera? A USB hub and switchers for USB devices can be helpful to quickly move all of your peripheral equipment to the backup computer. A KVM switch that allows you to use one keyboard, mouse, and monitor on multiple machines is also helpful. See "Resources" below for more information on setting up multiple workstations.

Resources

Box is a cloud-based storage app. https://www.box.com/

Dropbox is a cloud-based storage app. https://www.dropbox.com/home

GitHub is a cloud-based code storage app that can be used to store all kinds of files. https://github.com/

BitBucket is a cloud-based code storage app. https://bitbucket.org/

See tip 8 for additional information regarding these resources.

Challenges

- Do you have a backup computer? Is it another desktop or a laptop? Does it have all the required ports for peripheral equipment?
- Do you have a backup for your backup?

Prepare an hour-by-hour breakdown of your class to keep you on track.

Background

I started using this technique for new classes to help me gauge where I should be at any given time. It has proven so helpful to me for various reasons that I continue to do it for every one of my classes. A big part of a trainer's job is the management of the classroom, and part of that is managing the course content:

- Am I on time?

- Have we covered enough content for the time we spent?

- Will we be able to finish the remaining content on time?

These questions can be answered by having an hour-by-hour breakdown of how the class should progress, including break times. Now let's consider some of the other benefits of this hour-by-hour breakdown.

I complete a post-mortem after every class. In both the course content and my performance, the goal is to see what went great, was okay, or could have been done better. Clients also ask me to participate in post-class assessments. It's great to tell my client exactly what took place during class—what we covered on what day, and at what hour as well as what went smoothly, what did we have to skip entirely, and why?

I can do this because the hour-by-hour breakdown is based on the course outline that I'm expected to deliver. I can easily add notes to the course outline as to why we skipped an exercise, a topic, or a subtopic. I make these notes at the earliest opportunity during class while they're fresh on my mind.

Finally, I can use this hour-by-hour breakdown to reveal flaws in the class outline. For example, I might see that certain sections routinely get skipped. Maybe I should leave them out of the course. Some sections go on longer than anticipated. These notes tell me I need to reexamine the lesson and see why it's taking longer than expected. Perhaps it's not a well-written exercise or the lecture is lacking somehow. These insights are invaluable if I hope to improve my course offerings over time.

How to do it

I have built a standard template for this (see figure 9). The important parts include the following:

- Day/date of the training
- Hour
- Topic
- Breaks times
- Lunch break time
- Checkmarks to indicate whether or not that specific portion of the class was covered

Note: If I'm using a book or slide deck, referencing the page or slide number is especially helpful to keep me on track.

Course Outline

Client Information

Client:_____

TrainingProvider:_____

Location:_____

Date:_____

Course Info/ Books

1 _____

2 _____

3 _____

Class Hours:_____

Contact: _____

Total Number of Days: _____ # of Students: _____ # Remote Students: _____

Most Critical Subjects:
1. _____
2. _____
3. _____
4. _____

Day/Date	Time	Book/Chapter		Complete
Day One	< :30 to start	n/a	Confirm physical arrangement of class	
			Set up training aids: white board, markers, projector, flipo charts, presentation sw, class software	
			Set up learner supplies: books, paper, pens	
	1st :45 min	n/a	Advise learners re: schedule/breaks/etc.	
			Learner introductions and confirm prereqs	
			Reduce distractions, lighting, etc.	
			Introduce myself	
			Write day one agenda on whiteboard	

Page 1 of 4

Figure 8: Worksheet for an hour-by-hour breakdown of class. You can download this form at https://75-tips.com.

Challenges

- What do you do to stay on schedule?

- How do you quickly keep track of which techniques, exercises, and lectures are working and which are not?

7 | **Become familiar with your unique training style.**
There is only one you!

Background

As Oscar Wilde famously didn't say, "Be yourself; everyone else is already taken."[19] In my early days of training, I thought my personality needed to be molded into the persona of the archetypal trainer. It was only later, as I became comfortable with my audience, that I let myself be me. Okay, maybe I had to rein in the quintessential, fast-talking, fast-moving New Yorker. Still, I became a better trainer by focusing on professionalism and skills rather than mimicking my favorite trainers.

While conducting train-the-trainer sessions and mentoring vocational school new hires, I discovered something significant that I've never forgotten. Whether they were beginning trainers or had decades of training experience behind them, each trainer brought something new and exciting to me and, no doubt, their students as well. A significant amount of my mentoring is getting the trainer to see their attributes through my eyes and convincing them that their unique personality contains many strengths that can be utilized in knowledge transfer and to create a fun learning environment.

Everyone has a training style, whether they know it or not. "Like everyone, you have developed preferences in life how you give directions to strangers, how you explain a task to a colleague, how you clarify information for your spouse. You have developed a preferred way to do each of these."[20] The author of *Training for Dummies* goes on to indicate that "There is no right or wrong style."

I never said that.

While I agree with that sentiment, there is a guiding principle (also addressed in *Training for Dummies*) that your approach should be learner-centric. That is to say, whatever your style is, be sure that you can justify it in terms that favor the learner and not the trainer. For example, in the great slide-

---

19   Quote Investigator, https://quoteinvestigator.com/2014/01/20/be-yourself/

20   E. Biech, *Training for Dummies*, (Hoboken, NJ: Wiley Publishing, Inc.), p 123.

deck debate ("Is it better to use a slide deck or not?"), the answer lies in who benefits from it.

How to do it

Absent a coach to point out your positive and unique traits, what can you do? If your training sessions are recorded, watch them like a defensive coordinator analyzes last week's game film! Share them with other trainers and solicit their advice. Ask the people closest to you (spouse, best friend, relatives) what it is about you that stands out? How might that help a learner at any given point in class, like during a lecture or a coaching session during class time?

The other side of this is that you might discover some less-than-desirable traits for the classroom, like impatience. That's okay. We all have to work on these issues because training is such a personal occupation.

If you're a trainer, taking a realistic look at your personality is an undertaking you skip at your peril. Negative traits will come out in class eventually. So will positive ones, so the key is to expose them, learn from them, and become a uniquely gifted trainer just by being yourself. As Dale Carnegie said, "No matter what happens, always be yourself!"

Resources

All it takes is time, energy, and honesty with yourself. Don't disregard the traits that make you shine!

Challenges

- Have you asked someone who knows you well what positive traits you might bring to your classroom?
- Have you ever gotten feedback from a training coach or mentor?

Back up all of your materials in the cloud.

Background

We've all experienced a dreaded pre-backup computer crash. Maybe it was a manuscript at a point when your creative juices were flowing for fifteen solid minutes! Naturally, you didn't have the time to press Control + S and save; you were on a roll, brilliance emanating from your fingertips onto the keyboard when suddenly—crash!

It can and does happen at the most inopportune times. Whether you've lost the carefully crafted theory placed into your slide deck, the amazing code demonstration, or those flickers of genius in your lab exercises, you'll regret not backing up your files somewhere safe.

How to do it

Typical files to back up include workbooks, demonstration files, computer code, lab exercises, setup instructions, and so on. I would absolutely back up any file involved in the successful delivery of your class.

Resources

Here are a few locations that might suffice for backup storage:

A network access storage device (NAS) with backup software

- asustor (https://www.asustor.com/) provides a variety of solutions at a variety of price points.
- Synology (https://www.synology.com/en-us/products/DS220j) has an entry-level NAS.

You can find a review and description of NAS devices here: https://www.pcmag.com/picks/the-best-nas-network-attached-storage-devices.

A cloud-based online backup service

- Carbonite (https://www.carbonite.com/) offers subscription-based backup plans with multicomputer discounts,
- Backblaze (https://tinyurl.com/3eymwchu) offers similar plans to Carbonite.

Cloud-based storage sites

- Microsoft OneDrive (https://tinyurl.com/mw98nw7x) is included with Office 365 for backing up Microsoft Office documents. A OneDrive Basic plan includes 5 GB of free storage.

- Box (https://www.box.com/) has individual/team and business plans.

  o Free plans include up to 10 GB of storage.

  o Business Starter plans for business teams include up to 100 GB of storage and start at $5/month.

  o Personal Pro plans for individuals include up to 100 GB of storage and start at $10/month.

  o Box.com includes services beyond storage such as file sharing, note-taking, security features, Google workspaces, and more.

- Dropbox (https://dropbox.com) has personal and business plans.

  o Free plans are available with 2 GB of storage.

  o Dropbox includes services beyond storage, such as file sharing, file syncing, and file recovery.

- Google Drive (https://www.google.com/drive/) is free. Each new user gets 15 GB of free space, which is shared with other Google services, including Gmail and Google Photos, Google Docs, Google Sheets, Google Slides, Google Drawings, and Google Forms

There are several options for code backups:

- GitHub (https://github.com/) is arguably the largest repository of code in the world. GitHub has a free plan for individuals and organizations that includes the following:

  o 500 MB of package storage

  o Unlimited public/private code repositories

- Bitbucket (https://bitbucket.org/) code storage and management includes a free plan with the following:

  o 1 GB of storage

  o Unlimited private repositories

  o Up to five users

  o An upgraded standard and premium plan for $3 and $6, respectively

     ○   Additional services, including Jira integration, continuous integration, continuous deployment implementation, chat rooms, and more

Code sandboxes

- JSFiddle (https://jsfiddle.net/) is a playground for writing and testing JavaScript, HTML, CSS, and CoffeeScript.

- JSBin (https://jsbin.com/) is a playground for writing and sharing HTML, CSS, and JS with processors for Jade, Markdown, Less, Stylus, Sass Babel, TypeScript, and more.

- TS Playground (https://www.typescriptlang.org/play) is a playground that is helpful in understanding TypeScript vs. JavaScript.

- Python Playground (https://www.programming-hero.com/code-playground/python/index.html) playground for Python that includes a learning environment.

- Python Playground (labstack) (https://code.labstack.com/python) Simple Python code sandbox.

- rdrr.io Run R code in your web browser (https://rdrr.io/snippets/).

Challenges

- Where do you keep your original material?
- Do you have a preferred backup location?
- Do you have a backup for your backup?
- Do you keep any printed versions of your material?

Master the medium.

Background

In the live on-site classroom, we trainers are experts in our domain. We arrive at our session at least an hour before we expect students to come and wander around, checking out the environment and setting up our equipment. Where shall I stand, what's the best location for my laptop, do I need a mic? Are the learner's desks set up optimally for the type of work we'll be doing? Is there a whiteboard or a flipchart? Will I be able to make eye contact with everyone? Do I have room to walk around and see everyone's workstation? Where will the attendees eat if the event is catered? Does the client have any classroom rules I should know or communicate to the participants? The list goes on, and many of us have mastered it to the extent that we hardly think about it anymore.

The virtual classroom is another issue entirely, and it may take a day or longer to thoroughly acquaint yourself with all of the features. Most virtual classrooms have settings that change depending on several factors, including your internet bandwidth, audio, video, personal preferences, whether or not the class is being recorded, and much more.

Virtual classrooms have robust software that needs configuration. You also need to be aware of its limitations, such as the maximum number of breakout rooms, attendees, and so on.

How to do it

The learning curve can be steep, whether you use Zoom, Adobe Connect, Microsoft Teams, WebEx. GoTo Training or GoTo Meeting, Zoho Meeting, or BlueJeans Video Conferencing. I recommend spending as much time mastering the settings and features you're most likely to use first. Time permitting, look around with an open mind as to what else might be helpful. You must deal with some settings like selecting your mic, camera, and speakers. In addition, there will be features you must master for a seamless and professional class, such as screen sharing, chat, and recording if necessary. Finally, you'll want to see what other helpful features the virtual environment includes.

Once again, I recommend a checklist. Consider the checklist below. How many items are you comfortable checking? How well do you know the capabilities of your chosen virtual classroom software?

- ❏ As a host, I know what every button and menu command will do.

- ❏ I've logged in as a participant and know how to direct my learners when they need help.

- ❏ I understand and have set every configurable feature of the virtual classroom.

- ❏ I know how to share files with my participants.

- ❏ I know how to mute myself, others, and the entire group, if necessary.

- ❏ I've set all video options in my virtual classroom to their optimal settings.

- ❏ I've set all of the audio options in my virtual classroom to their optimal settings.

- ❏ I know how to share my screen in the virtual classroom, including multiple screens if necessary.

- ❏ I have printed (and am ready to copy and/or paste) all of the logistical details of my training, including the following::

  - ❏ URL for the virtual meeting

  - ❏ Passcodes

  - ❏ Meeting ID

  - ❏ Teleconferencing information

- ❏ I have an electronic copy of my courseware and all other training materials ready to share if necessary. Ideally, they're in a central location where learners can access them: a public storage location like Dropbox, code repositories like GitHub, or any accessible website. The virtual training software itself will also include a location to share files that you have previously uploaded to the software.

- ❏ I have the email and username of a technical support person who is knowledgeable about the virtual classroom and available to assist students via Slack, Microsoft Teams, or other communication software.

Resources

Consider bookmarking this documentation:

Zoom

- Support (https://support.zoom.us/hc/en-us)
- User guide (https://tinyurl.com/mr2nk3fn)
- Troubleshooting (https://tinyurl.com/26yccya2)

GoTo Training

- Support (https://support.goto.com/training)
- Organizer user guide (https://support.goto.com/meeting/new-goto-meeting-guide)
- Attendee user guide (https://support.goto.com/training/att-guide)

Adobe Connect

- User guide (https://helpx.adobe.com/adobe-connect/using/user-guide.html)
- Troubleshooting (https://tinyurl.com/3k5tz4yf)

Microsoft Teams

- Education guide (https://tinyurl.com/2p9x2zx8)
- Video training (https://support.microsoft.com/en-us/office/microsoft-teams-video-training-4f108e54-240b-4351-8084-b1089f0d21d7)
- Troubleshooting (https://tinyurl.com/2w7nssfp)
- **WebEx** (https://tinyurl.com/2p8jadhm)

Challenges

- With so much of your time consumed by creating course content, how do you find time to master the learning environment?
- What do you do to make up shortfalls in your learning environment knowledge? Workflow diagrams? Crib notes? Job-aids such as posters and cheatsheets?

10   **Look your best.**

Background

Trainers always want to look their best. We know that students will be distracted by physical tics, overly dramatic hand gestures, sloppy attire, and a whole lot more, so we present ourselves accordingly. We'd never dream of teaching in a dark, dimly lit room or lecturing in a whisper.

In today's virtual classroom, we're at the mercy of our equipment. A poorly placed camera and incorrect room lighting could make us look like we're in the witness protection program. We have to master our webcam from setup to delivery to look our best. And, as my wife pointed out in a not-so-subtle gift of a nose-hair trimmer, personal grooming or lack thereof is much more apparent when students are staring at a large close-up of your face!

Figure 9: Maybe not! Image from https://www.trekbbs.com/threads/the-ncc-82893-thread.310610/page-17.

How to do it

To look your best, you'll need a basic understanding of the following topics:

- Lighting
- Framing
- Background
- Clothing

- Cameras

- Filters

Lighting

Let's start with lighting. Without proper lighting, your learners will constantly be distracted. They won't make eye contact or have a sense of connectedness. In a perfect world, we'd be physically in front of learners. If we can't have that, we can get as close as possible, and a large part of that is proper lighting.

Use a reliable, soft, diffuse light source aimed directly at your face. Windows are an excellent source of natural light. Make sure the window is facing you and not behind you. Sitting with a window behind you will result in a dark appearance that may be so dark that learners can't even see your face.

The direct light of a strong bulb, like the ones you find in desk lamps, is not the best. If that's all you have to work with, try to diffuse the light by aiming the lamp so light bounces off a nearby wall, or drape some light fabric over the lamp to diffuse the light. If you can, aim the light behind the webcam and slightly above it. If it's still too dark, try aiming with two lamps on each side of the webcam, always making sure the light is soft and diffuse. Use daylight bulbs that mimic the natural light coming from your window.

If you are like me and train in a variety of time zones, you won't be able to count on natural sunlight. I've taught many classes that began at 2:00 am in my local time zone. Be prepared by purchasing an appropriate light before class.

Framing

Framing yourself on a webcam means adjusting the camera: its distance from you, zoom level, and aim. A good rule is to divide the visible area into thirds and position yourself so that your eyes are in the top third and your shoulders are visible.

Here are some basic best practices:

- Set the camera at eye level. You don't want the camera looking up or down at you, and both can create a negative impression on your learners.

- Position yourself so you're in the center of the camera frame. Find that sweet spot where you're not too far from the camera, which makes you appear distant from the learners, but far enough that if you lecture with moderate hand gestures, your learners can see your body language. It's important that your hand gestures are helpful and not just a distracting bad habit.

- If you teach standing up or use props, you'll need to adjust somewhat. It's helpful to mount your camera on a tripod that allows you to adjust horizontally and vertically.

- If you teach a subject that requires motion on your part like demonstrating scientific experiments, frame yourself so your movements are seen. Put yourself in your learners shoes and think about what you want them to see.

Background

Your background should be clean and uncluttered; you don't want to have anything visible that might distract your learners. You can slightly blur your background in some software like Zoom. I like to choose a calming background image that looks professional and collegiate. Virtual background images are effective, but they can awkwardly remove parts of your body as you move around.

Greenscreens can be extremely helpful when providing virtual background images. Web conferencing software can make a clean division between your moving body and the fake background image if you use a greenscreen. Software like Zoom offers a setting to check if you have a greenscreen. Other software, like Teams, can provide a background image without a green screen.

Clothing

I spent most of my training career conducting live on-site training, and I had an extensive wardrobe. My typical attire was a suit and tie. Long before the webcam became ubiquitous business equipment, I conducted a fair amount of virtual training.

It wasn't until the COVID-19 pandemic, when all my training became virtual, that I realized I really, really like striped shirts! Unfortunately, the camera did not. With the stripes plus a little bit of motion on my part I had the makings of an acid trip! It made me dizzy and, although no one said anything, it couldn't have been a pleasant experience for my learners.

Here are some essential clothing tips that have worked well for me:

- Assume the same dress code you'd use if you delivered the training on-site.

- Solid-colored clothing works best for webcams, but avoid solid white or black. They can be challenging because the webcam software will make lighting adjustments based on your clothes' reflective nature, which can cause you to appear washed out or too dark.

- Favor colors like blue, deep red, and green.

- But avoid green clothing if you use a green screen, or you'll be transparent!

- Avoid stripes and complex patterns.

- Avoid clothing with excess fabric that might move as you lecture; this can be distracting.

- Try to adjust the lighting to avoid reflections on your eyeglasses.

- Minimize accessories like bracelets that might make noise or be visually distracting.

- Even though your feet may never be seen, some trainers prefer to wear dress shoes. When I wear shoes, I feel more comfortable, and the session becomes more akin to a live on-site. Also, I stand up occasionally and I sure wouldn't want my students to see my bare feet!

Cameras

You have many choices when selecting an external webcam. There are budget and do-it-yourself options as well as more expensive DSLR camera options.

Webcam: Webcams are widely available at numerous price points and are designed to be compatible with today's desktop computers and laptops. A popular mid-range model is the **LogitechC920 and 922 Pro.** It offers an effective resolution of 1080 pixels (commonly known as 1080p) and is easy to use with webcam software that allows you to adjust settings like brightness, contrast, hue, saturation, and more.

DSLR camera: If you already own a DSLR camera, you may be able to use it as a webcam. If you're looking to purchase a DSLR to use as a webcam, popular choices include the **Canon EOS REBEL SL3 Digital SLR** camera (approximately $475.00). You can find many suitable used cameras at bargain prices that may not include the latest features but work well as webcams. I found my used camera (at a great price) at a local camera store with a knowledgeable staff. You'll need your DSLR camera to support the following features:

- **Clean HDMI out:** Some DSLR cameras and camcorders will display user interface (UI) elements on the output screen. You don't want attendees to see information like the camera's exposure, battery status, aperture, and so on. A camera with clean HDMI is one that's capable of sending a clean video signal that doesn't include these UI elements.

- **Power-supply AC adapter:** Classes that run for more than twenty minutes drain the camera's built-in battery. You'll need an AC adapter so that you can plug your camera into an outlet for the duration of the class. The AC adapter is attached to a dummy battery placed inside the camera where the battery would typically be. A dummy battery allows you to stream for hours, but you'll need to watch for overheating. Research reviews of the camera you intend to use to see if it suffers from overheating. Some cameras have an automatic shutoff to avoid overheating, which is typically a setting that you can disable as you become used to your new camera.

- **Resolution:** Check your camera's output resolution which refers to the size of the digital image the camera produces. An ideal screen resolution that's compatible with some of the other equipment you might use is 1920 x 1080, aka 1080p which means the camera will output an image that is 1,920 pixels wide and 1080 pixels tall.

- **Frame rate:** A rate of 30 frames per second is sufficient for most teaching environments. But if you're moving briskly or your training involves any fast-paced activity, look for 60 to 120 frames per second.

- **Audio:** I suggest capturing audio with a separate microphone because the internal mic on most cameras doesn't produce high-quality results, and you won't be able to situate the microphone and camera independently. If your audio is piped through the camera, you'll want a backup in case the camera mic fails.

- **Connection:** Check your camera's HDMI connection. You may need an HDMI micro or HDMI mini cable.

Camcorder: Consumer camcorders in the $250 price range make acceptable webcams. As you move up in price, you'll find better image quality.

Smartphone: Another option is to use your smartphone with software from Elgato called EpocCam (https://www.elgato.com/en/epoccam). You simply download the app to your phone, install the drivers on your desktop, connect the phone to your PC via wi-fi or USB. Then set the EpocCam as the webcam on your computer and you're good to go.

Android

To use your Android phone as a webcam follow the instruction below.

1.   Open a web browser and go to https://www.dev47apps.com/to download DroidCam Client.

2. Install the DroidCam Android app on your smartphone and grant it permission to access the camera and microphone.

3. Start the DroidCam app on your smartphone and note the wi-fi IP address.

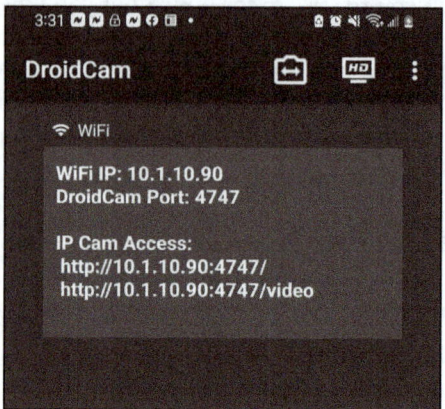

Figure 10: The DroidCam app after startup.

4. Launch the DroidCam client application on your desktop PC and enter the device IP from the DroidCam Android app (shown in step 3 above).

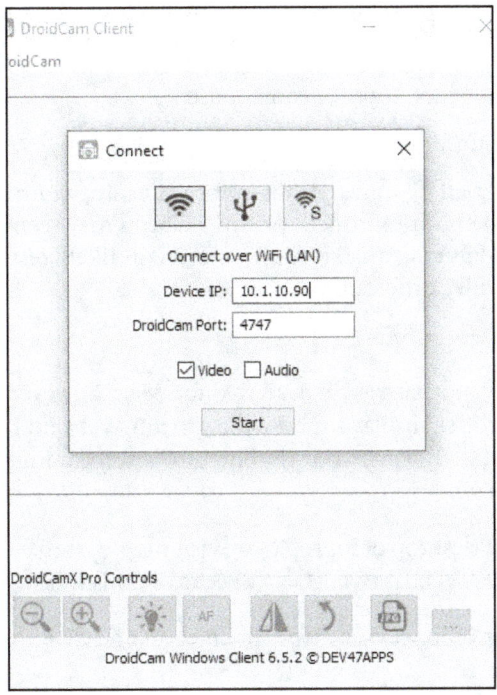

Figure 11: The DroidCam client application.

Apple

To use your iPhone as a webcam follow the instructions below.

1. To see if your iPhone or iPad is compatible with EpocCam software, visit https://tinyurl.com/2azstc49. Visit the iOS App Store and download EpocCam.

2. Launch the application and click Begin.

3. You will see "Step 1: Get the driver" with instructions for downloading a driver to your PC. Choose your platform, Windows or Mac, from the Get the Drive buttons at the top. If you choose Windows, you will be prompted to download iTunes to your PC. Don't do that. Instead, click the button to have the driver link emailed to you.

4. Return to your PC and follow the instructions in the email.

    Note: Don't close your phone because you use it in the next step.

5. Back on the iPhone, click Next. You can now start Zoom, OBS, and so on and choose the iPhone as your camera.

Here are some more tips for camera use:

• Keep your lens clean.

• Consider all of your options before choosing your built-in web-cam. The built-in camera on your laptop may seem easy to use, but configuring an external camera will likely result in a notice-able quality difference.

Mac

DroidCam is not currently available for Mac; however, there are alter-natives that offer similar functionality. Iriun Webcam runs on both An-droid and Mac. To turn your iPhone into a webcam using Iriun, follow the steps below:

1. On your desktop or laptop Mac, visit https://iriun.com/ and down-load the "Webcam for Mac" (v2.7.2 as of this writing).

2. On your iPhone, visit https://iriun.com/ and click Download at the App Store.

3. Download the Iriun software on your phone.

4. Launch the Iriun software on your phone.

5. Launch the Iriun software on your desktop, and you should see your iPhone camera's output displayed in the Iriun Webcam for Mac window.

HDMI, USB, and camera switchers: If your camera has an HDMI cable, you can run the cable to a multicamera switcher like the ATEM Mini Pro made by Blackmagic Design, which sells two popular versions (one costs $295 and the other, $495).

The **YoloBox** is another multicamera switcher. Both of these devices do much more than hooking up HDMI devices to your computer. They're popular with live streamers and gamers. You can find a comparison of the two switchers at https://tinyurl.com/f94php7r.

If you don't want to purchase a multicamera switcher, you can still use your DSLR with HDMI. You'll need a capture device such as Elgato's Cam Link (currently selling for approximately $130.00). The CamLink is a dongle that will convert the HDMI signal from the camera into a USB signal, making hooking up your HDMI camera as easy as plugging it into a USB port on your desktop or laptop computer.

Filters

Your virtual environment may offer options, including filters, to help you look your best. For example, Zoom has a Touch Up My Appearance setting.

Lights

Your room's natural lighting may be sufficient, and you may want to check it out before making any lighting purchases. Lamps that render a diffuse light should work if your office does not get natural light. Below are some examples of lights designed for video recording.

Ring lights: Ring lights range in price from $10.00 for small models that surround a smartphone to larger 14-inch models that sell for approximately $200.00.

Paper lights: This 24-inch paper light can be had for just $2.95 at Just Artifacts at https://tinyurl.com/2wh3296n and renders diffuse light similar to a ring light.

Figure 12: Paper lights from Just Artifacts. (left).

Figure 13: Ring light from https://tinyurl.

com/59mdkrhb (right).

Resources

Prices reflect the price at the publication date.

Webcams

Logitech C920S Pro, approximately $100.00 (https://tinyurl.com/2s34p6nz)

- Dimensions including fixed mounting clip: Height: 43.3 mm, width: 94 mm, depth: 71 mm
- Cable length: 1.5 m
- Weight: 162 g
- Compatible with Windows® 7 or later, macOS 10.10 or later, Chrome OS™

      o   USB-A port
- Works with popular calling platforms
- Max resolution: 1080p/30 fps –720p/30 fps
- Camera megapixel: 3
- Focus type: Autofocus
- Lens type: Glass
- Built-in mic: Stereo
- Mic range: Up to 1 m
- Diagonal field of view (dFoV): 78°
- Tripod-ready universal mounting clip fits laptops, LCD, or monitors (tripod not included).

Logitech C615 Webcam, approximately $50.00 (https://tinyurl.com/2p8b2twm)

- Compatible with: Windows 7, 8, 10 or later, MacOS 10.10 or later, Chrome OS™, Android™ 5.0 or later
- USB-A port
- Max Resolution: 1080p/30 fps–720p/30 fps
- Focus type: Autofocus
- Lens technology: Glass
- Built-in mic: Mono
- FoV: 78°
- Tripod-ready universal clip fits laptops, LCD, or monitors
- Cable length: 0.95 m

My DSLR camera

The camera and accessories that I use are listed below. I purchased the camera at a specialty camera shop that sold used cameras which is a cost-effective way to get a quality DSLR camera.

Sony A5100: with AC Adapter (https://tinyurl.com/459pw854)

Accessories: ZEISS Microfiber Cleaning Cloth
(https://tinyurl.com/mv2ccz3j)

11 **Sound your best.**

Background

Many trainers I know exercise their vocal cords by practicing volume and projection. Others are just gifted speakers whose voices project naturally. I rely on my natural voice in small groups, but I learned to use diverse types of microphones when speaking at large venues. That knowledge, however, did not translate entirely to virtual training where the microphones are very different (with the exception of the mic that is attached directly to your body or clothing known as the lavalier mic).

The use of microphones during virtual training can be beneficial. Some mics have features that can help us overcome some natural tendencies, such as being softspoken or simply born with a pitch that doesn't project as much as we might like. Unlike poor video quality (which, although annoying, can be overlooked), our learners simply can't overcome bad audio. If they can't hear us, all is indeed lost. Audio problems abound, and the possibility for things to go wrong is endless: too quiet, reverb, background noise, echo, buzzing, and feedback. They all contribute to an intolerable experience for our learners.

How to do it

Mic basics

Generally speaking, mics are either dynamic mics or condenser mics:

- A dynamic mic is often described as a little speaker in reverse. Dynamic mics are designed to have limited sensitivity for distance sounds based on the sounds decibels as referenced to voltage (dBV). They come in assorted styles such as ball mics (with built-in windscreens). A windscreen prevents the popping sound known as a *plosive* that's created by the air blown into the mic from pronouncing "p" words like "pop," "pencil," and "plosive." Common dynamic mic brands include the Shure SM and Beta series.

- A condenser mic is used for studio recording, acoustic instruments, and distance pickup.

One of the most notable features of a mic is the mic *pickup* or *polar patterns*, meaning the direction from which the mic picks up sound:

- The omnidirectional mic picks up sound from all directions.

- The unidirectional mic is designed to pick up sound from a specific area.

- The Cardioid-designed unidirectional mic has a medium pickup pattern capable of capturing sound for 100° around the front of the mic while rejecting sound from the rear of the mic, making it ideal for teaching from a home studio.

Background noise

Before purchasing and setting up a microphone, you must prepare the environment. For example, you may need to move halogen lamps because they emit a low buzz. You may need to turn off ceiling fans. If your training room is near a bathroom or kitchen, consider moving it. In short, remove as much "outside" sound as you can.

Room acoustics

Another concern is the surrounding area. If your room is fairly empty and devoid of carpet, furniture, and other items that affect sound waves, you may experience echo. A typical office will have desks, computer equipment and books that create a different kind of acoustical problem. Sound waves bounce off these items and ultimately make some parts of the room seem louder and others quieter. Experiment first with your studio as is. If you hear sounds that seem too close or too far way or echo, consider the effect that items in the room may have on your voice as you speak.

Which type of mic should I use?

Mics are built for different purposes, and the microphone built inside your computer should be the microphone of last resort. It's immovable, which means it can't pick up your voice if you turn your head or stand up. In addition to that, built-in mics can pick up sounds you'd rather not hear, like your computer's fan or hard drive. Fortunately, there are microphones on the market today that are designed for exactly what's needed in a virtual classroom:

- Some webcams like the Logitech 922X mic include two omnidirectional mics that are an improvement over your computer's built-in mic.

- You can also use earbuds with built-in mics. These can be easy to use and include helpful features like noise cancellation. I find them distracting and uncomfortable, but many trainers report using them with no issues.

Illustration 76115549 © Yael Weiss | Dreamstime.com

- Headset mics offer perfect mic placement and are available at various price points. Most have features like noise cancellation and provide a warm vocal quality.

- Lavalier mics are the ones you often see used by professional speakers. The mic attaches to your clothing (snaking it through your jacket makes for a nice no-see professional appearance). They offer similar quality to other high-end mics.

- Finally, you can use a stand-up mic that sits on your desk and connects via USB. See "Resources" below for more information about finding all of these mics.

Whichever mic you choose, give careful consideration to where you will place the mic. My mic is mounted to the ceiling inside of a shock mount. Low frequency rumbling called structure-borne noise results from your mic coming into contact with outside forces such as wind, a moving audio cable, footsteps on the floor or a passing train that causes your floor to shake. A shock mount is a mic fastener that holds the mic in place while isolating it from outside forces. The mic is mounted in a flexible elastic that prevents the mic from shocks and thereby limits structure-.

Choose your sound settings

After choosing a mic, you need to evaluate your sound settings. A good rule of thumb is to use noise meters to evaluate microphone volume. There are many high-tech and complex noise meters on the market, and many of them are free. I prefer simple-to-use meters that let me know when I'm speaking too loudly or softly. These are especially useful for recorded sessions. For a list of free noise meters, see https://listoffreeware.com/free-noise-meter-software-windows/.

You may also want to download a free VU meter, but first, here's a little explanation. A volume unit (VU) is a basic voltmeter that measures and analyzes sound signals through a simple average. It does this within a response-time range based on how quickly it responds to an incoming signal (known as the *attack time*) along with the time it takes the meter to return to its resting position (known as the *release time*). A typical Vu meter will execute in approximately 300 milliseconds. A Vu meter is ideal for assessing your volume because it was initially designed as a loudness meter.

My personal favorite is https://vumeter.en.softonic.com/. Simply connect to your microphone and begin testing your volume. Don't be concerned about the zero as you'll see it doesn't mean you can't be heard. You do want to avoid the red zone, though, especially if your session is recorded.

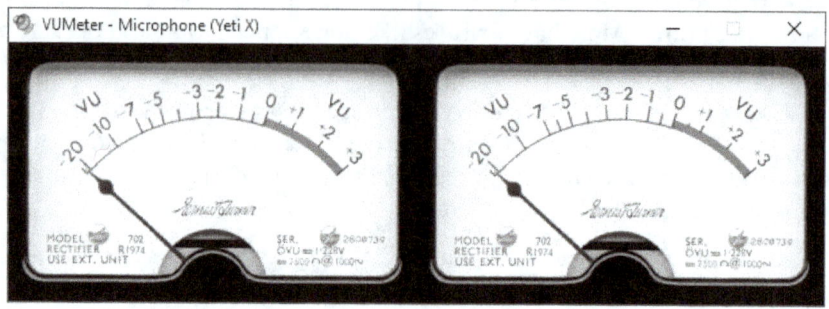

Figure 14: A VU meter showing the volume level of my Yeti mic.

Connecting a mic to your PC

When it comes to connecting your mic, you have a few choices, including these:

- Headphone/mic jack in your computer
- USB mic
- XLR mic

Let's look at each choice in more detail.

Headphone/mic jack in your computer: Most computers come with a headphone/mic jack. Most off-the-shelf products will work when purchasing equipment like a headset, mics, or combination headset/mic. If you have any issues, you may need to know what type of plug you have. It can be helpful for troubleshooting purposes if you have a basic understanding of the various TRS plugs available.

TRS stands for tip, ring, and sleeve. These plugs make three contacts that transmit a stereo or balanced signal. "TRS plugs come in different sizes ranging from 6.35 mm to 2.5 mm, the most familiar being the 3.5 mm plug, which is commonly used for headphones. The TRS-type plug can only be used for either microphone input or stereo audio input, and not both. It's common for headphones that use this type of plug to come outfitted with two, sometimes colored pink and green, to distinguish between audio and microphone input. Understanding the functions and differences between TS, TRS, and TRRS plugs is a step toward understanding how well they work with other socket types. Most of us may think that all audio jacks are the same and that you can simply use any audio plug with any jack. However, doing so can affect sound quality and can potentially damage your device."[21]

USB mic. These mics are very popular because they couldn't be easier to hook up. All you need is a USB port. You may need an adapter as there are several types of USB ports, including these:

- USB-A
- USB-B
- USB-B mini
- USB-B micro
- USB-C
- Lightning

Figure 15: Image from https://www.tripplite.com/products/usb-connectivity-types-standards.

XLR mic. XLR stands for X connector, locking connector, and rubber boot. I prefer the XLR mic for its richer, warmer sound. An XLR mic has several distinct types of cables, with the most popular being the XLR3 (or three-pin) style of cable. An XLR mic tends to be a higher-quality mic with a warmer tone. It sends a balanced signal that isolates noise. To use an XLR mic, you need an audio interface that accepts the XLR-mic cable connection or a mixer. A simpler solution is an adapter from XLR female to 3.55 TRS Male cable such as this one from Hosa at https://tinyurl.com/2p8succ2

For decades, I've used the Eurorack UB502, which you can find on eBay for under $30.00. I picked up a used Shure model 565SD from a local music store, and it works fine. See tip 80 for more information about hooking up an XLR mic to your ATEM Mini Pro camera switcher. My backup mic is a Yeti Blue USB mic.

Elgato sells an audio interfaced called the Wave XLR that accepts XLR microphones and comes with preamp, input gain, volume adjust, toggle for phantom power, Tap to Mute button, headphone output, and a USB-C connection.

---

21   Andy G., "Using Headphone Jack as Microphone: What You Need to Know," Sept. 3, 2021, https://www.headphonesty.com/2020/09/use-headphone-jack-microphone/

I like the proprietary Clip Guard technology that reroutes high-input levels through a second signal path that runs at a lower volume. You can learn more about the Wave XLR at https://tinyurl.com/yxcmpzh9.

Figure 16: Elgato Wave XLR audio interface (https://www.elgato.com/en/wave-xlr).

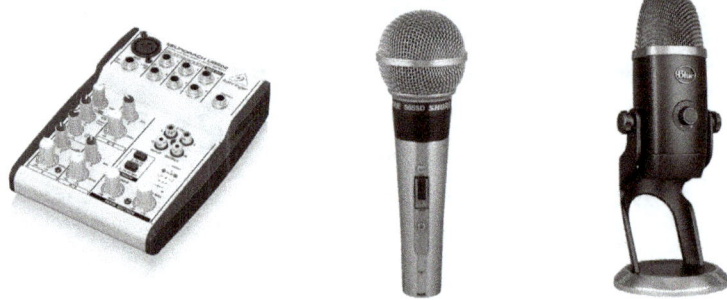

Figure 17: image from https://www.behringer.com/product.html?modelCode=P0218 and https://www.shure.com/en-US/products/microphones/565sd and https://www.pcmag.com/reviews/blue-yeti-x. (left to right: Mixer, Shure Mic, Yeti Mic)

Pop filter

The pop filter helps remove the muffled sound that our learners hear whenever we say a word that begins with the letter "p." You can purchase pop filters like the one below for around $10.00 or you can make your own with an embroidery hoop and black stockings. (Note: They don't have to be black; I simply find that black looks more professional.)

AxcessAbles 6-inch nylon studio microphone pop filter (for the recording studio, podcasts, and broadcasts) has a 14-inch gooseneck and clamp.

Figure 18: A pop filter with a clip for attaching to a mic stand.

DIY pop filter: You can make a pop filter using everyday materials found in your home. See https://

www.wikihow.com/Make-a-Pop-Filter for one example. I made several of my own using an embroidery hoop and a pair of stockings. A quick Google search with the words "DIY pop filter" should yield several dozen results. I like the one at Beatmaker Lab (https://beatmakerlab.com/articles/how-to-make-a-diy-pop-filter/).

Selecting your system microphone

To set the default sound-input device in Windows 10 via the Settings app, do the following:

1. Press the Windows key + I to open Settings.
2. Click System.
3. Click Sound on the left pane.
4. On the right pane, under the Input section, find the Choose Your Input Device option.
5. Click to reveal the drop-down and then select the input device you want.

To set the default microphone on the Mac, do the following:

1. Click on your Apple menu in the top-left corner and select System Preferences.
2. Double-click the Sound icon.
3. Click on the Input tab to see your microphone list.
4. Click on the microphone you want to use.
5. Adjust the input volume by moving the slider to the right.

Software settings

Your teaching environment (Zoom, Adobe Connect, GoTo Meeting, GoTo Meeting) typically includes audio settings that not only allow you to select the mic you'd like to use but also can have a significant impact on sound quality.

Zoom: Activate Zoom settings via the gear icon located beneath your profile picture. Most of the audio settings are self-explanatory. Here are a few helpful options that may not be clearly defined in the dialog box:

- The Automatically Adjust Microphone Volume checkbox makes your microphone softer or louder, automatically, and as needed, to normalize the volume and make it easier for other participants to hear you.

- In the Advanced section of audio settings, you'll find the Signal Processing by Windows Audio Device Drivers, which controls whether or not Zoom will further process your audio signal. The default signal processing setting is On (Windows–Default) because Zoom has identified certain devices that include their own audio processing. If your microphone includes its own audio processing or if you experience audio issues during class, try disabling this feature by choosing the Off (Windows–Raw) option. When signal processing is disabled, Zoom uses the raw output from your audio device.

If you're experiencing echo issues during class, visit https://tinyurl.com/bdfc-ccry for solutions and troubleshooting assistance.

The Echo Cancellation option will control how Zoom cleans up audio and tries to eliminate echo effects caused by your microphone. You need to test the options to see if choosing Auto will be sufficient. Choosing Aggressive may cause intermittent disruptions.

Adobe Connect: To learn more about audio settings, visit https://tinyurl.com/3x97tev7. To learn more about video settings, visit https://tinyurl.com/49s8dwnc

GoTo Meeting: To learn more about the in-session GoToMeeting controls, visit https://support.goto.com/meeting/new-gotomeeting-guide.

Purchasing a mic

Microphones come at a number of price points and with a variety of features. Before purchasing a mic, consider the following:

- What type of connection do I need (e.g., USB, XLR)?
- Will the microphone fit where I need to place it (e.g., on my desk, from the ceiling, with a desk mount)?
- Will it capture my voice at the distance at which I place it?
- Does it include a pop filter, or will I have to purchase one?
- Will the pop filter fit where I want to place the mic?
- Does it have a good rating for use as a vocal mic?
- Does it have a good rating for working with Zoom and similar environments?
- Will I need a shock mount?

Microphones

The resources included below are based on my own purchases.

Blue Yeti Mic with USB connector, approximately $100.00 (https://www.bluemic.com/en-us/products/yeti/)

- Power required/consumption: 5V 150mA
- Sample rate: 48 kHz
- Bit rate: 16-bit
- Capsules: 3 Blue-proprietary 14 mm condenser capsules
- Polar patterns: Cardioid, bidirectional, omnidirectional, stereo
- Frequency response: 20 Hz – 20 kHz
- Max SPL: 120 dB (THD: 0.5% 1 kHz)
- Dimensions (extended in stand): 4.72" (12 cm) x 4.92" (12.5 cm) x 11.61" (29.5 cm)
- Weight (microphone): 1.2 lbs (.55 kg)
- Weight (stand): 2.2 lbs (1 kg)
- System Requirements
  - Windows
    - Windows 10 or higher
    - USB 1.1/2.0/3.0
  - Macintosh
    - MacOS 10.13 or later
    - USB 1.1/2.0/3.0

Shure 56550 vocal microphone with XLR 3-pin connector, approximately $50 used (https://tinyurl.com/4y2kpxeb)

- Primary applications: Studio recording, broadcast
- Sound shield: Mono
- Operating principle: Pressure operated
- Capsule: Dynamic
- Polar pattern: Cardioid
- Orientation: End address
- High-pass filter: Yes
- On-board controls: High-pass filter, HF

- Windscreen: Foam (included)
- Output connectors (analog):1 x XLR 3-pin male (on mic)
- Audio mixer to hook up XLR connector mics

Behringer Eurorack UB502 2-Channel Mixer; approximately $25 used
https://tinyurl.com/cmb8t3vr

Challenges

- How do you evaluate your mic?

- Do you test locally or engage another instructor to dial in and give you feedback?

Read the training logistics sheet and background information as you receive it and once again before class begins.

Background

Most training firms share important logistical information about the training engagement. Sometimes changes are made that affect our delivery. For example, shortly before class begins, the client may decide to have three additional participants with zero experience or they may want participants with a decade of experience. In either case, you might want to change some content, add supplementary material, or use breakout sessions in response to this kind of information.

How to do it

You may want to reread logistical information related to your class because you might have overlooked some minor but very important detail that will change how you teach. For example, you may mistakenly believe the course will be delivered via your WebEx account only to discover it has been changed to the client's Zoom account.

My preclass checklist includes rereading the latest logistical information sheet for the class. In addition, I've made a habit of printing this material so I can physically check off each item. This serves as a reminder for any preclass issues I might need to address.

Technology

I keep the printed version in front of me before class. I also keep a digital version so I can easily copy and paste any logistical information that I may need to share with someone during class.

Challenges

- What type of logistical information is vital to have at your fingertips before class, during class, or after class?

- What format do you keep this information in (e.g., digital, Print)? Where do you keep it?

Solicit feedback.

Background

Exploring feedback is an influential selling tool and an effective learning aid for trainers. Reviewing feedback early on can help sell the training in several ways:

- It evokes a sense of accountability.

- By calling for feedback, the training company is sending a message that they care about the effectiveness of this training and want feedback that proves the training was successful.

- Ultimately, training is purchased to increase productivity. That may mean removing bottlenecks and providing a workplace where workers feel they're growing their skills. The goal may simply be to increase output per day per worker.

When it comes to teaching programming skills to engineers, architects, or software developers, accountability is often determined by their direct reports: supervisors, lead architects, team leads, and management all of whom may track time spent versus money saved and so on. A technique that bakes this accountability into the training while simultaneously providing valuable information about classroom content is invaluable.

How to do it

One technique is sometimes referred to as the *360-degree feedback process*. In this process, employees receive anonymous feedback from a predetermined group including coworkers, supervisors, managers, subordinates, and sometimes even clients). The input may be in surveys, questionnaires, or brief phone interviews.

To be successful, the participants must remain open-minded and respectful, always acknowledging the process as a collaboration designed to bring out the best a worker has to give in a trusting environment. The learner provides their feedback and then makes a plan to grow and develop new skills based on all of the input. The training takes place and the results are measured again with feedback from all the participants.

The process can help create learning objectives for the training and provide a measured result.

Challenges

- How do you determine if your class is successful?

- What type of follow-up do you do with the learner's direct reports? Can you use that information to determine what parts of the course were successful and what parts were less than successful?

Tips for Starting Class

""Excellence is an art won by
training and habituation."

— Aristotle"

14 Focus on the learners, not the presentation.

Background

I spent days perfecting my presentation in one of my earliest training sessions. Every nuance was rehearsed, and the verbiage accompanying every slide was deliberately composed. After much rehearsal, I felt I had perfected it. The slides were compelling, and the stories were well thought out.

Figure 19: It's difficult to see this reaction when your focused on yourself.

Then came the morning of the class, which was a live on-site session. After slide number fifteen, I could see the pain on the attendee's faces. It was grueling for them. I could see they were eager to do something, anything other than listening to me recite slides almost word-for-word. My focus was entirely on the presentation as a whole. But was I meeting my marks? Did I tell the story correctly? Did my voice have inflection at the proper times? All of my energy was on the presentation. None of my energy went toward the learners. I can't call them participants because they sure weren't participating!

How to do it

As I slowly realized this, I decided to take a break. I gave myself a half-time pep talk! When I returned to the classroom, I hid a few slides and made a simple decision: focus on the learners, not the presentation. I didn't disregard the slides entirely; I still showed a pertinent slide from time to time. The shift in focus to the learners was dramatic. At first, it caught them a bit off guard, but they all, one by one, came on board quickly and enthusiastically. I asked probing questions, solicited opinions, and cut all lectures short in favor of hands-on exercises. If I didn't have a hands-on activity, for example, when presenting a demonstration, I made it a hands-on exercise. I asked a student to come up and finish the demonstration that I had briefly started.

Challenges

- What specifically do you do that puts the focus on the learner?
- Is it always appropriate to put the focus on the learner?

Open your virtual classroom one hour before the official start time of the class.

Background

After nearly 30 years of training (for vocational schools, community colleges, university extension programs, corporations, and more), I've come to realize, somewhat to my surprise, how often students are nervous about attending class. Now add to that the fear of having equipment failures. Today's learners have to be sure their cameras and mics work, that internet connections are reliable, and that they have all required software for class. It's a lot to think about on top of an already busy work schedule. Many students arrive early to test their equipment. By not opening your classroom early, you deprive learners of this opportunity.

Equally important are your tests. Going through your preflight checklist (see tip 1) often depends on having the classroom open and ready, ideally before students arrive.

I like to test everything the day before class as well as to open class one hour early, mainly for the students' benefit. Even though I've already tested my equipment, I know from experience that what worked yesterday may fail today. I'm much more confident testing right before class as well as during the day before. Be sure to test your equipment long before the workday ends so that if you have to notify anyone of a problem, you're not in a panic about disturbing them after business hours.

Technology

Set the alarm and then set a backup alarm! When I used to travel for training engagements, I often used my cell phone as an alarm clock, putting it across the room from my bed, setting the alarm by the hotel alarm clock, *and asking for a wake-up call*! Wouldn't you know, my internal alarm clock would ring before all of the others almost 100 percent of the time!

Challenges

- What special tips have you created to ensure you're on time for class?
- How often do your participants arrive early?

Make a first impression that deliberately conveys a positive and welcoming message.

Background

We all want to make great first impressions. Trainers, in particular, understand the impact of the first few minutes on the remainder of the class. I know you all strive to make that first impression a great one!

Some of my earliest classes included a lot of mumbling, fumbling, and rambling about my background and credentials. In hindsight, I realize I was reading technical training material and trying to shoehorn it into my personal style and against my better instincts.

These class introductions occurred during live, on-site instructor-led training. I'm glad I struggled through that period because it taught me a lot and provided an excellent foundation for transferring to virtual instructor-led training. I learned from watching my students during these rambling introductions that I was setting the wrong tone for the next five days. They arrived eager to learn, and I delayed the learning process. I also made the class about me and not them. Add more than a few irrelevant slides (yes, even the course-objective slides), and you have a recipe for disaster. My poor students. "When is the training ever going to begin," they must have thought.

Eventually, I summoned the courage to ask my students how they'd like a class to start. What could an instructor do or say that would make them feel eager to participate, comfortable, and confident in their decision to attend my class? Almost unanimously, their answers contained some form of the statement, "Start quickly!"

In addition to that statement, I've learned that there are several things my students want to know pretty quickly after they arrive:

- Will I be bored today?
- Will I learn what I need to learn?
- Will I have a say in any of this training?

Whatever I can do or say to answer these questions as quickly as possible will set the right tone for the remainder of the class. Remember, you can't not make a first impression. What do you want yours to be?

As soon as students arrive, engage with them, giving them a warm and friendly welcome. Make it short and quick, leaving them with time to set up and get comfortable. Let them know you'll check on them again before class starts.

If a student arrives late, put them at ease immediately. Remind them not to worry; you'll get them caught up at the next break (and be sure to keep your promise). This simple statement not only eases the mind of your late arrival, but it lets the rest of the class know that they're in a safe place, and you'll lend a hand with them as needed.

Everything you say after this point should evoke a welcoming environment. Immediately inviting learners into the conversation can help set the tone for engagement.

How to do it

While preparing for a train-the-trainer session, I sought the help of motivational speaker Lou Heckler. Lou was well versed in the technical training arena as his son is the owner of Accelebrate Inc., a technical training firm based out of Atlanta, Georgia. The session's theme was "From good to great," and the goal was to get already excellent trainers into the realm of greatness and near-perfection.

Lou gave me an extensive reading list that I soon discovered included more than a few books about hospitality. What an inspiration that was! What a perfect way to make a first impression and set learners' expectations regarding their instructor for the day: I'm here for you, I'll help you in any way possible, and I'll be patient as you learn this new material.

In *Setting the Table: The Transforming Power of Hospitality in Business*, restauranteur, and CEO of Union Square Hospitality Group Danny Meyer shares about his successful restaurants through the lens of feedback and criticism. Throughout the book, we learn how he leverages focus groups with a select group of chefs, general managers, and a few loyal clients. Constant feedback from restaurant guests combined with self-acknowledged hubris leads to numerous changes that turn fledgling restaurants into flourishing establishments bursting with excitement. By soliciting feedback, Mr. Meyer uncovers many flaws from lack of preparation and seating issues to wine selection, late reservations, and more.

One compelling and consistent theme throughout his career is the distinction he's made between service (as the technical delivery of a product) and hospitality, which he defines as a dialogue.

"To be on the guest's side requires listening to that person with every sense and following up with a thoughtful, gracious, appropriate response. It takes both great service and great hospitality to rise to the top."[22]

This quote resonated with me, and it's the motivation behind this tip: to make a great first impression, you must first put yourself in the learner's shoes and identify with how they feel from the moment they step into your virtual classroom.

It's been proved that while some stress at the time of learning may enhance memory formation, stress impairs memory retrieval.[23] This is why it's so important for trainers to create a relaxed and safe environment for learning. . A surprising number of students arrive at our training sessions with a fair amount of stress. Many will admit to sometimes feeling out of control and captive with no way out.

We need to dispel these thoughts as quickly as we can. Let attendees know that they have a say in what will occur during the learning. Let them know that their feedback is not only welcome but required regarding course content, length and frequency of breaks, and how we can all help one another learn.

Greetings like the following can help convey the right message (feel free to expand on this greeting but be sure you allow yourself enough time for any additional responses from the student). "Good morning, Anne! Welcome to class."

Be sure to send the message via the chat window to everyone and by name. I've found it helpful to send these greetings privately. I discovered this after realizing that some students use this opportunity to express any preclass anxiety. Personally and privately greeting participants gives them the chance to be more forthcoming.

A personal and private greeting is also my attempt to re-create the live instructor-led, on-site experience. Typically, I've lingered by the classroom's front door and greeted the students as they've arrived. I let them settle into their seats undisturbed while they boot up their laptops or get acquainted with their workstations.

Once I see that they're settled in, I stop by and ask them how their morning is going. Before I leave, I ask them if they have any questions or concerns about setting up and getting ready for the class. I repeat this process for every new

---

22 D. Meyer, *Setting the Table*, (New York: HarperCollins Publishing), p. 65.
23 S. Vogel, L. Schwabe, "Learning and memory under stress: implications for the classroom," npj Science Learn 1, 16011 (2016). https://doi.org/10.1038/npjscilearn.2016.11.

arrival at a slow, deliberate pace. If you move too quickly, it looks like you're making a polite gesture instead of actively seeking to know their concerns. You must show them you have time for them and any concerns they may have) right then and there. This type of greeting is admittedly a bit more challenging in a virtual class, but it can be done.

The science

Do you remember the role the hippocampus plays in both learning and re-call? If not, reread "A Brief Overview of What Happens to Your Learners while You Teach" in the introduction. Now consider the impact stress has on students as they arrive to class uneasy.

"While moderate stress can improve memory formation, severe or chronic stress can produce the opposite effect. Chronic childhood stress is associated with memory impairments in adulthood[5], while chronic exposure to stress or glucocorticoids has been shown to produce spatial memory impairments in laboratory settings[6,7]. These effects may be due to the damaging effects of stress on the hippocampus. Chronic stress and exposure to high amounts of glucocorticoids can reduce LTP [long-term potentiation]in the hippocampus and cause atrophy of the dendritic spines that these neurons use to receive signals from each other[8]."

Technology

Keep a text document available with common chat messages like your morning greeting. See tips 23 and 24 for the greeting for subsequent training days. See tip 80, which shows how to use software to send a single chat message to all participants simultaneously.

Challenges

- How do you start your classes?

- What is the first thing you say and the first thing you ask your students to do? How do you think these actions make them feel about the remainder of the session?

Engage your learners immediately at the start of class.

Background

If technical trainers had a genie that would grant them three wishes, many of them would wish for students who participate early and often and remain engaged for the duration of the class.

I've had countless conversations with trainers who bemoan, "Nobody was talking but me…Ugh!" A successful trainer is hyper-aware of each student's level of participation. I greatly admire the instructor who starts class and remains concerned whether it's a two-hour or two-week session. It's not an easy task, but you can make it easier on yourself by kickstarting the idea of near-constant engagement as quickly as possible.

How to do it

The quickest way to communicate any class message is to put it into action immediately. If you want your learners to talk during class, get them talking immediately. Send the message that asking and answering questions is not merely allowable; it's encouraged.

In the book *Financial Times Guides: Business Training*, authors Tom Bird and Jeremy Cassell ask the question: "Why is it that some trainers can engage a whole audience right from the start of a session and maintain that engagement throughout the training?"[24] The authors spent over 35 years working with organizations around the world to design and implement training programs. In their analysis of excellent trainers, they found the answer to that question involved a structure with two distinct features, "engaging all participants from the start and maintaining engagement for the duration of the training."[25]

There are several effective techniques for engaging students immediately. Asking the students to introduce themselves is perhaps the most common, and this is because it provides numerous benefits. (See tip 22 for some of the additional benefits of student introductions.)

Another way to engage students is to ask a thought-provoking question relating to the course topic. I like to use the chat window for this. After everyone

---

24   T. Bird, J. Cassell, *The Financial Times Guide to Business Training*, (Harlowe, UK: Pearson Education Limited)

25   T. Bird, J. Cassell, *The Financial Times Guide to Business Training*, (Harlowe, UK: Pearson Education Limited)

responds, I read the answers aloud to elicit more comments. I take the time to provide positive feedback for everyone's response. This interaction sets the tone that learners are significant contributors and their feedback is valuable. Be specific, not just complimentary. Tell each learner why their answer resonated with you.

Finally, you can conduct a poll so that you can use students' answers to help you prepare for future classes.:

- What does a typical day look like in your job role?
- What are some of the hardest things to learn about this subject?
- What skills would make your job easier?
- What should be taught to other people who will be doing what you do?

Bottom line: Encourage learners to do something immediately! It instantly sets the tone for the entire training engagement.

Challenges

- When is the first time you ask your students to do something?
- What do you ask them to do?
- Does your first request set the tone for engagement?

Provide your cell phone number at the start of the class.

Background

With so much on our plates while we conduct technical training, the last thing we want is an emergency. Those situations are often entirely out of our control, which is a feeling no trainer likes. We're managers; after all, we manage the content, learners, environment, and so on. Unfortunately, emergencies happen from time to time. While we may not be able to eliminate these situations, we can have a plan for when they occur. That plan begins with communication.

We teach in a time when there are many ways to communicate with our clients. We have software like Slack, chat apps, and of course, good old email. Without access to the internet, these methods will fail us. Even a telephone landline can go offline during a storm, and a cell phone is the closest thing we have to a fool-proof form of communication.

Storms, power outages, equipment failure, and more can cause a loss of internet access, leaving your learners confused and unsure of what to do next. I've experienced a power outage on more than one occasion. Immediately following the power outage, I received a text message from one of my students. I told him the situation, and we made a plan. He forwarded that information to the class, and I was back online shortly after that. In the meantime, I could rest assured that the students had an activity to work on while I was offline. It would not have been impossible for my students to reach me if I hadn't provided my cell phone number, but it would have taken a team of individuals to relay the message.

How to do it

Provide your cell phone number via the chat window at the first class meeting. Ask at least one attendee to write it down. Verify that the student will be the official caller and keep your number in case there's ever a problem. You may want to designate an alternate student who will also note your cell phone number.

Technology

Be sure to have your cell phone fully charged and ready for class. Don't forget to add this task to your preflight checklist.

Challenges

- Have you ever lost internet access during class? What happened?

- How did your students manage the situation?

- Was there a protocol in place?

- Did you have the correct client contact information to relay to all what was happening?

19 Set expectations regarding student behavior (and add this to your preflight checklist).

Background

Can you recall a positive experience you had as a student at any age? Try to remember what made the experience so pleasant for you.

My wife's favorite teacher was her first-grade teacher, Miss Honey. When I asked her what made Miss Honey so unique, she found it challenging at first to put it into words. She quickly recalled many attributes, most of which began with a pleasing smile and the ability to respond positively to even the unruliest children. She'd gently remind a particularly rebellious child of how things are done as if the child had merely forgotten the rules as opposed to willfully disobeying them. Each day, my wife remembered, started as if taken for granted that it would be a wonderful day full of positive experiences, and that positivity emanated from Miss Honey.

I've had similar experiences right up through adulthood in training classes taught by experienced professionals. We may not have wild students running about our classroom wreaking havoc, but we do encounter circumstances that can derail our class right from the start. Faulty equipment, attendees who haven't met the prerequisites, difficult attendees of all kinds, internet problems, and more can lead to a shaky start for any class. If we can remember to respond positively and convey that positivity, it not only puts everyone at ease, but it also puts everyone in the right frame of mind for learning.

Miss Honey had a lot of rules, and she delivered them directly but with kindness and respect. The one implied rule was that the children would have a wonderful time once made aware of the expectations. Our adult learners, of course, are not children, but they do benefit from knowing what is expected of them. As adults, they should have a say in classroom guidelines and expectations as well.

See tip 19 for information about learners' expectations. This tip will pay dividends throughout your session.

How to do it

So, what do I mean by "student behavior"?

It's everything you need your students to do: ask and answer questions, provide feedback (positive and negative), participate in conversation with others, and so on. If you want engaged students, you absolutely must let them know how to engage with you as well as their classmates.

At the start of class, in no uncertain terms, let your learners know that you'll be asking questions and expecting responses from each of them. It's equally important to tell learners how to respond. I ask all my students to unmute and shout out an answer for short answers. I'll request they answer via chat for more extended and thoughtful questions. I then quickly identify the learner by name and read their response, give my feedback, and ask for more input from the students. I'll note anyone who hasn't answered a question and ask for their feedback directly. It's no longer me teaching the class now; it's the students themselves. I'm merely a facilitator. Remember, you are instructing adults who have a vast array of knowledge, and they have valuable input that could benefit everyone.

I also set expectations around using the webcam, both mine and theirs. I explain the how, when, and why of my webcam use. We then agree to their webcam use.

We briefly discuss the microphone and confirm those users who are not in a position to unmute. For those instances, we produce a reasonable alternative for answering questions, often the chat window.

Another area that would benefit from some ground rules is how to get the most out of lab exercises. I've learned from my students that it's best to spend a few minutes setting expectations for activities to avoid confusion. My courses consist of the following exercise categories: guided, practice, challenge, extra credit, and homework. Students find it helpful when I let them know that they'll be doing the guided exercises with me. The practice exercises are for outside of class, such as during breaks. They do the challenge exercises entirely independently, but we'll review them together. Extra credit exercises are for fast learners who complete the challenges with time to spare, and homework exercises are for the learner to complete before the next class.

Finally, I lay some reasonable ground rules for stepping away from your computer during class. Typically, this is simply a request to let me know via chat that you're stepping out. This simple announcement makes all of us accountable for our presence in class, and, of course, I promise to do the same.

Just one or two reminders of these expectations at the appropriate moment are typically all that's needed to get the class off on the right foot. The students now freely and confidently participate thereby getting the most benefit from the course.

When setting expectations, remember these two points:

- Setting expectations is a two-way street. Be sure to remind your students that their expectations for you are equally important. You can do this by reminding your learners that you consider the goals they stated during the student introductions to be their expectations of you and the course content. At this time, it can be helpful to ask via the chat window if they have any other expectations for the course.

- Expectations should always be learner-centric, and they have to be doable. In other words, you have to maintain these expectations throughout the session. Be sure to keep them reasonable in terms of time constraints, predefined course objectives, and so on.

Remember that you are collaborating with adults, and they appreciate it when you respect their prior experiences.

Note: Start class with a promise; a promise that you will engage and encourage learners throughout the class, you will hold their interest and make it fun. Encourage them to remind you to make good on your promise. In short, expectations go both ways!

Challenges

- How would you expect your students to behave if you were describing the perfect class? What type of interactions would you find ideal?

- How do you communicate these expectations to your learners?

- How do you make your learners aware of the benefits of these expected behaviors?

- How do you encourage learners to ask questions?

20 Always wait until everyone is ready before beginning class.

Background

Trainers are an enthusiastic bunch, eager to share our knowledge and increase worker productivity. So many of my colleagues have shared with me the sense of satisfaction they get from knowing that their career choice has genuinely changed the lives of their learners. I've personally had students from many of my public open-enrollment classes email me to tell me how the knowledge they acquired in the class took them from unemployment to a well-paying job.

One student told me he could leave a position he held for over ten years where he used an old and obsolete technology (he was kept in that position because he was the only one who knew the technology). His class skills allowed him to stay at the company he loved but with a new, challenging, and exciting position.

Figure 20: If we could see the student that wasn't ready when we started, he'd look like this guy.

Sometimes we're so eager to get started we forget that our learners may not be ready! No one likes to be left behind or to be busy setting up while the rest of the class takes off without them. It's incredible how many classes I've witnessed in which an instructor starts an exercise only to have several students chime in that they weren't ready due to a software or materials issue. I learned this lesson when I walked around the room to check on everyone and found three students who had not even started the exercise that everyone else had completed. When asked, they all said, I wasn't ready when you started and couldn't catch up.

This lack of preparation can be incredibly frustrating to motivated students ready to begin. This delay causes those learners to check out, such a class isn't only mismanaged; it's not being managed at all. Now the instructor has to reengage those students and reset expectations to counter lost momentum. While this may seem trivial—especially if you can get the student up and running in less than a minute—it can still take a toll on learners. We must control every aspect of virtual training that we can, knowing that there will always be issues beyond our control that impact the success of the course.

I've been guilty myself of forgetting this essential but straightforward check. That's why I add it to my preflight checklist!

How to do it

Ensure all students have answered the question below affirmatively in the chat windows.

They must type yes or no so you can quickly review the responses and make sure everyone is ready:

- They have the required software.
- They have the courseware they need.
- They have all the course-related materials at hand.
- They can access another browser window if needed.
- You can do a mic and webcam check when they introduce themselves and also use this time to confer with anyone who had earlier video or audio difficulties.

Challenges

- What do you say or do to ensure that everyone is ready to begin class?
- How do you get feedback?
- Is your method foolproof?
- What can you do in advance of class to help unprepared students?

21 Complete a flight check with your students.

Background

Many years ago, during one of my first virtual outings, I'm sorry to say that I began a lesson by lecturing nonstop for almost ten minutes. This class was pre-Zoom and long before the great virtual classrooms we have today. Unfortunately, no one could hear me. How embarrassing! Admittedly, it's unlikely that is going to happen to you now, but just in case, I conduct a preflight checklist with my students. I'm not just checking my equipment at this time, but I'm creating an opportunity for attendees to check their equipment as well.

How to do it

Confirm that all students can hear you and see your webcam and screen. Also make sure that your screen is an appropriate size.

Introducing a slide devoted to this is perfect because it serves several purposes:

- Firstly, it quickly informs your learners what's happening. Remember, even if people turn away from the screen very briefly, it's enough time for them to miss pertinent information in the virtual environment. Or they may have missed your last statement because they're having audio issues or there are too many distractions in their environment. Students stepping away is a compelling reason to have a slide deck so that you can display a slide while students are working on a lab or taking a break. Should a student briefly step away from their screen, they can simply read the slide upon their return and know what is going on.

- Secondly, it provides reinforcement early in the class that issues will be addressed in real time. This slide is also an ideal time to ask your students if they'll be missing any portion of the class due to prior commitments, meetings they have to attend, or personal matters. Note these commitments and provide each learner with a time before the next session when you can bring them up-to date regarding what they missed.

Technology

See tip 80 for more details on your classroom hardware and software.

Figure 21: A slide showing flight-check questions.

Challenges

- What do your learners need in order to participate in class?

- How do you confirm with your learners that they're ready to partici-pate in class?

- Have you explained all of the communication methods available in the classroom such as a question box, chat window, emoticons, and hand raising?

Help students introduce themselves quickly by focusing on relevant questions.

Background

Farmers Insurance provides an excellent example of the effectiveness of structuring questions during student introductions. The renowned insurance company offers an extensive training program: "When participants first arrive, they're assigned to a red, blue, or green group. The red group is instructed to go **meet people** in the room. The blue group is instructed to go **learn three things about somebody** in the room. The green group is instructed to **ask another member of the class about his or her family, prior occupation, favorite forms of recreation, and what he or she enjoys most**. When the class reconvenes, they share what they have learned about others, and it is quickly evident that the green group, which had a structure for talking to others, learned much more than did their peers."[26] [Added emphasis is mine.] The information gleaned is hereafter referred to as FORE (family, occupation, recreation, enjoys), and it's used throughout the remainder of Farmers Insurance training.

These are some of the questions I use during student introductions:

- What background do you have with the topic of our class?
- What are your goals for after class?
- What would make the next five days a success for you?
- What can we cover that makes your investment of time worthwhile?

I always have students introduce themselves. I made this decision after a few huge classes with over 25 students. I felt there wasn't enough time for lengthy introductions. I found that the entire class felt "off" to me. I lost confidence in my ability to reach learners based on their past experiences because I didn't know their past experiences. Ultimately, I learned more about them as the class went on, but that was time-consuming too, perhaps more so than it would have been if shared in the first class.

It can be tempting to skip the introductions for very large classes. But instead of ignoring them entirely, I suggest spending more time during the preclass needs assessment. There are several ways we can get the information we need:

26 P. Brown, H.L. Roediger III, M.A. McDaniel, *make it stick*, (Cambridge: The Belknap Press of Harvard University Press), p. 243.

- If possible, arrange a preclass conference call with all attendees or with a representative who knows the attendees well.

- Circulate a preclass questionnaire where the students can identify themselves by answering the same questions you would ask during in-class introductions.

- Create an online poll that queries the student's current skill set and background.

Most public speakers live by the simple mantra: know your audience. This is especially important when training adult learners. How can we use reference points that resonate with our learners if we don't know their backgrounds? Trainers need to use suitable analogies, something we can't do without knowing where our learners are coming from and what prerequisite knowledge they have. And there are numerous times when we can use this information in the ongoing struggle to engage our learners.

Consider the following comments:

> John, I know you write C++. Can you tell us how this code differs from how you might implement this feature in C++?

Repeat this with several of your attendees and you start an engaging dialogue. More often than not, learners will immediately engage with John and the group as a whole, indicating that John's analogy between the current language and his experience with C++ was beneficial to them.

Or there's this:

> Lee, you mentioned that you had solved this design problem with the only solution available to you two years ago. Do you think what we just learned could be used instead?

Once again, other learners with backgrounds similar to Lee's are invested.

There's no point in discussing topics already familiar to the group. How do I know what those topics are? We identified them in the student introductions at the beginning of the class.

How to do it

Consider gathering this information via the chat window, where you provide the topics that learners need to address (background experience, goals, and areas of interest). Students can answer the questions in the chat window as well.

Here are some excellent questions to put in the chat window for students to answer while waiting for all your students to arrive to the class:

- What does a typical day look like in your role (straight coding all day, scrum meetings, testing, and so on)?

- What are some of the hardest things to learn about for your current role (CSS and designing, unit testing, and so on)?

- What area of knowledge would make your job easier ? (e.g., I need to know more about async programming and performance; our website is really slow; I need to know more about normalizing tables, and so on.)

- What should be taught to people in your role?

During the introduction phase, use your notes page to jot down their background in the course topic (see tip 2 for information about taking notes as students introduce themselves). It can be helpful to simply jot down the letter next to their name using the chart on the followingn page

Abbreviations	Description
A	The student is aware of the subject matter and can recognize some terms and concepts.
F	The student is familiar with the subject matter and has some recall of several of the class topics.
C	The student is competent in the subject matter and recognizes gaps in his or her knowledge and understanding but can apply that knowledge capably.
M	The student has mastered the material and can transfer his or her knowledge to others.

Technology

Use a word cloud from Slido.

Go to https://www.sli.do/ and create an account.

Create a word cloud via the instructions at https://tinyurl.com/48xc5dxp.

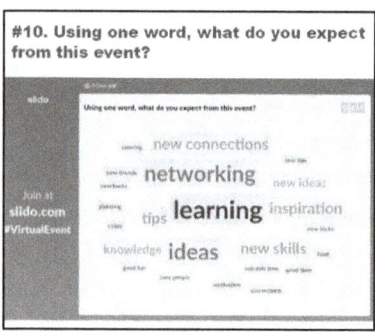

Figure 22: A word-cloud example from Slido.

Challenges

- What would you like to know about your learners before class starts?
- How will you get the information you need from your learners?
- Do you poll students regarding their subject matter knowledge *before* lecturing?

Start your class with a welcoming and professional message.

Background

Think about an online seminar that you attended that you especially liked. How did it start? What was it that made you feel you made the right decision by joining? Did it have a professional look that made you think the presenter made you feel welcomed and well-informed about the schedule and was also respectful of your time? These small nuances have a profound effect.

Whether your virtual classroom uses sophisticated broadcasting software like Open Broadcaster Software (OBS) or simply screen sharing for a PowerPoint presentation, you can implement this tip. You can show a simple graphic at various times right before class begins. Use your creativity and make sure that your welcome graphic accomplishes the following:

- Students feel welcomed because the graphic is positive and inspiring.

- The students know they're in the right place because you are showing the course title and, if appropriate, a description of the audience. Example: "Welcome to Introduction to Python for Data Scientists."

- Let them know how much time they have before class starts. My students have told me time and again how much they appreciate seeing a timer (not only at the class start but during all breaks). Your welcoming message shouldn't read: "Class will start in five minutes" because it doesn't answer the question "Five minutes from when?" or "Class will start at 9:00 a.m." without providing the presenter's time zone. Instead, use a timer as shown in the example below.

Technology

OBS graphics

One of the benefits of OBS is that you can create background graphics. You can choose to hide or show OBS scenes during your class. A scene may consist of a particular camera view, computer screen, background image, and the like. Each scene may contain sources including a video source (such as a camera), an audio source (such as a particular mic), text, a slideshow, a web browser, window capture, and more. A source may also be a simple graphic. This graphic can overlay any screen that you might be broadcasting. For example, you may have your webcam on and show a graphic that shows your name and some related class information when class starts, as shown in figure 23 (following page).

Figure 23: Lecture slide with background.

H2R graphics

H2R Graphics by Here to Record is software available for Mac or Windows that lets you lay graphics over your shared screen in virtual classrooms. You can use the free version or pay for the Pro version, which supports multiple projects and includes more graphics like timers and animations. They're ideal for lower-third graphics (shown above), ticker-type messages, animated timers, and more. Here are some sample graphics created with H2R Graphics.

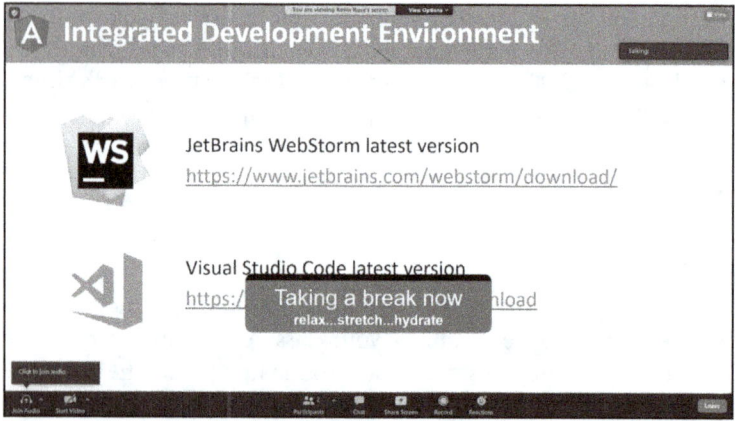

Figure 24: An H2R Graphics break message.

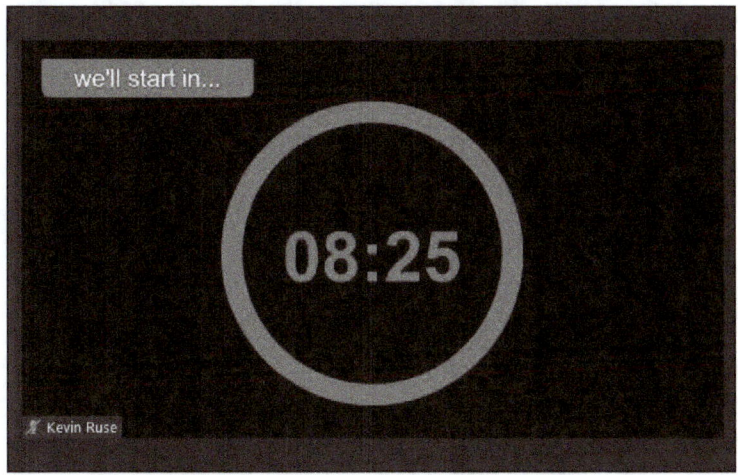

Figure 25: An H2R Graphics timer.

To get started with H2R Graphics, follow the steps below.

1. Visit https://h2r.graphics/ and download the software.

2. Launch the software to open the Launcher where you can change app settings and open a graphics project. You will store each graphic you'd like to display during class in a graphics project.

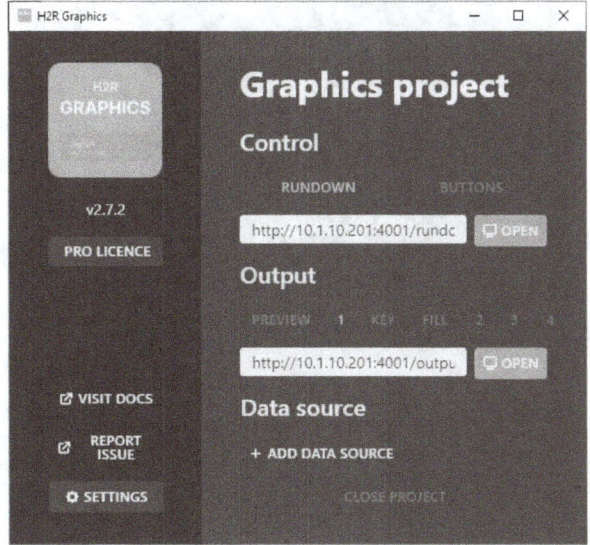

Figure 26: The H2R Graphics Launcher where you can open the Rundown and Button sections

3. First, you'll have to create some graphics in the Rundown section of the software (shown in Figure 27). You can learn more about Rundown at https://tinyurl.com/2nc38jsb.

    a. Click the plus sign to add a graphic. You can choose from Lower third, Image, ticker, Webpage and more.

4. Return to the Rundown screen where you can click on the left column to make the graphic visible on your screen while you teach. You can edit or delete the graphic from this screen as well. You can also select which video outputs can show the graphic.

    Note: you may import your own graphic files into H2R from the Media tab.

Figure 27: The Project Rundown window in H2R Graphics. Note the red rectangle indicating the Countdown timer is running and visible on the screen.

5. To avoid creating multiple graphics for multiple clients and classes, you can use variables such as a company or class name when you store text information. For more information about using variables, see https://tinyurl.com/ky96w43y.

6. You can learn more about using H2R with OBS at https://tinyurl.
   com/2p9da7k6. Here are the basic steps:

   a. Launch OBS and H2R Graphics.

   b. Open a project (the graphics project introduced above).

   c. Copy the output URL (see image below).

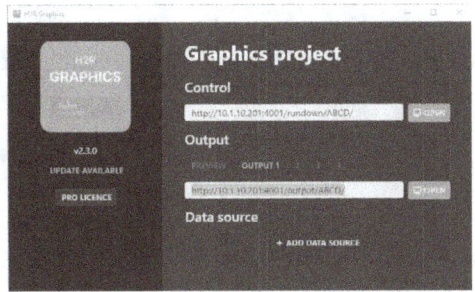

Figure 28: The Graphics Project showing the output and data source addresses.

   d. In OBS, add a new Browser Source to your scene, setting the URL
      of the source to the URL you just copied in step 3. Set the browser
      width to 1920 and the height to 1080. Then press the OK Button.

7. You can set the color of the output graphics in H2R settings under
   Output → Background Color.

You can learn more about using H2R with the ATEM mini-camera switcher
at https://tinyurl.com/2p94yekn. Here are the basic steps:

1. Connect your computer running H2R Graphics to your ATEM switcher. Typically, you can do this by running an HDMI cable from the
   computer and to one of the HDMI inputs on the ATEM.

2. Enable Extended Desktop mode on your computer.

3. Open an output window within H2R Graphics and drag it onto the
   extended desktop display (the window appears on your ATEM Multi-
   view.

4. Make that a full-screen window.

5. Next, you'll need to set the output window's background color. For the Chroma keying to work, the background of the output window must be green or some other solid color.

6. By default, the output's background color is set to green. You can confirm the setting by going to Settings > Outputs > Launcher.

7. Now open up ATEM Software Control and navigate to the palettes on the right.

8. Click on the on the Upstream Key 1 to expand the section and open the Chroma tab.

9. Set Fill Source to your H2R Graphics laptop or PC input you are using.

10. Open the Chroma Sample option and set the color to green by sampling an area.

11. Turn on Upstream Key 1 to see the graphics in action.

Challenges

- How do you greet your learners?
- Do you greet them individually or as a group?
- Do you greet them verbally or via the chat window or both?

Check in with all your students individually (via private chat) at the beginning of each class day.

Background

If we wait for end-of-class evaluations to help us course correct, it will be too late to benefit the learners we have now. That's why it's so helpful to get individual feedback from participants at the *start* of each class day. Once again, the chat window is very effective in eliciting candid and helpful critical feedback.

How to do it

Here are some examples of feedback questions to ask at the start of each class. I like to send these questions out to the group as they arrive and before everyone is in attendance:

"Hi Mary, how did class go for you yesterday?"

"Good morning Mike, how did class go for you yesterday? Did you learn anything you didn't already know?"

"Good morning Mark, how did class go for you yesterday? Did you learn anything you can apply in your current position?"

"Hi Christine, How did class go for you yesterday? Was the pace okay?"

Challenges

- How do you check in with your learners?
- How often do you check in?
- What specifically are you asking when you check in with your learners?

Use effective icebreakers.
(See tip 22 about student introductions.)

Background

Time is almost always of the essence during our training sessions. We never seem to have enough of it. Between managers who are reluctant to lose workers for a week's worth of training and tight budgets, class duration seem to get shorter and shorter. What should ideally be a 5 day class becomes a three day class. With that in mind, we must budget our class time like a financial budget with zero waste.

The teaching process begins with introductions, which can take up a lot of time in a large class. Many trainers and public speakers are taught to use icebreakers, which have been touted for years as an effective way to get conversations started. The implementations vary and can run fifteen minutes or longer; they include scavenger hunts and "people bingo" to posing simple questions about where attendees are from or a "fun fact" about themselves, their favorite hobby, and so on.

The effectiveness of icebreakers is debatable. According to Amina Temkin of the Center for Care Innovations, "Whether you're in a five-person department meeting or a multiday conference with hundreds, it seems that the activity designed to bring participants together and ease tension is the very activity that tends to drive most people's anxiety or boredom levels through the roof.[27] In short, Amena says that typical ice breakers don't work and are pointless and that people don't like them.

While I don't entirely agree with that sentiment, I do believe that, given time constraints, icebreakers must be brief and informative. I find the best ones are those that help facilitate the class after the learning has started. See tip 22 to learn how Farmers Insurance uses their icebreaker to gain valuable information that ultimately benefits the trainer and the trainees throughout the course.

How to do it

In tip 22, I provided some of the questions I use during student introductions. Here are some additional class start questions that are more akin to ice breakers.

---

27   A. Temkin, "Why Everyone Hates Icebreakers," *Customer Care Innovations*, Oct. 13, 2016, https://
www.careinnovations.org/resources/why-everyone-hates-icebreakers/

- What is your favorite part of your job?
- What is your least favorite part of your job?
- Briefly describe your most interesting project and what made it interesting for you?
- Tell us about the most recent roadblock you hit doing your job that represents why you think today's class will be beneficial?

Questions like the following can be beneficial:

- What is your favorite part of your job? What work task do you enjoy the most?
- How did you end up in your current job title?
- What is the most frustrating part of your technology?

Avoid ice breakers that add little value during the class. Try to choose content-related ice breakers but still allow for personal identification. A good ice breaker helps the trainer understand the learner's relationship to the course topic and enables a relaxed environment to share personal information.

Finding popular ice breakers and tweaking them a bit can be very effective. For example, a common ice breaker is the game "would you rather." By substituting technical terms you can learn a lot about your students. Example: "would you rather acquire data or process and clean the data?" Here's another one for software architects: "would you rather gather requirements or make high-level design choices?"

Challenges

- What is your favorite ice breaker?
- How long to your ice breakers typically last (per student)?

Tips to use during class

"I never teach my pupils; I only attempt to provide the conditions in which they can learn."

— Albert Einstein

Remind your students to stretch.

Background

I began my career as a typesetter and have been typesetting, writing, and coding for nearly forty years. I was diagnosed with tendinitis about five years ago, and it was only then that I hired a specialist to examine my office and work habits. He redesigned both to be ergonomically correct. Fortunately, today's generation of coders is well aware of the importance of a safe workplace.

I'm still tempted to escape my office environment occasionally and head toward the more scenic parts of my house like my balcony, deck, and so on. The pain quickly reminds me that I'm making a mistake.

I'm afraid the pandemic may catch many off guard. On my first physical therapist visit, he asked what caused the tendinitis, "There's always a reason," he proclaimed. Well, I wanted to ask him the same question! I'd been doing this for decades; why now? He was correct; there was a reason. I realized that for almost twelve months prior, I'd flipped my training-to-writing workload to 50 to 75 percent writing and 25 to 50 percent training. It took that period to tip my arms over the edge. Once I returned to a heavier training schedule, the pain subsided.

I've also developed bursitis in both shoulders that requires cortisone injections. Who knew typing was going to take such a toll on my body? I sure didn't. I'm hopeful when I hear students prioritize their health. Ergonomics is common knowledge today, and I'm happy about that.

How to do it

The last thing I want to get caught doing is preventing my students from exercising workplace best practices. Today's students are very knowledgeable about workplace safety and the toll their job takes on their overall health. Here are some stretch break reminders:

- Stand up and stretch your entire body.
- If your job involves a keyboard, be sure to stretch your arms and rotate your wrists.
- Check in with your body: are your neck, shoulders or wrists sore? If so, check out some ergonomic resources. Provide these resources to

the class in the chat window. See tip 80 for setting up hardware with chat messages that are ready to copy and paste.

- Focus your eyes on an object that's much further from you than your computer monitor.

Finally, don't forget to take care of yourself as well. Start class well-hydrated and maintain hydration throughout. Some instructors report benefitting from light full-body stretches before class.

- Consider hourly stretch breaks or try to incorporate them into your normally scheduled breaks.

Resources

- Mayo Clinic: Office ergonomics how-to guide https://tinyurl.com/48vcdstz

- Syntrio: The 4 P's of Creating an Ergonomic Home Office Workspace: https://tinyurl.com/2s3u4we4

- The BackStore: Do's and Don'ts of a workplace ergonomics: https://tinyurl.com/mpdprpaj

Challenges

- How do you encourage your learners to stretch?

- How often do you think it's necessary to provide this encouragement?

Make eye contact.

Background

Eye contact is something most trainers learn to apply quickly. It's common knowledge how effective it is at keeping learners attentive. Most of us have experienced people who don't make eye contact, and we know first-hand how uncomfortable it can be.

You can make this tip more effective by periodically scanning the room, looking at the attendees in the back, and so on. It's an easy skill to master during live, on-site instructor-led training, but it can be challenging to do in a virtual classroom mainly because of our virtual-training technology.

How to do it

A quick Google search provides numerous techniques for making eye contact using a webcam. Here are a few ideas for solving the eye-contact problem. (See Resources below for information about purchasing the equipment.)

- You can use a center cam that places the cam in the center of your screen. I find it distracting to see it on my screen, but it may work for you. It's a tiny camera that can be purchased or you can set up a complex DIY setup:
    - https://tinyurl.com/4b9rezym
    - https://tinyurl.com/5apajtuy
- You can use a teleprompter (https://tinyurl.com/mr2fv2fh).
    - Complex setup(https://tinyurl.com/hhxrypp5)
    - A bit easier (https://tinyurl.com/2p8b9rdj)
  You can use an iPad or tablet instead of the dedicated monitor used in this tutorial.

Resources

- Center Cam (https://www.thecentercam.com/)
- Glide Gear Teleprompters (https://glidegear.net/collections/tele-prompters)

Challenges

- How important do you consider eye contact?

- Have you ever taken an online class with a live instructor? Did they make eye contact?

- What do you do to ensure you make eye contact with your learners?

- In what part of the class do you think eye contact is most important? Lecture? Lab?

Ask for your student's attention.

Background

We've all experienced it—the student who fell asleep in our class! Yikes, how could this happen to me? I'm so entertaining and enthusiastic, not to mention suave and debonair! Yet there he snores!

At least during live on-site training, we can see who's asleep and address the situation. In one memorable class, I spoke to the student privately, and he apologized profusely, explaining that he commutes to work every day except Friday. The commute is three hours each way (four with traffic). Upon arriving home, he attends night school classes three days a week online and one day in person. Wow! My heart went out to him, and we decided to make a plan whereby I checked in with him periodically, which I did with complete empathy. He was an exception, but let's face it, paying attention is challenging even if you're passionate about the topic. If you have a "drowsy" student, it's far more helpful to have a discrete conversation than to address it during class.

Training classes can be everything from one to two hours total to several weeks or more. No matter the length of the whole class, our lessons can be structured to correspond to the learner's attention spans. Depending on what study you read, our attention span is five to ten minutes long. At that point, we tend to tune out and succumb to nearby distractions like email or chat. This study (https://tinyurl.com/5n8nxtv4) reports an attention span of seconds! While as this site (https://tinyurl.com/2vx6j7uc) suggests, there is more to understand about attention spans.

No matter which study you believe, we trainers seem to develop a sense of when a learner's attention is waning. It's a gut feeling we get, and we're often right! I believe that gut feeling is still a good indicator even during virtual training and with or without webcams.

How to do it

There are many different ways to address the problem, and you may already be practicing one or more of them. Many years ago, at a training seminar I attended, a demonstration I saw suggested that our learners only pay attention for about twenty minutes and only focus with awareness and understanding between seven to ten minutes of a lecture.

The obvious solution to me is to cease lecturing after ten minutes. Curbing lecture time is something I've tried to practice to the extent that I rarely have to think about it. I do glance at my desktop clock frequently while lecturing. If I'm past the ten-minute mark, at the very least, I'll start asking questions and encouraging comments and, at best, switch gears to a guided exercise, quiz, or something else. Course content sometimes prohibits us from changing gears at will (for example, perhaps the topic requires more content, and it's too soon to start an exercise).

At this same seminar, I was introduced to a technique called "the reset." Here's how it works.

The reset is simply any attention-getting device that sort of jolts your students out of their disengagement. Resetting can be achieved in many ways. You can, for example, use statements like these:

> "This next topic is important, so I'll wait half a minute in case anyone has to step away and then I'll begin."

> "How about a quick water or stretch break so we can hit this next topic refreshed and ready to go!"

Another reset method involves changing the environment of the learner. Prompting students to leave their computers to get a beverage is one way to accomplish this.

If I've lectured for more than ten minutes, sometimes I simply, without warning, stop talking. I wait for someone to tell me that I'm muted and then let them know that I was just checking on everyone!

In their technical trainer verification exam preparation book, *How to Be a Successful Technical Trainer: core skills for instructor certification*, authors Terrance Keys and Andrew R. Zeff recommend that "every couple of minutes we must prod people to participate. People want to be included in the process. A bystander will not cognate and think about the concept at hand nearly as much as a participating player." They go as far as to suggest the "we must solicit interaction every couple of minutes to keep the class moving ahead."[28]

A good rule of thumb is to deliver limited amounts of information; provide no more than can be absorbed and understood before adding more details. Again, student feedback at these times is critical. That's how you know you're delivering too much information or that it's time for a reset. Finally, a simple "May I have your attention, please" goes a long way!

---

28   T. Keys, A.R. Zeff, *How to be a successful Technical Trainer*, (New York: The McGraw Hill Companies), p. 174.

Technology

I have various sound effects at my immediate disposal (see tip 80 for more information about using a broadcasting system). Some are humorous, and others are just subtle noises that are excellent at getting everyone's attention. One of my favorites is the sound of crickets when no one is answering a question. I'll intentionally ask a question when I think I've reached the attention span limit, play the sound effect, and then announce a quick break, followed by an explanation as to why we're breaking and setting expectations for everyone's return. The whole reset takes about two minutes and should be delivered in a humorous and nonjudgmental manner.

Resources

- You can find free sound effects at https://www.audiomicro.com/free-sound-effects

Challenges

- What do you do to "reset" learners who may have lost interest or gotten distracted?
- What techniques do you use to get your learner's attention?

Make smooth transitions between showing your slide deck and showing a new screen such as your workbook or your software screen.

Background

Sometimes in our enthusiasm to share information, we inadvertently change screens too quickly or slowly or both in the same lesson. The problem is born directly from virtual training where it's common to have multiple windows open at once. In an attempt to be prepared, you open every window or file you might need access to teach the class, leaving you with extra windows to cycle through until you reach the correct one. Haphazard screen sharing looks unprofessional and makes the trainer appear unprepared.

Also, part of a smooth transition from one screen to the next is the logical transition between subject matter topics. Part of presenting a cogent lesson includes the successful closure of the previous lesson. This is especially important if one lesson builds upon another. It's equally valid when giving a high-level overview to transition to a deeper dive into the same material. It's also crucial to make that kind of transition as smooth and logical as possible: "Effective teachers achieve closure to their lessons. Effective teachers plan how to bring a lesson to a close and how to make the transition into the adjoining lesson."[29]

How to do it

One of the easiest ways to change screens with limited extra technology or software is to hide the "changing" part. One quick and familiar way to cycle through multiple windows on a Microsoft Windows machine is to hold down the alt key and tap the tab key. The first tap on the tab key displays a thumbnail view of your open windows. Attendees don't need to see that screen, so be sure that you're not sharing your primary screen because that's where the thumbnail appears. Subsequent taps of the tab key cycle through the screen thumbnails. When you then select a thumbnail, that screen appears for your learners. In this way, your learners don't see multiple screens flying or crawling by (depending on their internet connection), which can be very distracting.

---

29 N.L., Gage, & D.C. Berliner, Educational psychology, (1984), Boston: Houghton Mifflin.

In short, arrive in class fully prepared to change screens. If you intend to share a password-protected screen, make sure you have logged into that site before class begins. Likewise, if you want to share documents, have them open and ready to share before class. If you use multiple monitors, consider moving all the shared material to one monitor. If you share a website, be sure you've closed all unnecessary tabs and windows.

Note: You can set the main screen in Windows in Settings → Display as shown in the screenshot.

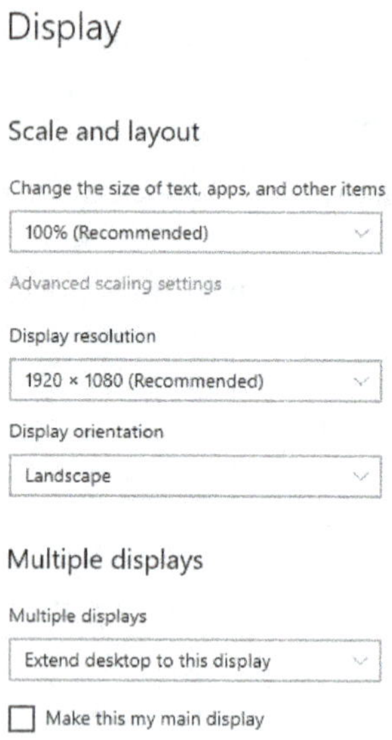

Display

Scale and layout

Change the size of text, apps, and other items

| 100% (Recommended) | ∨ |

Advanced scaling settings

Display resolution

| 1920 × 1080 (Recommended) | ∨ |

Display orientation

| Landscape | ∨ |

Multiple displays

Multiple displays

| Extend desktop to this display | ∨ |

☐ Make this my main display

Figure 29: Display settings in Windows 10.

Switching between slide deck slides

After teaching a class several times, I'll notice areas of content where the students have additional questions or demonstrate a lack of prior knowledge that I have assumed they have based on their background and experience. If I may or may not need supplemental material, I'll put the extra slides in the Appendix section at the end of my slide deck. When we reach the slide with the material that needs more explanation, I link that slide to the Appendix content. I leave the current presentation and move to the supporting materials slides with one click—the appendix slide links back to the original location in the slide deck; again, one-click back. For the students, this appears to be a seamless transition, and it presents much better than fumbling around for supporting material or bouncing around showing slides inadvertently while you try to find your way back to the original slide. Remember, in a virtual class, if you bounce from screen to screen or slide to slide, your students see it all at varying rates of speed based on their internet connections

Challenges

- How do you move from screen to screen?
- How do you share your screen? Do you share more than one screen?

Give recognition.

Background

One of the joys of completing a successful training session is reading the end-of-course student evaluations. Who doesn't like receiving a ten out of ten for their job performance? I'm sure our learners feel the same way, yet I'm still somewhat surprised at how effective simple recognition can be.

The American philosopher and psychologist William James said the "deepest principle in human nature is the *craving* to be appreciated."[30] He did not say we merely desire appreciation; he chose the word, crave. That's right, we crave it, and when we trainers supply it with sincerity and specificity, it's greatly appreciated. I've been in environments where I was pulled aside by more than one student who told me how much it meant to them to have their contributions noted and their opinions respected.

How to do it

We've all heard the expression, "Imitation is the sincerest form of flattery." One of the simplest ways to recognize students is to read aloud their answers in the chat window. Quoting students helps the trainer better manage time: students won't be answering verbally but will still be recognized for their contributions. During these times, I add "Good answer" or "Very well said" followed, of course, by the student's name.

The majority of the conversation in class is done verbally and outside of the chat window. There are numerous opportunities to provide recognition: during lab exercises, code reviews, debugging, and question and answer sessions. None of us would give false praise, but it can be easy to provide ambiguous or perfunctory praise. Our learners can sense when we're just being polite because our recognition lacks specificity. Phrases like "Great answer" and "Nice work" are phrases I use often, but I also try to include why I think it's a great answer or what it was about the task the student completed that was exceptional.

Providing this type of recognition comes with practice. You have to get used to thinking on your feet. An effective compliment begins with a genuine understanding of why you want to give the praise. What is it specifically that the student is doing correctly?

---

30   D. Webb, "All-About-Psychology.com," https://www.all-about-psychology.com/the-craving-to-be-appreciated.html

To understand what I mean, compare the following feedback.

Good	Better
Good answer!	Excellent answer, Ann; I really like how you focused on the problem before deciding how to fix it.
Nice catch!	That was excellent debugging, Pete. You saved a lot of time by using the tools supplied in the software.
I like the finished architecture. Very well done.	Lisa, I can see by the way you diagrammed the network that you'd complete the analysis quickly and thoroughly.

By being specific with your praise, you teach others what success in a given task looks like. It's just like the sales mantra: "always be closing; always be teaching"!

This tip goes beyond recognition, especially when a response seems "not worthy" of praise or is incorrect. Try to remember that most answers are seldom entirely wrong. We must try to find something positive about the response and note it.

Positive reinforcement encourages all learners to participate. Now is the time for encouragement. Sometimes, the only thing we can reward is the student's willingness to try, which is well worth rewarding. If you can, turn the negative into a positive. Guide the learner toward finding the correct answer on their own. If you must correct a wrong answer, point out what was positive about the response first.

Here are a few more tips on giving recognition:

- Mix up the times you give recognition. Don't be predictable by making a routine of it at a particular time in class.

- If you find yourself personally connected to the student's exemplary behavior, don't hesitate to let them know. I often teach long boot camps for new hires that last for a month or more. If you get to know the students well, there will always be examples of stand-out behavior such as helping other students or going above and beyond to contribute to their respective team members. It's typically not long after noting and encouraging this behavior that the rest of the group follows suit.

- Try to recognize a student's preferred method of affirmation. Some students would rather not be called out in front of the group, even for something positive. You may sense this by their behavior or response to your compliments. If this is the case, simply compliment them through private chat.

Challenges

- How do you reward learners for completing a successful task?
- How do you recognize correct answers?

Read the (virtual) room.

Background

Back in pre-COVID-19 days, we could read a room by glancing around from our podium. If that didn't work, we could wander amongst the attendees noting their facial expressions and, in some cases, what was on their monitors. We looked for body language from head to toe, and like me, I'm sure you all became very adept at sizing up your learner's mood and attitude. You learned to make on-the-fly adjustments based on rolling eyes, wandering feet, crossed arms, yawns, and so on.

In the virtual classroom, this is more difficult to do but still possible.

Figure 30: Reading the virtual room is challenging at best. Occasionally asking participants to turn on their camera's will help.

The challenge in either environment isn't necessarily an engagement problem but to find out what's causing the pain. Do they already know this material and are therefore bored? Ask them! Are they thoroughly confused? Ask them! Do they need more challenging material? Are they hungry? Do they just need a break? You get the idea—ask them! As a new trainer, I was initially very hesitant to do this. Little did I know that dealing with the elephant in the room was the fastest way to solve the problem, and my students respected it.

Scott Berkun, writing about public speaking, says, "It's impossible to teach well without learning something along the way. Good teachers listen as much as they talk, improving their material based on what they hear and studying to see if it had the positive effects they hoped. A bored teacher is merely someone who's forgotten he must keep finding ways to learn from his students, even if it's simply to learn where he has failed them as a teacher."[31]

Reading the virtual classroom is more challenging than reading the physical room. After all, a big part of "reading the room" is seeing our students. In the great webcam debate—should we or shouldn't we request that all webcams remain on at all times?—I'm in favor of noting my preference for keeping them on while showing respect for the learners who can determine for themselves when it's appropriate to turn the webcam on or off.

It's been said that "Zoom fatigue" isn't so much about seeing other learners' faces on a computer screen but seeing our own faces; knowing that we're always "on," can be stressful. There are times when a student wants to munch on a snack or sit at an unflattering angle, so at these times, they prefer to turn their webcam off. I tell learners that I'd like them to keep their cams on at the very least during introductions when they're asking questions and, after that, for as long as they're comfortable.

I also tell them why I feel this way and how we'll all benefit from this. At the same time, I defer to them and clarify that I respect their feelings. I remind them that I hope that when, from time to time, I ask them to turn their cams on for a group discussion, they feel comfortable complying. The trainer's webcam is equally important and subject to the same debate—do we keep our cams on for the whole class or just at certain times? Again, I prefer to turn it on when lecturing and as often as possible after that. I like to keep it off when the students are completing lab exercises so that I'm not a distraction. I also like turning it on and off for emphasis. See tip 53 about zooming in and out for emphasis while lecturing.

How to do it

So, absent a webcam, how do we read the room? Checking in with students is imperative. If we can't see a student, we may not sense their frustration. In this case, the virtual classroom might have an advantage over the physical classroom. Have you ever suspected a shy student is having difficulty but not letting you know? You sense the frustration, but you also feel the learner's fear of being discovered.

Being reluctant to share their exasperation is a handicap suffered by more adult learners than you might think. These students want to learn and are

31   S. Berkun, *Confessions of a Public Speaker*, (Sebastopol: O'Reilly), p. 136.

highly motivated, but their fear gets the better of them. It can be challenging to be discrete in the physical classroom. However, the virtual classroom provides an excellent solution: the chat window. A private chat can do wonders here. I've seen the positive reaction enough times to report positively that this technique works. Sometimes it works so well that the student feels safe enough to ask questions more often and verbally let me know if they're behind and need more time to catch up.

What are some other ways to read a room? Feedback is invaluable, and you must be specific about your concerns if you hope to read the room accurately. Here are some feedback questions that can help you read the room:

- How's the pace of the class? Too fast? Too slow? Just right?
- Was that last exercise a beneficial use of our time? Too easy? Too difficult?
- Rate that last lesson based on whether or not you learned something you didn't already know, on a scale of 1 to 5.

These are questions I frequently ask the group during live on-site training. I quickly discovered that students were far more forthcoming and helpful if I asked them privately. I made a habit of doing this every morning. I would walk around the room, kneel beside a student's desk, and ask how the previous day went for them. Standing above them seemed implicitly intimidating, and I decided that kneeling so that I was below them may have had an empowering effect on them. I would ask if there was anything they wanted me to do differently. Often the questions were tailored to the student. For example, when talking to a more experienced student, I'd ask, "Given your extensive experience, did you learn anything new? Are there any additional topics I can speak to that would make the class more valuable for you?" I now do this in the chat windows, and it's every bit as effective, if not more so virtually, than in an on-site training.

Technology

See tip 80 about keeping common chat questions ready to copy and paste.

Challenges

- What specific techniques do you employ to gauge the learner's understanding as you teach?

- What methods do you use to measure attention and engagement?

- How often do you deploy these methods?

32 **Practice active listening.**

Background

Do you have a favorite friend or relative that you confide in or from whom you seek advice? What is it about that person that makes you feel so comfortable? One of the traits that comes to my mind is that the person makes me feel genuinely heard. They listen with intent, and that intent is to understand me. They remain quiet while I speak, nodding in agreement as they come to understand what I'm saying.

If we wish to instill trust in our learners, we need to master this skill. Active listening is an absolute requirement for answering students' questions. Sometimes just the act of paraphrasing and clarifying can result in the learner answering their own question. That may be the ideal way to address learners' questions—let them answer them themselves!

One pitfall of teaching a topic for a long time is that you feel you can anticipate a learner's questions. I guess that's because we often can. But for the times we haven't anticipated the question but proceed anyway, often by interrupting the student, we can leave the student frustrated because they haven't been heard.

The vast majority of learners I've taught are incredibly polite and often don't complain at that moment. I began to realize this when a learner returned to a topic with a "new" question—I hadn't really answered or understood their previous question. Sometimes the student was very clear when returning to a previous topic, saying, "What I really meant to ask earlier was...." After a few such occurrences, I became convinced that I had a problem in this area and needed to fix it before it got even more out of hand.

How to do it

My first attempt to get better at active listening involved a four-step process:

- Make a mental note not to speak while a student is talking!
- Try not to subconsciously answer the question while a learner is still talking!
- Answer the question.
- Confirm with the learner that you've answered the question.

I did this many times until it became a habit. The only part I tweaked was the last step. It became mainly unnecessary to confirm with the student, except on those occasions where their body language or our follow-up commentary made me question whether I had indeed answered their question.

The art of active listening should involve the following characteristics:

- A nonjudgmental attitude
- Eye contact (see tip 27)
- An effort to clarify the learner's question
- Positive nonverbal feedback such as leaning into the camera and nodding your head in agreement

If you practice active listening, the entire class will also reap benefits because you'll have demonstrated a genuine interest in them and any challenges they might be experiencing. You send the message that you want to understand and are ready to help, all while building trust and establishing rapport with the entire group of learners.

Challenges

- How do you practice active listening?
- What specific actions do you use to let your learners know that you're listening?

33 **Remember that attendees are counting on you to manage the class.**

Background

I was a young instructor in my early corporate training days, often teaching attendees much older than myself. I come from a generation where respecting your elders is close to the golden rule. For this reason, difficult students who were significantly older than me were a challenge. This scenario was especially tricky when the class didn't include a supervisor or manager.

Did this make me the de facto manager for the day? I wasn't sure. Managing students is not the only issue we trainers might encounter. Frequently, it's the management itself that presents the problem. I've had students leaving the classroom repeatedly because their bosses kept calling them out of the room via email requests. In some cases, I learned from the students that management was against holding the training in the first place.

If you experience something like this, keep in mind that as soon as students leave their normal workplace and arrive in your class, they expect you to be in charge and to lead. Let's not disappoint them.

Initially, I avoided confronting situations that were clearly detrimental to the students but seemingly beyond my control. I did that at my peril. There were occasions when the client voiced dissatisfaction with the training results on the post-class follow-up call. I learned pretty quickly that these situations were indeed my responsibility. I learned to solve the problem by escalating the situation to those in charge of the training. If you're a contract trainer, you can discuss the problem with the training company that hired you. Either way, issues that arise that hinder the success of the class must be dealt with and quickly.

How to do it

I encountered a situation like this once on a trip to Florida. I was teaching application development for a medical company working on a sizeable and very critical datacentric application. In attendance was the entire web application development department. As the students began leaving the room, first one, then two, then three, I stopped class immediately. I approached the team lead (who, surprisingly, was not one of the students who left) and asked if there was a production issue. I suggested that perhaps we should take an early lunch or break. He told me to wait while he looked into the matter.

Indeed, a significant server issue had arisen and needed to be dealt with, and it was an all-hands-on-deck situation. We planned to end class immediately, and I proceeded to spend a delightful afternoon at the beach. We agreed to resume class with a new schedule that would allow us to make up the missed hours. I stayed later than expected each day and made myself available earlier than usual.

Successful technical trainers are flexible and accommodating. We have one shot at making our training successful, and sometimes issues arrive that are beyond our control. My patience was rewarded with more classes from this client, and the purchaser made it clear that my willingness to work with them through this production issue made all the difference.

Managing students can be challenging, but this tip's focus isn't necessarily just to address difficult students or adverse situations. The good listeners, the enthusiastic and engaged learners, the robust company processes, and so on should be perhaps not only managed, but leveraged as well.

As trainers, we may begin our class in the leader role, but the sooner we change that role to the facilitator, the better. We show respect for our adult learners when we defer to those students who take a leadership role by offering suggestions or helping us understand how the material being taught relates to the company.

In short, our learners are equal to us in the role of trainer and typically have more knowledge than we do about the company's inner workings, products, and services. You can leverage this information and encourage quieter learners, make more connections that reinforce learning, generate enthusiasm, and much more.

The "sage on the stage" is sometimes exactly what a group of learners need; it can also be the dreaded instructor who drones on and on, never coming up for air and leaving little room for participants to engage. Remember, our students/attendees are called participants for a reason—be sure to let them participate! And do that, not just once or twice a day but as often as *practically* possible.

See tips 54 and 55 for more information about encouraging participation.

Challenges

- Have you ever experienced any classroom management disasters?

- Who did you think was at fault?

- How did you fix the issue on the spot? This is different from the question, "How did you overcome the issue so your students never experience the problem again."

Lighten the mood with humor.

Background

I wouldn't be the least bit surprised to learn that some of my fellow trainers are stand-up comics—they're genuinely that funny. If you're laughing, you're happy, and if you're happy, you're probably free of stress. Stress is a learning blocker. You can still learn while stressed, but it typically won't last. In the worst-case scenario, your cognitive abilities are impaired by stress, and you simply can't learn the material. In addition, everyone appreciates a little fun in an otherwise dense technical training session.

How to do it

But I'm just not funny, Kevin! How can I make my students laugh?

Adding humor to training is a difficult tip to write because humor can be subjective. What's funny to some is not amusing to others, and the last thing we want to do is offend. If you're funny, you probably know it, so just master the art of being funny in a very safe, PG sort of way. Also, humor that's not at anyone's expense is a must.

Even if you think you're not funny, you can probably tell a joke or two. Computer jokes, also known as "geek jokes," are kind of like dad jokes: they're corny but they work.

This website (https://tinyurl.com/a56m9ayt) offers the following:

- How many programmers does it take to change a light bulb? None, because it's a hardware problem.

- How many types of people are there in the world? There are ten types of people in the world: those who understand binary and those who don't.

And here are a few more that I've picked up from other jokesters I know:

- There are only two hard things about computer science: cache invalidation, naming things, and off-by-one errors.

- Why do Java developers wear glasses? Because they don't C#.

- Why did the programmer quit his job? Because he didn't get arrays.

- What is the most used language in programming? Profanity.

- How do you know when two functions have broken up? They stop calling each other.

- Why did they break up in the first place? They were having constant arguments.

You don't have to be a comedian to inject humor into your class because being funny isn't the same as having fun, and we should strive to have fun in class. Having fun means being able to laugh at yourself. We trainers always make mistakes during class. Rather than trying to hide or excuse them, which never works anyway, give the group a laugh at your expense. Fix the problem and move on. The mistake you made will soon be forgotten, but the feeling of fun and levity will continue.

I challenged the students with a complicated problem in one of my boot camps. If they got it right, I would dance for them. That dance was pretty funny, and we all got a good laugh! We know that unhappy employees are less productive than they could be; unhappy learners are the same—they learn less and thus make the session far less valuable.

Humor that's related to the training is the best. Sometimes I'm just in the groove, and I manage to adlib a funny story related to the current topic. If it lands and I'm successful, I make a note of it, eventually refining that story like a professional comedian until I can tell it with ease. The best part is the students never forget that part of the lesson and often remind me by repeating the punchline at the appropriate time.

So, feel free to cut loose and have fun. Your learners will benefit, and the class will be far more enjoyable.

Challenges

- How do you introduce humor into the classroom?

- What type of humor is inappropriate?

Tell students when you need a minute to prepare.

Background

I think most trainers would agree that most of our learners are polite, patient, and respectful students. That's why the "difficult student" story can be so interesting to us, because it's a rarity.

Sometimes I forget just how patient students can be and, as a result, I may fumble around for a document on my desk or a file on my system, assuming I can find it much faster than I really can. If I mute my microphone to avoid the noise, the learners silently wonder what's happening. Did they lose their internet connection? Has their speaker stopped working?

How to do it

I have to remember how patient my learners are and, just as importantly, show respect for both their time and their patience. It's much easier and more respectful to simply let your students know that you'll need some time to prepare the next lesson. If possible, it's best to let them know precisely how much time. If it's just a minute or two, let them know that. If it's longer, consider taking a break.

Be sure to announce what you're preparing and when you expect to be ready. Having a slide or an H2R graphic ready to display on the screen can be very helpful. Combined with a stream deck, you're one button away from showing the students a graphic that lets them know you're preparing a file and will be ready in one minute. Make a habit of explaining to your students why you'll be disengaged.

Technology

See tip 80 for more information about using a stream deck.

See tips 23 and 45 for more information about displaying on-screen graphics with H2R.

Challenges

- What specific situations might cause you to leave your computer for a moment?

- What specific situations might cause you to lose focus and attention on the class for a moment while remaining at your computer?

- How can you let your learners know what's happening?

Show students where to find emojis.

Background

Imagine you're teaching a class and not only can you not see your students' faces, but also, their voices are streamed through a device that makes them sound like robots. With absolutely no visual or audio feedback, how could you possibly know how participants are feeling? They could be delighted with your lecture style, frustrated with an exercise, or experiencing any number of human emotions.

Fortunately, teaching virtual classes doesn't remove all traces of feedback from participants. We can see, hear, and infer mood from the learner's responses. I wonder how often trainers ask themselves, "How are my students feeling right now?" Maybe we sense something is wrong, but we're not sure.

I'm guessing trainers ask that question of themselves frequently but rarely ask the attendees. I've found it very helpful to ask attendees point-blank: "Please let me know how you're feeling in the chat window, privately if you prefer."

One of my favorite speakers, Dr. Ray Jimenez, is fond of saying, "Show me some love!" or "Maybe you're feeling frustrated; either way, let me know!" I like to use Dr. Jimenez's prompts right before a break and give students an extra three minutes of break time to respond.

The problem is that the virtual environment can remove us from direct knowledge of the learners' moods. One way to solve this problem is the use of emojis. Emojis are small digital images that express an idea or an emotion. Many emojis represent emotions like happiness, confusion, frustration, and more. Show your learners how to locate emoji's within the learning environment. Typically, you'll find emojis available in the chat window.

How to do it

Encourage learners to use emojis, when you ask certain questions. Here are some examples.

- How is everyone feeling? Tired? Ready for a break? Want to plow ahead? Respond with an emoji.

- Is everyone done with the exercise or are you still working or have questions? Respond with a thumbs up.

- Was that last exercise a good use of our time? Respond with a thumbs up.

Technology

When you ask them how they are feeling about a specific topic, encourage learners to use their emoji's.

Adobe Connect

1. You can access emojis on a Windows computer with this keyboard shortcut. Press the Windows and Period keys concurrently to access the Emoticon dialog box.

2. You can now scroll through the emojis and select one.

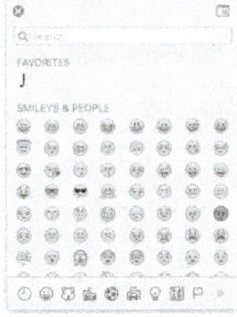

Figure 31: Adobe Connect emoticons.

Zoom

You can access emoticons on Zoom:

1.   In the Chat tab, select a chat thread.

2.   Hover over the message to which you want to react and click the Reaction icon.

Figure 32: https://tinyurl.com/yc4v6m7v.

3.   Select an emoji. It will appear below the message.

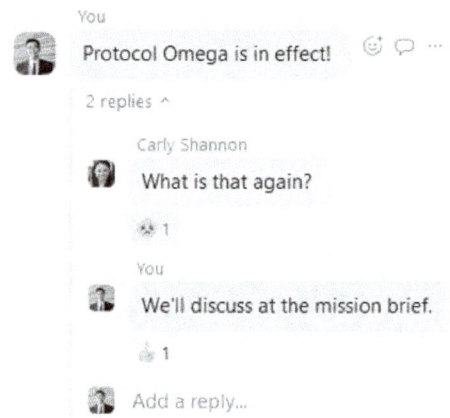

Figure 33: https://support.zoom.us/hc/en-us/articles/115004789183-Replying-and-man-aging-chat-messages.

WebEx

1.   You have access to a large library of emoji and can choose from various categories and color palettes.

2.   When writing a message, select emoji , choose the emoji that you want to add, and send the message. You can also search for an emoji using the search box.

3. You can copy and paste emojis from the message area to add them to space or team names. Emojis that you choose often, appear in the Frequently used section

4. You can also type an emoticon into your message, leaving a space after the text, and Webex App automatically changes it to an emoji.

5. You can also use emoji shortcodes to instantly add emojis to your message.

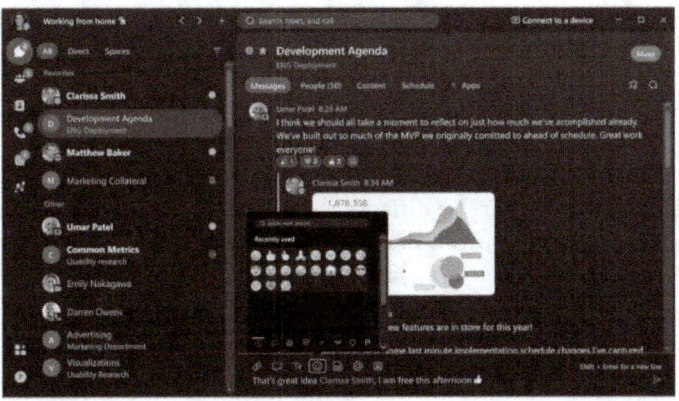

Figure 34: How to add emojis. https://tinyurl.com/7nv3hd4c.

Challenges

- What methods do you use to get emotional feedback from your learners?

- What techniques do you use to get a sense of how your learners are feeling—if they're stressed, overworked, overwhelmed, way ahead of their classmates, and/or bored?

- Would you prefer a text response, an emoji or both?

 **When teaching or using software, synchronize your settings to those of the learners.**

Background

Technical classes typically involve software and hardware that both the trainer and the trainees are expected to use. Frequently, there's some discrepancy between the tools used by the trainer and the those used by the attendees. Ideally, hardware and software requirements should be determined and agreed upon before class. One of two scenarios typically plays out:

- Each student may choose their own software to complete the exercises, noting that the instructor may use different software. These differences may become part of the class content. Alternatively, it may be determined that the differences in tooling would be detrimental to learning and confuse the learners as they try to follow the trainer's instructions.

- All attendees agree to use the same hardware and software as the trainer.

How to do it

Here are some tips for working with software related to your class.

First, make it clear from the beginning of the class what software the attendees will be using and that to be used by the trainer. All too often, we hear that using different software is perfectly okay with the learners, only to read the end-of-course evaluations and discover that it wasn't okay. Addressing the use of software in the needs analysis will help avoid comments like, "I couldn't keep up because the instructor and I were using different programs."

In addition to using the same software, it's sometimes imperative that everyone is using the same versions of the software and operating system.

Finally, even if you're using the same software, the trainer or trainee's settings may be customized, resulting in a distinctive look and feel. Most configurable software allows users to export their configuration settings in a separate file. You can then export those settings and share them with your learners.

Using a shared configuration file ensures that their screen matches yours and brings them a level of comfort and security. They can focus their energy on the significant differences between your screen and their own and not on the trivial settings that are different but not pertinent.

The concepts you teach often apply to a variety of software. If using various software is part of the course objectives, then allow students to use different software and make the differences part of the class. But, if possible, always use the same software as your students. If you're teaching beginners, it can be distracting to them to have different software even if the software they use is industry standard and capable of completing all the tasks required in class.

Challenges

- How do you ensure your learner's software matches your own?

- How do you minimize the differences?

- Do you make a special announcement at the beginning of class or do you point out the differences throughout the class?

Favor an andragogical approach over a pedagogical one.

Background

Merriam-Webster defines pedagogy as "the art, science, or profession of teaching." Its origin can be traced specifically to the teaching of children. According to vocabulary.com, "Pedagogy and pedagogue come from the Greek *paidos* ("boy, child") plus *agogos* ("leader"). Thus, we often think of a pedagogical approach as appropriate to the teaching of small children. A common phrase for this approach is "treating the learner as if they were a child or an empty vessel to be filled." We can all remember highly structured kindergarten classes; we had no say in the subject matter and were even told when to take a nap!

It's still possible in today's learning environments (and advisable in some misguided management styles) to teach with a pedagogical approach. The proverbial "sage on the stage" talks incessantly and presumably fills our heads with knowledge in these classes. Such teachers take a break only when they deem it appropriate, and they never ask questions. To be clear, the "sage on the stage" teaching style has merit; an excellent example of this approach is the invited expert at the lunch and learn class. Many scientists prefer this approach to learning.

But what I'm calling the pedagogical approach is not appropriate for adult learners. Indeed, the vast majority of the tips in this book take an exceptionally andragogical approach, that is, one for the teaching of adults. The andragogical approach is learner-centric as opposed to teacher-centric. Unlike teaching children, the andragogical method is all about teaching adult workers: self-directed and autonomous problem-solvers. This means the trainer respects their prior knowledge, understands that they typically know more about their company process than we do, and are capable of discovering their solutions. I would argue that we don't teach at all: we're all colearners, and our role is to facilitate or be the guide on the side.

How to do it

A few simple guidelines ensure that you're taking an andragogical approach:

- Negotiate the curriculum with learners rather than conforming with strict adherence to the course outline.

- Empower learners to take control of their learning by allowing them to share their knowledge and answer questions freely.

- Throughout the class, consult with and involve learners by asking questions relevant to how they do their jobs.

- Respect that each learner brings a unique perspective to the subject matter by virtue of their education and job experience. Show that respect by encouraging learners to share their experiences and rewarding them with recognition. See tip 30 for more information.

- Discover each learner's motivation for attending class. Are they trying to pass an exam, solve a particular problem, or broaden their knowledge? Armed with this information, you have a much better chance of making the material relevant.

Challenges

- What do you say to learners to indicate that you recognize their body of knowledge?

- How do you encourage learners to share their subject matter knowledge?

- How do you encourage learners to share their corporate knowledge, corporate culture, and processes?

- When is it advisable to discuss corporate matters such as communication tools, culture, and processes?

Teaching Methodology Tips

"I am not a teacher,
but an awakener."

— Robert Frost

Choose a lecture style geared to long-term memory rather than working memory.

Background

Whether we're conducting training for a company as large as Google or as small as a start-up firm with fewer than five learners, we often encounter similar challenges. Two of the most common ones happen when class attendees have disparate skills sets and learners are learning at different rates

In a perfect world, our learners would have very similar backgrounds and skillsets and identical working-memory capacity. In the real world, a class full of students with the exact same background and experience happens rarely, if at all.

Regardless of the student population, our goal is the same: to transfer knowledge so that newly trained employees return to their jobs with excellent skills and capable of greater productivity, arguably the end goal of all corporate-sponsored technical training.

The introduction described how neurons form new connections to each other in the brain's neocortex (long-term memory) when learning takes place. We must aim for the neocortex to send our learners back to their jobs with more knowledge!

Unfortunately, some of our current training methods miss this mark with the result that learners are storing new information in the part of the brain known as the working memory. The problem with working memory is that information goes in but doesn't stay. So when information resides only in working memory, learners return to their jobs unable to recall and implement the knowledge gained in our class.

Connections between neurons can be made stronger with active focusing on a new topic—as learners do in class—but sometimes that's not enough to form links in long-term memory. Thus, only the appearance of understanding is gained. This false sense of security regarding what has been learned can last long enough to give instructors a ten out of ten on course evaluations but not enough to increase on-the-job productivity. The problem with working memory is information goes in, but it doesn't stay.

From an andragogical perspective, we have two jobs as trainers:

1.   We must transfer knowledge as we teach using our favorite tried and true methods such as lectures, practice, writing code, and so on.

Neural connections are being formed wherever these kinds of learning are taking place. Chemical signals pass from neuron to neuron as axons reach out to touch the dendrite of a nearby axon creating a new synapse, and thus a learning connection is made.

2. We must ensure that these new connections are strengthened and stored in long-term memory so that learners return to work able to recall newly attained knowledge as needed. Adult learners have a significant advantage over children that trainers must exploit. Linking prior knowledge to new information helps learners make stronger connections, and adult learners can draw on a lot of previously acquired knowledge!

The challenge for trainers occurs early in our lesson when our words, ideas, and concepts are in a learner's working memory. Suppose I begin my lecture with the difference between programming variables and constants. As long as my learners are focused on these ideas, they're available to them from their working memory.

But like a juggler spinning objects in the air, the average adult's working memory can hold only about four pieces of information at one time. This isn't true for all people, some can hold much more (in fact, this difference explains why there are fast and slow learners).

The question is, what can we do as trainers to reduce this disparity?

Working memory capacity is believed to be fixed by adulthood. Capacity is relatively small for toddlers but it grows to reach its peak (typically four pieces of information) at age 15. It's also thought that some teaching methodologies can enhance working-memory capacity. One effective method is to bring learners' prior experience into play.

For example, programming languages are ripe with shared principles and concepts. It shouldn't be challenging to use previous knowledge of one programming language when learning a new and different language. If you're not familiar with the learner's current skill set and therefore find it difficult to make analogies, don't hesitate to ask learners about the similarities or differences between what you are teaching and their current understanding. Their responses will help you make connections that are stronger.

When learning is very fresh, the best way you can strengthen neural links is through practiced retrieval of the information. "The use of retrieval practice as a learning strategy, by teachers and students, has been shown to increase students' long-term retention and transfer of knowledge to new situations."[32]

Fortunately, there are many ways to encourage your learners to practice retrieval. The most obvious one is asking questions frequently. In coaching trainers, I've found infrequent questioning to be the most common trainer mistake. I recommend lecturing no more than five minutes (ten minutes maximum) without asking a question. Finally, when students can retrieve and practice independently (as during lab exercises), the neural links have been strengthened, and the knowledge is linked in long-term memory.

For more tips on implementing practiced retrieval, see tip 41 on no-stakes testing, the anti-lecture, and quizzes.

How to do it

These are two of the most effective techniques for teaching to long-term memory:

- Practiced retrieval

    o   Ask questions frequently.

    o   Be sure to call on all of your students regularly.

    o   Before you instruct students, ask them to provide the instructions instead.

    o   Use quizzes that encourage learners to reflect on what they've just learned.

    o   Provide frequent lab exercises that challenge the learner to perform tasks independently.

- Spaced repetition

    o   Ask short but frequent questions regarding previously taught material.

    o   Periodically, ask more-extended reflection-type questions that cover material previously taught.

    o   Add one or two questions to quizzes that cover previously taught material.

32   Pooja K. Agarwal, Jason R. Finley, Nathan S. Rose, and Henry L. Roediger III, "Benefits from retrieval practice are greater for students with lower working memory capacity, Memory," DOI: 10.1080/09658211.2016.1220579, (2016)

Many trainers are hesitant to ask too many questions during class because they feel questions are too time-consuming. While questions they can be time-intensive, the payoff is learning that sticks.

It helps to know a bit more about questions so you can determine which are and aren't time-consuming and which will be most effective.

Fact-based questions

These questions prompt for factual information as a response and can be memorization-type questions. Combined with spaced repetition (such as those asked at the beginning of each new class as a form of review of the prior material), fact-based questions can be both helpful and quick. They're common in software classes. Examples include: "How do you change the security setting?" and "Where is the configuration file located?"

Experienced-based questions

These help gauge a learner's current understanding of a topic and also set the stage for connecting prior knowledge to new knowledge. Examples include: "How would you implement this feature without introducing a security vulnerability" and "Why do you think this solution might degrade the performance of the application?"

Opinion-based questions

These may be the most time-consuming of all questions types. Use these sparingly when time is limited. While value judgments can be appropriate, use them only when you think they'll solve a problem for the group as a whole. Examples include: "what are the pros and cons of this technique" and "Now that we've learned two different ways to solve this problem, which one is best and why?"

Challenges

- How do you know your learners will retain what you've taught when they return to work?

- Do you follow up with your learners?

- Have you asked your learners what they think might help them retain new information? Have you offered suggestions such as a follow-up class or job aids?

Bring emotion into your lectures.

Background

Emotion plays a role in cognitive processes in a typical training environment. These processes include learning, memory, reasoning, and problem-solving, and all of these are vital to the transfer of information in technical training.

From the "Influences of emotion on learning and memory" published in *Frontiers in Psychology*, "Emotion also facilitates encoding and helps retrieval of information efficiently. However, the effects of emotion on learning and memory are not always univalent, as studies have reported that emotion either enhances or impairs learning and long-term memory (LTM) retention, depending on a range of factors."[33]

The paper goes on to state, "In addition to elucidating the memory-enhancing effects of emotion, neuroimaging findings extend our understanding of emotional influences on learning and memory processes; this knowledge may be useful for the design of effective educational curricula to provide a conducive learning environment for both traditional 'live' learning in classrooms and 'virtual' learning through online-based educational technologies."[34]

How to do it

Fortunately, there are a vast number of ways to add emotion to our training, including these:

- **Provocative questions** These can encourage learners to show their emotional responses. The neuroscience of learning tells us that socialness being sociable helps make strong links during learning. Use this fact to your advantage and set the example yourself by telling emotional stories of your own technology struggles. Be sure to allow time for reflection or ask for examples from your learners and have them put their answers in the chat window right before a break.

- **Storytelling:** This is another straightforward method that's both easy to understand and implement. Telling a story about a frustrating situation or the opposite, the joy of solving a complex coding problem can encourage similar emotions in your students. Linking the feeling

33   C. M. Tyng, H. U. Amin, N. M. Saad, and A.S. Malik, https://www.ncbi.nlm.nih.gov/pmc/articles/PMC5573739/, The Influences of Emotion on Learning and Memory

34   C. M. Tyng, H. U. Amin, N. M. Saad, and A.S. Malik, https://www.ncbi.nlm.nih.gov/pmc/articles/PMC5573739/, The Influences of Emotion on Learning and Memory,

to the learning context is enough to make a stronger connection for the student in long-term memory. See tip 57 for more information about storytelling.

There are less obvious but equally effective methods for adding emotion to your sessions: Q and A sessions, exercises and lecture.

- **Q and A sessions:** It is easier to introduce emotion to questions with answers that lean toward understanding than questions with merely memorized answers. You ask understanding types of questions when you favor higher-order thinking during the learning session. What does this look like? Asking students to remember something is a quick way to deal with a concept that needs no further explanation, such as parts of a programming language's syntax: it falls into this memorization category, is easy to forget, and has little emotional connection.

  Remembering is a form of lower-order thinking, while understanding requires more explanation and more opportunity to start using analogies, examples, and dramatic stories. Your learner's input at this time is invaluable because that's where the emotion comes in. For example, asking a learner how to declare a variable in a programming language involves memorization, and asking a learner what to name a variable requires understanding. The understanding question opens up the floor to debate, leading to anecdotes with emotion.

- **Exercises:** You continue by having your students apply knowledge in guided or independent exercises. (See tip 39 about the anti-lecture for more ways to engage users during the lecture portion of the class.) Applying their knowledge is still a form of lower-order thinking that provides little opportunity for emotion. After an exercise, you can ask the learners to explain the code they wrote, which will help reinforce what they've learned, especially if you let them do all of the talking. It's often inferred from Edgar Dale's Cone of Experience that students remember as little as 20 percent or less of what we instructors say, but more than 70 percent of what they say. The theory has been revisited, most recently by Will Thalheimer, who states, "There is no scientific evidence to back up the percent-remembering numbers."[35]
  I believe the notion of students reiterating what they've learned has merit, if not for retention, then for engagement. When a learner has to explain their answers in their own words, there is a deep emotion-

35   W. Thalheimer, "Debunk This: People Remember 10 Percent of What They Read," March 12, 2015, https://www.td.org/insights/debunk-this-people-remember-10-percent-of-what-they-read

al connection with what is being taught. Typically the other learners benefit as well as the answer is often told in the context of the worker's organization. The idea of giving new information meaning by expressing it in your own words, a process known as elaboration, lends itself to the notion that there is no limit to how much you can learn. Elaboration helps foster a growth mindset in your learners. This notion becomes evident to all participants when learners see and hear their co-workers in the act of learning: it is the old adage "if they can do it, I can do it" in action.

- **Lectures:** Now it's time for the higher-order thinking that brings emotion to the newly learned concepts. Present the learners with a scenario and ask them to analyze both the problem and the solution. They can compare their thoughts through an evaluation, which should be done verbally. Remember, you're the facilitator, and you must encourage this verbal evaluation process by questioning your learners.

  This is higher-order thinking! They're using their working memory to reach into their long-term memory to solve a coding problem. Higher-order thinking inherently brings with it a degree of emotion. You can enhance this with short stories or scenarios. Don't be afraid to add drama; even if it's contrived, it will be memorable, and that's what makes it stick!

For example, you can show your learners a finished feature of an application and elicit solutions for implementing that feature. Ask other learners to evaluate the answers and analyze the potential solutions. Adding detail and real-world drama to the fictional scenario will paint a picture for your learners and help them retain both the problem and the solution.

When creating scenarios, I've gone as far as to ask my learners to close their eyes and think about a particular company project they've worked on—to create a mental image. I provided additional guidance as to what I was looking for to tie it into the upcoming lesson.

Sometimes I'll ask a learner to share what they're thinking, with surprising results. After one such experiment, several learners chimed in and said, "I was thinking of that same project!" After a bit of laughter, the group decided that it was unanimous, and they were eager to hear more about the topic. They had all come to the same conclusion: that project presented problems and they wanted answers. Successful scenarios create tension and then break the tension.

Challenges

- How do you sense if your learners are making an emotional connection with the material in a virtual learning environment?

- What can you do to add emotion to the content?

Use testing as a tool for learning.

Background

In 1885, Hermann Ebbinghaus posited that "just 20 minutes after learning, we can only recall 60% of what we have learned. After one hour, only 45% of what has been learned is still in our memory, and after one day, only 34%. remains. Six days after learning, the memory has already shrunk to 23%; only 15% of what has been learned is permanently stored,"[36] a finding he dubbed "the forgetting curve." We now know significantly more about learning and memory, but the forgetting curve remains a challenge we trainers must tackle.

We know that practicing retrieval is the best way to get information into long-term memory. In her excellent book *A Mind for Numbers*, Barbara Oakley tells us that "Testing in itself is a powerful learning experience. It changes and adds to what you know, also making dramatic improvements in your ability to retain material."[37]

In a 2020 video—*Making (Low-Stakes) Practice Tests More Effective*—Edutopia (https://tinyurl.com/584u54m5) makes a case for practice tests. Many teachers and trainers use practice tests to find learners' knowledge gaps. Based on what we've discovered about the neuroscience of learning, we now know that practice tests can do more than that—they strengthen memory, which is exactly what corporate technical training requires. Public school teachers know this as well. "Frequent, low-stakes quizzes help boost memory. In a 2014 study, students who simply reread material for an upcoming exam scored 50 percent, on average. But students who took practice tests did much better— scoring 66 percent on the exam."[38]

The Dallas Mavericks are known for their extensive tracking of performance data on their players. When the Mavericks signed Dorian Finney-Smith to a contract, he was one of the NBA's worst 3-point shooters. Because the Mavs track the practice shooting numbers to quantify progress, it became evident

---

36 T. Tietz, "Hermann Ebbinghaus and the Experimental Study of Memory," Jan. 24, 2022, http://scihi. org/hermann-ebbinghaus-memory/

37 "Retrieval practice produces more learning than elaborative studying with concept mapping," 2011 Feb 11;331(6018):772-5. doi: 10.1126/science.1199327. Epub 2011 Jan 20..

38 https://www.edutopia.org/video/making-low-stakes-practice-tests-more-effective, Making (Low-Stakes) Practice Tests More Effective, January 24, 2020, Both Multiple-Choice and Short-Answer Quizzes Enhance Later Exam Performance in Middle and High School Classes Kathleen B. McDermott, Pooja K. Agarwal, Laura D'Antonio, Henry L. Roediger, III, and Mark A. McDaniel Washington University in St. Louis. Journal of Experimental Psychology: Applied © 2013 American Psychological Association 2014, Vol. 20, No. 1, 3–21.

that Finney-Smith was getting much better over time. Maverick's owner Mark Cuban said, "I think I threw him one of my old lines. Practice till you can't get it wrong." Mark Cuban's wise advice is worth passing to our learners, and we can set the tone by using practice quizzes.

There are too many studies to count that verify this simple fact: frequently tested students learn and retain information far better than those who are not tested.

How to do it

Testing students is an excellent way to implement practiced retrieval. However, it must be done correctly. It's too easy to do it wrong and get a result the opposite of what you intended.

So, how do you get it right? First, let's look at the ways you can implement testing.

Quizzes

Randomly ask students questions throughout class (this works nicely with tips 65 and 66, for keeping students engaged).

The student writes the code, and the trainer types it for all to see and discuss.

Before we learn how to implement the ideas above, let's lay some ground rules for testing that apply regardless of what type of quizzes you choose to implement.

- Quizzes should be easy to access.
- Quizzes should have a short URL. (Consider using TinyURL [https://tinyurl.com/app] to create these short URLs.)
- Learners' access to quizzes shouldn't require additional work:. signing up for accounts and creating a user name and password are all impediments to reaching the quiz.
- Consider embedding quizzes inside your presentation (seehttps://www.classpoint.io/interactive-quiz-in-powerpoint/).
- Implement no-stakes quizzes.
- Make quizzes anonymous. Online quizzes for example, should not record any information that identifies the student such as their name or email address.

- Your learners should know that these aren't quizzes in the traditional sense, nor are they graded. They're a learning tool, and no one but the learner will know the results.

- Educate your learners briefly about the effectiveness of practiced retrieval. Remind them that these are "no-stakes" quizzes. In contrast to their experience on the job, they're not being evaluated. There aren't any grades, or consequences for passing or failing— for example, there's no need to worry about failed experiments or broken code!

- You must ask the right questions in the right way!

- See tips 63, 65, 66, and 71.

Now, let's learn how to implement testing in class.

Online Quizzes

If you follow the ground rules above, quizzes can be an excellent form of practiced retrieval. You can have these quizzes hosted online (see "Resources" below) or you can host them on your website. Once students understand that these quizzes are learning tools and not assessments, they'll want to take quizzes frequently.

That's how hosting quizzes online is an improvement over embedding the quizzes in your presentation. Learners can easily bookmark the quiz in their favorite browser. Remind them of Mark Cuban's quote: "Practice till you can't get it wrong."

Online flash cards are excellent for practiced retrieval and students usually provide positive feedback . Many websites are available that create flash cards for you and also gamify them (see "Resources" below, at the end of this tip for these websites.

Randomly ask students questions

This approach is excellent because it accomplishes several goals:

- It allows you to engage students on an individual basis. My general rule is to check in with each student before fifteen minutes of class time have passed. Challenging? Yes, but it's rewarding when each student's feedback is positive because of all the individual attention they've received.

- It satisfies our goal to allow students to practice retrieving information, and it enables us to do so frequently and quickly, unlike taking quizzes and other alternative methods.

Here are some helpful hints for randomly asking students questions:

- Call students by name.
- *Always* provide positive feedback after a correct answer, as in these examples:
    - "Great answer, Joe!"
    - "Well said, Diane!"
    - "That was a perfect explanation, John!"
    - "I like the way Samantha said…"
- Always provide encouraging feedback after an incorrect answer, as in these examples:
    - "I think you're on the right track, Bob. Can you expand your thoughts on…?"
    - "Jill, can you rephrase the question the way you understood it?"
    - "How did you come to that conclusion Diane?"
- Consider inviting other students to add to the prior student's answer.

Before I implemented the techniques described above, my end-of-course evaluations contained a lot of comments like these:

- "The instructor was very informative and provided a lot of additional knowledge."
- "Kevin's training was great. He knows the subject well."
- "Instructor was very knowledgeable."

Flattering? Yes, in a way, but the point of the class is to help the students become more knowledgeable! In light of that, the positive evaluations aren't all that flattering!

Later in my career, when my training became more learner-centric, comments changed. Implementing this tip and drilling students repeatedly during class has consistently rewarded me with end-of-course evaluation comments like these:

- "The instructor could keep us motivated and engaged."

- "Somehow, Kevin made it interesting; I was never in danger of nod-ding off."

- "Kevin kept us engaged the entire time."

The difference between my earlier career (where I did most of the talking) and my later career (where the students did most of the talking) is compel-ling. Subsequent follow-ups with students also leads me to believe the learn-ing sticks when the students are given more of an opportunity to speak and participate in various ways.

The antilecture pattern

In this scenario, you've completed a lesson and are ready to enter the applica-tion phase. Typically, you might walk your students through a solution or ask them to complete a lab (e.g., maybe you've just taught REST API design, and now it's time for learners to write URI segments. Or perhaps you've just dis-cussed functional programming, and now it's time for them to refactor code).

Before you assign the lab exercise, you have an ideal opportunity to imple-ment the antilecture pattern because, ultimately, you want your students to perform the task independently.

Follow the steps below to execute the antilecture pattern:

1. Set up the training scenario as you typically would (e.g., open a code file for editing).

2. Pick a student to walk you through the following steps; I often say, "you talk, and I'll type."

3. Encourage other students to chime in with their opinions. Call on some students by name to open the floor for discussion.

4. Follow the exercise through to its logical conclusion to one of two results:

    o   The student could have gotten everything right, and the attendees didn't debate the answer much. Now you have the other learners catch up to the point the original learner fin-ished their lecture and the exercise continues on.

    o   Alternatively, the code or exercise could fail. Open the floor for discussion, debugging, and so on until all of the learners solve the problem.

If it's a guided exercise that the students must key in answers, they can do so after the discussion and final code is completely worked out.

Games

Games are different than *gamification*. Games are by far the most recalled parts of my classes and get the most upvotes on the end-of-course evaluations.

I'm not a particularly hard-core gamer, so I hesitated before seeing the value of incorporating games in the class. Instead, I thought games might be perceived as kind of hokey. I was surprised to learn that learners of all ages and genders seem to really enjoy these games. I've coded a few myself and also use canned versions from various companies (see "Technology" at the end of this section for websites that can help you quickly build games and game-like quizzes).

If you teach front-end web development, the following websites may be helpful:

- **Mastery Games** (https://mastery.games/)provides an excellent example of topically related games.

- My students also like **Flexbox Froggy** (https://flexboxfroggy.com/). It's a game that helps students learn the CSS flexbox. See https://flukeout. github.io/ for lessons on CSS selectors.

- **Pixactly** (https://pixact.ly/) teaches the fine art of working with pixels.

- **The Command line** Murders (see https://github.com/veltman/clmystery) for learning the command line interface.

- **Hex Invaders** (http://www.hexinvaders.com/) helps students learn hexadecimal colors.

- Run a Google search for popular programming languages such as JavaScript. Also use "learning games" in the search. This should result in several free and paid options.

Reflection

This is an incredibly effective technique because it involves higher-order thinking. However, it's time-consuming, so factor in the effect it will have on your training schedule. Here's the implementation process:

1. Provide a scenario that represents the completed state of the concept. For example, in a web development class you could provide a screenshot of a completed feature (e.g., a lookup table of physicians that ac-

cept a particular insurance plan or a complete database and requirements but no queries).

2.   Next, ask a student to reflect on completing the assignment:

    o   The web application example must list all of the work needed
to execute the lookup table.

    o   For the database example, students must consider the queries
that will be required and write them. To do that, they'll analyze what's needed to complete the task and reflect on what
they've learned—all without assistance.

Reflection is one of the best types of retrieval practice. By not helping students work through this challenge, you've introduced a short-term impedi-
ment that results in more substantial learning. The notion behind challenging students in this way is called *desirable difficulty,* and you must present these
difficulties throughout the class (see the introduction for more background
on desirable difficulties).

Although I suggested earlier in this tip that you randomly ask students questions, note that you could have students ask you questions. Don't miss this
opportunity to put the question asked by one learner out to the entire group.

It's equally important to set the right environment for questions. Jane Vella
writes about this idea in her book *Learning to Listen, Learning to Teach*: "Set the
norm that any question that arises has priority over the task at hand. This
means that adult learners are invited to interrupt the learning task to ask
their questions or raise their burning issues. This is not easy to accept, as it
can look like the proverbial red herring. But in my experience, one adult's
question is often the unasked question of the whole group. It is useful to refer
questions to the group by what I call a bouncing question. 'Before I respond,
what do you think of Mary's question?' This continues the vital peer learning
while leaving time for you to respond in full. You as teacher are thus developing a relationship for learning among peers."[39]

Resources

There are many websites that create quizzes and gamified quizzes. Here are
a few:

- **Quiz Maker** (https://www.quiz-maker.com/) offers a free but limited
account. It provides a robust set of features for making quizzes.

---

39   J. Vella, *Learning to Listen Learning to Teach,* (San Francisco: Jossey-Bass, a Wiley Company),
    p. 98.

- **Quizlet** (https://quizlet.com/) offers quizzes and flash cards. It can also turn your quiz into an asteroids-type game.

- **Free Online Surveys** (https://freeonlinesurveys.com/) offers online surveys, quizzes and polls.

- **EddApp** (https://www.edapp.com/) offers online course creation tools.

The Science

The resources below relate to tests as assessments:

- *Evaluation Basics*, **Donald V. McCain. ASTD/ATD Press, 2005.** (https://www.td.org/books/evaluation-basics)

- *Test Development: Fundamentals for Certification and Evaluation*, Melissa Fein. ASTD/ATD Press, 2012. (https://tinyurl.com/2p94bhxw)

- Brain science: Testing, testing–The whys and whens of assessment, Art Kohn. *Learning Solutions Magazine*, April 20, 2015. (https://tinyurl.com/tf4hmx7k)

- These "testing" blog articles by Connie Malamed https://tinyurl.com/44pfawf8

Challenges

- How do you implement quizzes–verbally, via your slide presentation, using external websites?

- In addition to a list of task-related questions, do you also maintain a list of reflection-type questions that require critical thinking?

Twenty-four hours after the training, send your students something to remind them of a concept and/or topic.

Background

We know that spaced learning has proven more effective than massed practice, but why is this so?

In the introduction, I described how the learning process results in new connections between neurons in the neocortex (long-term memory) and that spaced repetition strengthens these connections as they move from working to long-term memory.

We know that we can practice spaced learning during class, but what happens after class?

How to do it

Spaced learning is a suitable time to introduce *microlearning*. The definition of microlearning and of its many implementations are beyond the scope of this book, but for our purposes, we can define microlearning as Ray Jimenez did in his YouTube interview (https://tinyurl.com/3ac8jayz). Jimenez borrows his definition from Dr. Theo Hug (professor at University of Innsbruck) and says that "micro-learning is a way of learning with answers and solutions that is low in effort, easy, fast, and ready to use and finally useful in order to fix, solve, and improve things at work."

Ray goes on to focus his definition with emphasis on the learner: "A way of helping workers and learners at work in order to fix, solve, and improve things." In this way, he's turning the definition's emphasis away from content and more toward learners' benefits.

There are several ways we can incorporate microlearning designed to help the learner retain and use what they learn in class:

- You can periodically send the learner real-world work scenarios that present a problem.
- Then, let them recall a solution using information delivered in class.
- Follow that with reminders at one week, two weeks, one month, and three months.

According to Jimenez, we must distinguish content- versus application-driven; material prompted by the need of the worker. On the job, workers learn in small chunks instead of implementing all of the learning that took place over a week-long course. They learn by completing simple tasks. We can put these tasks in an email or a text message and deliver them to the learner when they need it most—on the job!

The website Arist provides a perfect example of microlearning designed to reach and teach learners on the job. Using their software, you can send a "mock" text message from a "pretend" colleague with a problem and ask the learner to solve it by texting the correct solution back. In this way, Arist software can facilitate the automation of microlearning tasks.

Technology

Predefined microlearning lessons can be distributed automatically via software. Here are some of the services that provide this automation:

- **Arist** (https://www.arist.co/)
- **Qstream** (https://qstream.com/)
- **Surge9** (https://surge9.com/surge9-app/)

Challenges

- How do you follow up with your learners after class?

Answer public questions publicly and private questions privately.

Background

A vital component in keeping students engaged and participating is providing a safe environment where the instructor is a trusted confidant. Associating your classroom with a trusted space can be challenging to convey to your students, but you can do so with a series of consistent and respectful actions.

This tip addresses respecting your student's right to privacy, and it requires a watchful eye.

How to do it

In a live instructor-led class, a shy or reluctant student can pull you aside during a break to ask a question or deliver some feedback (such as, "I think you're talking a bit too fast for me.").

In a virtual class, trust can be established through private chat.

Private chat is a chat feature that allows students to communicate with you without the rest of the class knowing about it. It isn't a simple one-click action—the learner has to go a little out of their way to ensure their question or comment is private. Unfortunately, it's all too easy for us trainers to simply read that private question aloud or answer it by responding to everyone!

For this reason, be extra careful when reading messages sent to you via the chat window: confirm that a message has *not* been sent to you privately before you respond publicly! If you feel the class as a whole would benefit from the question, ask the learner if they'd mind if you shared the question while assuring them that you won't mention them by name.

Resources

Double-check your virtual training environment settings to be sure private chat is enabled. Here are resources for a few of the more common apps:

- **Zoom documentation** (https://tinyurl.com/277ewyd7)
- **Teams video** (https://tinyurl.com/46rbvn97)
- **Supervised Chat in Teams** (https://tinyurl.com/57bxy7p4)

- **Adobe Connect** (https://tinyurl.com/mryrf8um)
- **GoTo Webinar** (https://tinyurl.com/3j875p2j)

Challenges

- How do you keep an eye on the chat window during class?
- Where do you place the chat window?

Incorporate planned repetition of concepts.

Background

We saw in the introduction how students learn from a neuroscience perspective. From that point of view, it's easy to see that our job as trainers is to help strengthen the new connections made in the neocortex. If we can support the process known as consolidation, learners will be able to recall at will what we teach them in class when they return to their job.

This strengthening of connections can take place in the classroom if we give our learners the opportunity to employ spaced practice: "studying information more than once, but leaving considerable time between practice sessions."[40]

Certainly, the gap of time we provide will be limited by the duration of our class. A three-day class doesn't leave time for a considerable gap, but the technique can still be successful.

Any training methodology you want to implement during class, including spaced repetition, begins with a plan and ends with the media responsible for the transfer of knowledge. The delivery format can include anything from notes shared by the instructor to a 500-page workbook.

Many trainers, especially those in high demand, find little time to prepare for their classes because they're constantly training. The result is a haphazardly put together class with little thought given to pedagogical principles. The bulk of their efforts comprises preparing lab exercises and training materials. They don't understand or take the time to prepare each class from the learners' point of view. Essentially, they're preparing courses from their perspective. For example, trainers often prepare materials that present information without building into the courseware the checks and balances that ensure the student has assimilated the information correctly. Trainers may also present material out of order by starting with the details of a complex topic instead of the broader subject matter. In short, trainers provide new material with little thought to pedagogical best practices. Finally, when determining content or the course outline, the curriculum and delivery style must match up to the learning objectives from a business perspective. The worker needs to leave the class with certain skills intact and those skills should be given priority throughout the class.

---

40   P. Brown, H.L. Roediger III, M.A. McDaniel, *make it stick*, (Cambridge: The Belknap Press of Harvard University Press), p. 74

What's needed, even if at a very fundamental level, is a deep understanding of the learning process and the motivation for the class from a corporate training perspective.

How to do it

I'll very broadly define the steps to creating a learner-centered class. It's only from this starting point that you can begin to implement planned repetition of concepts. There are volumes of work done on class preparation (see "Resources" below). In the interest of brevity, I'll define basic steps here:

- **Assess the training needs:** Why is training necessary? What is the problem the training is expected to solve?

- **Define the performance of objectives:** What should the learner know how to do after the class is completed?

- **Write the course outline:** What outline meets the learning objectives?

- **Write individual lessons:** Do the exercises agree with the course outline. Does each individual lesson build upon prior skills?

- **Confirm that these lessons satisfy the performance objective:** Do the lessons effectively teach the skills addressed in the performance objectives?

- **Refine the learning approach:** Are the lessons taught in the correct order? Do any of the tasks presuppose knowledge that the course has not yet addressed?

- **Support consolidation:** Do the lessons allow enough time for some degree of consolidation?

Let's look more closely at a few of the challenges in meeting these objectives. First, understand the performance objectives of the class. Many trainers overreach in terms of what can be accomplished within a given period. It took me a long time to understand this: In an effort to make sure I left no stone unturned in my classes, I inadvertently delivered too much material. Too much content has the potential to leave a learner confused and overwhelmed after class. It also makes planned repetition nearly impossible because there is not enough time.

Therefore, the first question to be considered while creating courseware is, "What kind of information do our learners need to be able to do their jobs?" The answer is rarely, "all of the information that can possibly be supplied."

Something amazing happens in virtual technical training when it's done right—our learners are captivated and eager to learn. Now, give them just enough to keep them engaged and allow enough time for spaced repetition. The more time you spend delivering ancillary or extra background information, the less time you have for consolidation to take place. You want learners to experiment on their own, both mentally with concepts and hands-on with concrete tasks. Put anything helpful but extra in the appendix of your courseware or in a job aid or handout.

Now that you've planned for spaced repetition during the course preparation phase, let's look at how to implement it by using the ideas expressed above.

In "How Learning Occurs" in *Make It Stick*, the authors describe consolidation:

> An apt analogy for how the brain consolidates new learning may be the experience of composing an essay. The first draft is rangy, imprecise. You discover what you want to say by trying to write it. After a couple of revisions, you have sharpened the piece and cut away some of the extraneous points. You put it aside and let it ferment. When you pick it up again a day or two later, what you want to say has become clearer in your mind. Perhaps you now perceive that there are three main points you are making. You connect them to examples and supporting information familiar to your audience. You rearrange and draw together the elements of your argument to make it more effective and elegant.[41]

Apply this to writing your training materials. If you approach your lessons with the same mindset, you'll naturally add spaced repetition:

- By revisiting ideas during the revision process, you connect your ideas seamlessly.

- When you reevaluate, reexamine, and reconsider, you're repeating.

- When you allow for time gaps between these ideas, you're spacing the learning.

- The gaps between these main points can be filled with brief lectures, demonstrations, question and answer periods, and so on.

- The result is planned spaced repetition.

Now for the science:

---

41   P. Brown, H.L. Roediger III, M.A. McDaniel, *make it stick*, (Cambridge: The Belknap Press of Harvard University Press), p. 74.

> The process of learning something often starts out feeling disorganized and unwieldy; the most important aspects are not always salient. Consolidation helps organize and solidify learning, and notably, so does retrieval after a lapse of time, because the act of retrieving a memory from long-term storage can both strengthen the memory traces, and at the same time make them modifiable again, enabling them, for example, to connect to more recent learning.[42]

Use this to your advantage by intentionally planning for and employing spaced repetition.

What does spaced repetition look like in the classroom? There are several ways to achieve this vital objective. In a typical technical training course, concepts build upon one another. Database design, for example, may begin with first understanding the purpose of the database (a rather broad subject) to finding and organizing the required information, dividing the information into tables (a new concept), and then slowly working down to the details of creating columns, specifying primary keys and relationships, and perhaps ending with the idea of database normalization

Rather than go from topic to topic at a quick pace, spaced repetition can be achieved by deliberately returning to a previous topic before, during, and after introducing a new one. Allow time to pass, then return to the previous topic (pop quiz anyone?). Mix up the delivery style when returning to an earlier topic. Make it a challenge by applying desirable difficulties. How might you do that? Put a spin on the original lesson; throw a monkey wrench into the actual scenario. Ask questions like these:

- "Where do you see this working? Where do you see this not working?"

- For our database example, you might ask, "What would happen if you named this table [insert a poor name here]" or "What would happen if you used one table to hold all the domain values here?"

Another technique is to provide simple quizzes after each topic where several questions on the quiz revisit a previous topic. If you don't feel you have the time to introduce a formal quiz, try some verbal quizzing.

Alternatively, let the group know that you'll be going around the virtual room, presenting each learner with a topic. They must then cite one thing they know about the subject. This is an incredibly challenging, and there-

---

42 R. Barr, Notes for Make it Stick, http://scaling4growth.com/wp-content/uploads/2015/10/Make-it-Stick.pdf.

fore effective, retrieval practice method because you're not giving them any clues.

For example, here's a possible dialogue from a beginning JavaScript class:

Trainer: Joe, tell us one thing you know about variables?

Joe: They are placeholders for information.

Trainer: Sue, your turn.

Sue: You can declare them with the keywords "var" or "let."

Trainer: Steve, what can you add?

Steve: If you don't provide a value, the variable is considered "undefined."

Sometimes the learner's answer will be wrong, and this is where you help facilitate the correct answer, *but you don't provide it.* First ask the learner to rethink their response and if necessary, provide a clue to help them figure out where they went wrong. Oftentimes, this is all you need to do. If the learner is still struggling try another clue before putting the question out to all learners to respond.

Finally, when practicing spaced retrieval, be sure that you're not practicing memorization (resulting in the illusion of subject knowledge). Memorization is not a helpful indicator that your learner has learned or will recall the material later. This is why a simple question with a simple answer is not as effective as adding a twist to the question that requires some critical thinking.

That's not to say that simple queries and responses are ineffective in some cases. Programming syntax is a terrific opportunity to reinforce simple facts. You must, for example, end your code statements with a semicolon, capitalize this letter, and so on. Flash cards work great here, but you can implement the idea of a flash card in a class by frequently asking your students to fill in the blank or suggest the next step in a process or write the following line of code and so on. Even after your learners have answered these questions correctly for some time, don't stop asking the same questions; just put a little more space between the questions.

Note: You may want to remind your students that you're not asking as a form of assessment. You're not trying to "see if they get it." You're using the questions to support more profound understanding and retention.

Challenges

- How do you plan for the repetition of concepts within your class?
- How do you know if you're overdoing planned repetition?

Give students reliable break times.

Background

I'll never forget the time a student implored me to cover a specific topic related to their particular question. I wrote the question down so I wouldn't forget to address it, and I knew the perfect time and context to introduce the discussion. I dove headfirst into the subject and did what I thought was an elegant and complete answer to her question. Another student jumped in to add more clarity, and another student highlighted how the process could be implemented within the confines of the corporate culture.

"Did that answer your question, Sarah?" I asked confidently. "Sarah?" She was gone. She missed the entire discussion! She returned to her computer just when I asked for a final time, "Sarah, are you there?"

Learners often leave the classroom to take a needed break because they don't know when the next break will come. If attendees are forewarned, they might wait for that drink of water or stretch break because they know a break is coming in five minutes.

There is much debate about the appropriate duration and frequency of break times during virtual classes. I like five minutes every hour, a fifteen-minute break in the morning, and a fifteen-minute break in the afternoon. Other trainers prefer five to ten minutes every ninety minutes, which works equally well.

But what I (or my fellow trainers) prefer is of little importance to learners. As a group, they can decide what they need. Of course, as facilitators, our job is to make sure that nothing impedes our learning objective, including breaks that are too long or too frequent.

How to do it

The challenge in a large class is in coming to a consensus. I poll the group right before a break and ask the students what they need—five or ten minutes. Or I split the difference and go for seven minutes. I ask them to respond in the chat window and suggest they do this privately.

Eventually, a pattern emerges. It often goes like this: the first break is the longest. We've just got through a significant amount of talking: class setup, class outlines, ground rules, introductions, and so on, and they need a long break. After that, the breaks get shorter.

This method varies from class to class so I also ask students for explicit feedback about our break schedule (private responses in the chat window are more effective here, so I explicitly ask for them). I get varied but forthcoming answers such as, "I don't like frequent breaks because it breaks my concentration" or "I prefer longer breaks because I can't really do anything in five minutes." I use these private conversations to acknowledge the learner's feelings.

Based on the total feedback, I make some suggestions for the break schedule. Inevitably, you can't please all of the people all of the time, but I get as close as I can so that most if not all learners are satisfied. By allowing learners to decide on their break frequency and duration, I've found that they feel less captive and more in control of their day.

The only strict rule I have is that everyone keeps their word. If you say you'll break at a specific hour, make sure you do so. If you tell students the break is for only five minutes, start promptly after precisely five minutes. A quick tip for getting students back on time after breaks is to promise to reveal "a little known" feature of the software or introduce a free tool designed to make their jobs easier. Be sure to let students know you'll promptly reveal this special news after the break.

After a break, one of my classic on-site training tips for reengaging enthusiastic students is to dim the lights or shut them off completely, wait half a minute, and then turn them back on again. This simple signal gets the group's attention, and they stop chatting amongst themselves, return to their seats, and are ready to resume class.

In the virtual classroom, I use a similar technique. It's most effective with Open Broadcaster Software (OBS) but can probably be pulled off with just your slide deck:

- Make a scene in OBS or make a completely black slide.
- Display the screen immediately after your break timer goes off, wait half a minute, and then resume class.
- Welcome each student back by name audibly after every break. A friendly and straightforward roll call like this makes everyone

accountable for returning on time and serves as a reminder that everyone's presence is important.

Technology

There are several ways to utilize timers in class seamlessly. I use them for timed exercises, short breaks, and lunchtime. Several ways to add timers to your online courses follow.

Add timers to PowerPoint slides

In the screenshots below, I've added a progress-bar timer Ito a PowerPoint slide. It allows students two minutes to answer the question shown. The green bar is animated over a time period equivalent to the break time.

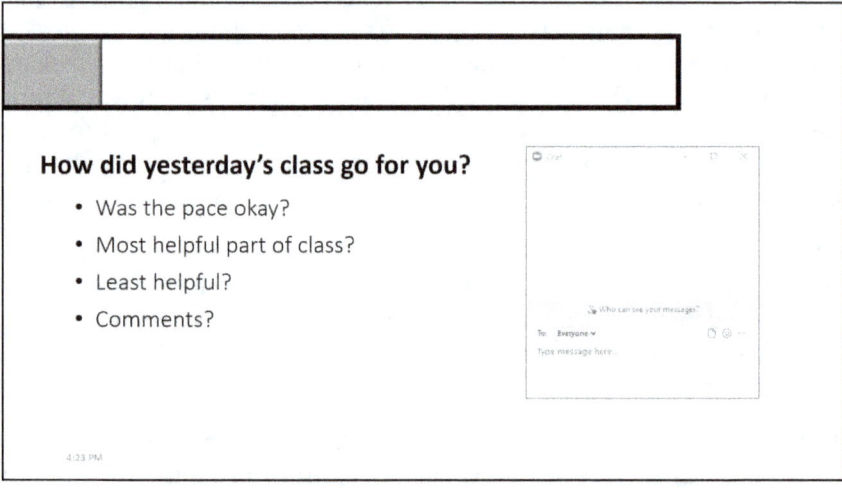

Figure 35: Sample PowerPoint slide showing a countdown timer in the upper-right corner.

There are tutorials online that show how to create these timers:

- https://tinyurl.com/yc5v72cb
- https://tinyurl.com/v4a88hwa

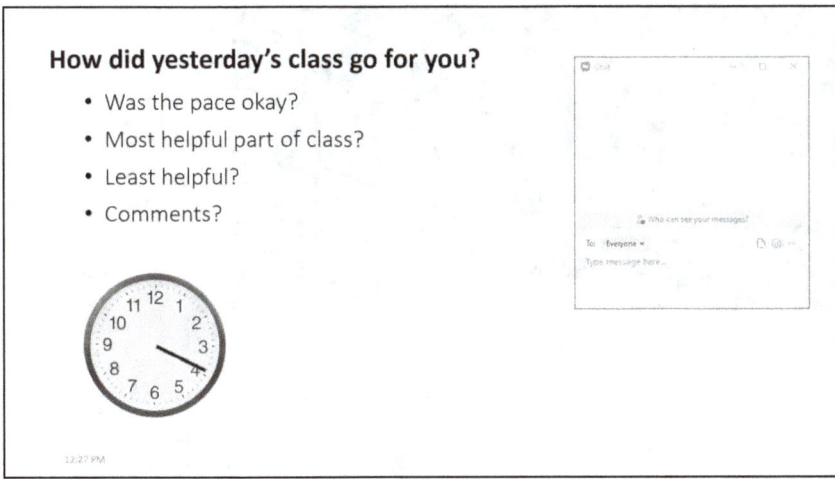

Figure 36: A timer from https://www.tutor2u.net/search?q=powerpoint+timer.

H2R graphics

The software comes with a predefined timer that you can display as overlays on the screen you're sharing. (For more on this software, see tip 23.)

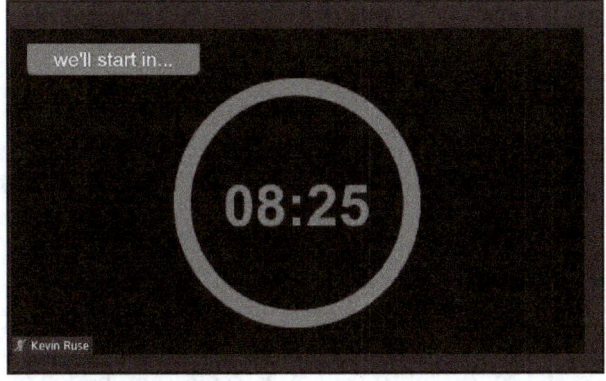

Figure 37: A countdown timer from H2R Graphics.

OBS scenes

OBS, the Open Broadcasting Software, uses scenes to display to attendees. Combine OBS with a stream deck and you're one button away from displaying a timer to your students. Scenes in OBS can come from a variety of sources, including web pages. I set a scene in OBS that uses the following web page as its source.

Figure 38: My favorite timer website from https://timer.onlineclock.net/.

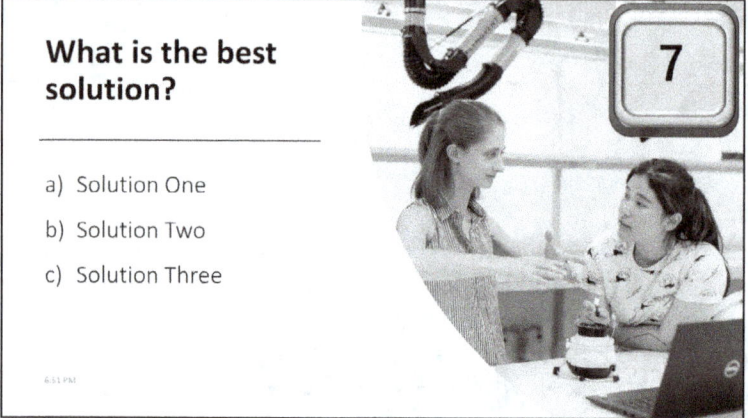

Figure 39: Another slide showing a timer in the upper-right corner. Clicking the timer activates it for the specified time.

Challenges

- How often do you give breaks?
- Do you give breaks at a consistent time or after a consistent period of time passes?
- What do you think is the ideal time interval between breaks?
- What do you think is the ideal duration of time for a break?

Replace some of your show-and-tell with guided exercise.

Background

Ask any employee what they'd rather do when learning a new skill: watch someone execute the new skill for anywhere from fifteen minutes to several hours or perform the task themselves under the watchful eye of an expert who intercedes only when necessary.

What would you rather do—watch me as I set up a Kubernetes cluster or set it up with me? Would you rather watch me apply learning algorithms for a smart device or help me figure out the formula? Watching activities like this is considered passive learning, and too many trainers think it's a necessary evil, but it isn't. There are alternatives. My favorite is the guided exercise.

Sure, there are times when a quick show-and-tell is the best form of knowledge transfer. For lengthier topics, passively watching someone complete a task is one of the least effective ways to learn and retain new information. "By mimicking th challenges of practical experience, these learning strategies conform to the admonition to 'practice like you play, and you'll play like you practice,'" improving what scientists call transfer of learning, which is the ability to apply what you're learning in new settings."[43]

Isn't that exactly what the corporations that hire us expect? "Guided exercise allows students to transfer new material from their working memory to long-term memory."[44]

How to do it

If a lecture or a demonstration goes on too long, you risk losing your learners, so I've replaced many of my show-and-tell sections with guided exercise. Doing so allows me to easily employ other techniques like the antilecture (see tip 41). It also allows me to ask the students before we type code or analyze a task what they think the next step should be, which is an excellent form of retrieval practice.

Without a doubt, the most prominent positive comment in most post-class evaluations is the overwhelming appreciation for hands-on exercises. The

43 P. Brown, H.L. Roediger III, M.A. McDaniel, *make it stick*, (Cambridge: The Belknap Press of Harvard University Press), pgs. 85-86

44 R.W. Pike, *Creative Training Techniques Handbook*, (Amherst, MA: HRD Press Inc.), p. 100 (Rosenshine, 1988) (Reynolds, 1992, p. 20)

guided exercise is a perfect activity format because it's too early to expect your learners to complete the task without some assistance.

At the same time, we've learned that asking learners how to do something *before* the subject is addressed has many benefits. It improves cognitive processes by introducing that desirable difficulty that helps learning stick. It makes it emotional and memorable as when you're called upon to answer a question and, after some reasoning, you provide an answer that while perhaps not perfect is recognized as a great start! Now that's motivating!

Challenges

- What's the most prolonged period of time for which you've lectured?
- How long does your demonstration take to complete?
- What's the most extended period during which your learners aren't doing anything active, regardless of the training method?
- Can you convert any lengthy activities into guided exercise

47   **Give your learners time for reflection.**

Background

"The act of taking a few minutes to review what has been learned from an experience (or in a recent class) and asking yourself questions is known as reflection."[45] There are several ways to allow your learners to reflect. Even the tried-and-true practiced retrieval we've spent so much time reviewing is a form of reflection.

Elaboration is another excellent way to entice your learners to reflect. After asking a question and having it answered, ask another student to elaborate on the first answer. Change the scenario in the first question and then ask for elaboration, putting a different spin on the original question.

Questions, in general, make for excellent transitions to reflection. Most trainers have been exposed to the different types of questions that can be asked during class, but here's a refresher:

- Knowledge questions: The learner responds with factual or recalled answers. Sometimes these are procedural-type questions that require a solution to a problem, a missing step in a process, and so on.

- **Comprehension questions:** The learner must answer by interpreting or explaining information in a way that demonstrates that, given a scenario or facts and figures, the learner understands the problem or solution.

- **Application questions:** The learner can solve a problem using the skills they've just learned.

- **Analysis questions:** The learner must employ critical thinking. Perhaps you've given them two possible and viable solutions to a problem, and they must choose the best one.

- **Evaluation questions:** The learner must render a judgment or opinion and justify their position.

- **Synthesis questions:** The learner uses higher-order thinking that provides a unique and creative solution for a given issue. The trainer must supply the necessary background information so that the learner can synthesize the answer by combining several topics you've taught into a coherent explanation.

---

45 P. Brown, H.L. Roediger III, M.A. McDaniel, *make it stick*, (Cambridge: The Belknap Press of Harvard University Press), p. 88.

When using guided exercises, you can choose from many of the question types shown above. The learning objective combined with the exercise objective dictates which question is most appropriate. The best questions cause the learner to reflect on what they do with the knowledge while they are on the job.

How to do it

Questions that effectively elicit reflection include open questions like, "Why is it helpful to know the relationships within the collection of data items?" Closed questions like "What is the maximum number of records supported by this database?" are memorization questions. While they may be helpful, they typically don't evoke a period of reflection.

The same is true of leading questions versus probing questions. A leading question like "What part of the application would allow me to configure a version control system?" can be very effective in building confidence but doesn't prompt a deeper understanding of the topic. Probing questions like "What do you think would be the best way to integrate version control for all stakeholders?" allow for reflection.

Another effective technique that engages the entire group while simultaneously allowing different answers to the same question is to use a round-robin approach. In this method, ask a learner to answer a question and immediately but randomly follow up with another learner who must provide their take on the answer without using the original learner's verbiage. If your second learner gets stuck, you can prompt them by asking them to expand on a single point from the first learner's response.

Challenges

- What types of topics leads to in-class reflection?

- How can instructors prompt learners to reflect on a given concept or process?

48   Convert "on-the-job" learning to "in-class" learning.

Background

To fully comprehend this tip, it helps to review where learning takes place for most workers. The first time a learner is introduced to new information, such as a new technology, it's typically through planned and scheduled training. These classes are the type technical trainers deliver on-site or virtually through an introductory course.

Additional or advanced training is frequently overseen by a supervisor, team lead, or in-house subject matter expert (SME). Sometimes after the initial class is delivered, formal follow-up training is provided internally; other times, mentors are assigned or informal training takes place in a "lunch and learn" session.

Absent a formal and planned advance course, the bulk of the learning takes place weeks or months after the initial training under several circumstances, including the following:

- A problem arises, and it's time to implement the skills from class.
- Circumstances change, and there's a new workflow process or technology, or perhaps there's an alternative or advanced use of the existing technology.

This type of learning takes place long after we trainers are gone. However, we can help the learner by introducing hypothetical scenarios during class. Many tips in this book can be used for this purpose; you can ask questions, set up fictitious scenarios, and, most effectively, you can anticipate and present problems in class to be solved via group activities and independent exercises.

How to do it

Devote a portion of your learning material to the future. You can accomplish this by putting yourself in the learner's shoes. Imagine you're on the job and think about what problems you might encounter. It's imperative that while you may use some of your own experience to uncover these issues, it's much more effective if you truly take on the persona of your learner. Where do they work? What have you learned about their on-the-job experiences to help you anticipate the specific issues they might encounter? It's tempting to rely only on your own experience, and it would be a much quicker task if you did. It takes more time to gather the information about learners, their technology, their management, but the experiences you uncover will be more realistic.

Challenges

- How do you introduce in-class challenges that mimic the learner's real job?

- How do you input those "desirable difficulties" that are needed to make learning stick?

Practice silence.

See what I did there?

Find learning opportunities wherever you can.

Background

I review my recorded sessions with both joy and regret—joy at the parts of the training that went even better than I realized and regret over missed opportunities. My missed opportunities are the learner's missed opportunities. My digressions, the questions I didn't ask, the times I supplied the answer instead of introducing that "desirable difficulty" that's so important to the learning process—all of these things robbed students of learning opportunities. They missed the chance to cement a concept in their mind so well that if they encounter the issue when back on the job, they can instantly recall the solution.

How to do it

Here are some common missed opportunities.

Answering questions

When a single student asks a question, you provide the answer while focusing your attention on only with that student, implicitly allowing everyone else to check out.

What to do instead: When a single student asks a question aloud, repeat the question for everyone to hear and ask other students to answer the question. You've now involved everyone in a learning experience. It's often cited that students remember 20 percent of what we instructors say but as high as 80 percent of what they say. (See tip 40 about the reliability of such statistics!) Remind them of that fact and don't deprive them of the opportunity to make learning stick!

Failed lab exercises

A student shares a failed exercise (code error, missing code, or some demonstration of a lack of understanding), and you fix the error.

What to do instead: Ask the student to describe the error (while the student shares their screen). Let the other students know it's their job to locate and describe the error. Now it's a group project! Everyone is thinking, not just the learner who asked the question. Sharing diagrams and code is also a fun time to remind everyone to use their annotation tools!

Introducing new topics

You begin a new topic by lecturing, live-coding, or using another demonstration technique.

What to do instead: Before a new topic begins, ask some exploratory questions: "Is anyone familiar with...?" "Does anyone know the meaning of...?" and the like. It's imperative to ask these questions of adult learners who come to class with a vast array of prior experience. Acknowledging this is respectful and helps us trainers adjust pace and not lecture on topics the group is either already well-versed in or can relate to from other programming languages and concepts.

In the early part of my career, I realized that I was losing students, not because they didn't understand the material but because they already knew it. Don't waste students' time. Find out what they know about every topic before you teach it from the ground up. It's tough when teaching virtually to "see" students checking out, making this point very important indeed.

Challenges

- Have you ever reviewed a recording of one of your sessions? Did you find any missed learning opportunities?

- What was your most common mistake? What can you do differently to avoid that mistake in the future?

51 Break all the rules.

Background

That's right, break the rules! All that matters is that your learner's needs come first. I encourage you to take any of these techniques that I've learned and implemented over the last twenty-five-plus years and twist 'em up, spin 'em around, and make something new. We only know what works by trying it. In my research over the years, I've seen that what was once considered gospel in the realm of training techniques has now fallen by the wayside in favor of a more modern approach with numerous sound and legitimate studies to back up the training approach and its validity in the workplace.

How to do it

It can be helpful to keep a journal of your teaching experiences. If you put something new into practice, write it down quickly while it's fresh in your mind. Take some additional notes regarding how you might improve the technique. Write down what you thought worked well and also what didn't work. I referenced random notes and journals I'd squirreled away for ten years or more in writing these tips. It was fascinating to revisit how my training approach has changed over the years.

Deciding between two choices

Throughout the book you may encounter a tip that conflicts with your understanding of how to best conduct a class. Perhaps your technique is the polar opposite of mine. In deciding the best approach, I am reminded of an excellent programming tip from consultant Kevlin Henney. Although Henney is discussing making a software architectural decision, the advise works well for trainers deciding between two techniques.

> When a design decision can reasonably go one of two ways, an architect needs to take a step back. Instead of trying to decide between options A and B, the question becomes "How do I design so that the choice between A and B is less significant?" The most interesting thing is not actually the choice between A and B, but the fact that there is a choice between A and B.[46]

---

46 Kevlin Henney, 97 Things Every Software Architect Should Know, (Sebastopol: O'Reilly, 2009) 48.

Challenges

- How have you broken some of the tips in this book?

- What have you done to change or reverse the tips that proved successful?

Consider the practice of "workflow learning."

Background

Training must always take into account what happens to the *worker* before and after the training. You must avoid the "workshop" mentality and always remember that these learners must return to their day-to-day jobs ready to implement what has taken place in class.

The best way to do this is to frequently refer to the worker's job. Incorporate real-world on-the-job experiences into everything you do: lectures, questions, and exercises. When creating lab exercises, ask yourself, "What goes through a learner's mind when they're at work?" This questions is especially helpful when working with subject-matter experts.

Workflow learning is often described as on-the-job training because the learner doesn't leave their workplace. They simply go about their work and rely on job aids, experts, or mentors to help them do their jobs better. This definition may cause you to wonder how you can implement on-the-job training in a classroom. Technically, it isn't pure workflow learning but it can pull out some of the method's benefits.

The workflow is based on getting workers trained during the workers' five moments of need:

- **The moment of apply:** Workers need to apply the knowledge.

- **The moment of change:** Workers need to change their approach based on new information.

- **The moment of solve:** Workers solve a work problem using new information.

- **The moment of learning new:** Workers need new information to solve a problem.

- **The moment of learning more:** Learners have contextual experiences but need additional information.

The key to applying the benefits of true workflow learning in a traditional classroom setting is to address these specific moments of need while in class.

How to do it

Use on-the-job scenarios as often as possible. Ask your learners for more of their on-the-job scenarios. It's okay to ask them, "How might you implement this in your current project?"

You can also ask learners to work on their current projects in class. If that's not possible, provide finished or starter projects and ask your learners how they'd work them out to completion.

Ask learners specific on-the-job questions like these:

- "How would you build out this feature?"
- "When would you apply this technique?"

Being specific can help prompt learners while still allowing them to reflect on their own workflows as in these examples:

- Provide multiple scenarios and ask for a solution that fits them all.
- Provide a scenario where the solution involves a topic you haven't covered yet.
- Provide a scenario and a solution and ask for a new solution.

Challenges

- How do you incorporate a learner's current workflow into class?
- How do you prepare for class so that you understand the learner's current workflow?
- How do you incorporate the five moments of need in class?

Tips for Engaging Learners

*"Presentations aren't about the presenter
they're about the audience and
what the audience needs."*

— Simon Raybould

Zoom in and out with your camera when training.

Background

When teaching live on-site, we have many small luxuries that impact learners' ability to pay attention: We sit down at a desk, often behind a computer. We stand up and lecture, perhaps at a podium. We stand by a whiteboard or a computerized smartboard. We walk among the learners weaving in and out between desks. These micromovements (if not overdone) help reset a learner's attention. Contrast this with learners in virtual classrooms who see nothing but your face from the shoulders up all day long, which introduces tedium.

This tip goes hand in hand with tip 62 for the same reason. It subtly but definitely breaks up the monotony of a lecture. I've seen it done in online classes I've taken and can confirm that this small gesture helps a lot. **Note**: Don't overdo it or you risk it losing impact.

How to do it

I use three zoom settings:

1. I use the following setting before making a statement of extreme importance. I zoom on my face and make it larger than usual. This hides my body and exposes my face from the neck up. I use a dramatic documentary-style black background. I then make the statement and zoom back to a standard distance from the camera.

2. I use another setting to tilt back. This merely breaks the monotony and sometimes help settle the discussion into a more extended one.

3. I use a third setting when a learner has the floor. I alternate this one: I turn my camera off completely, allowing everyone's full attention to be on the speaker. Or I move back far enough that I'm not the center of interest but still close enough for the speaker to know that they have my complete attention. It's best to experiment with your environment to see what feels right.

Technology

Use OBS to create at least three zoom effects. Overdoing zoom can be distracting to learners.

Challenges

- What do you do to break up the visual monotony that sometimes takes place during our training sessions?

Engage students often as in every few minutes.

Background

I've traveled by plane for most of my training engagements and often play a little game on the flight home. Whether my class had three or thirty students, I'll try to recite each student's name and draw a mental picture of their face.

With a particularly large group, I'd do this with the tray table down, writing on a notebook that I always have handy. I try to remember as hard as I can, often imagining the learners in their seats during class (fortunately, most students don't switch seats after day one). Eventually, I'll finish. If I can only produce 14 out of 15 names, I note that. Next, I access the end-of-course evaluations.

A not-so-surprising trend emerged over time. The less-than-perfect post-class evaluation score would come from the student whose name or face I simply couldn't remember. Why did this happen? Clearly, I engaged less with that student than all others or I wouldn't have forgotten them. Remember tip 2, where I emphasize the significance of calling students by name? So, why couldn't I remember these particular students after class? I needed to be brutally honest with myself if I wanted to improve.

In some cases, I decided they had a thick accent, making it challenging and time-consuming to unpack their answers. Equally responsible is my accent and how it prevented learners from understanding me. I had to make an effort to speak more slowly and clearly and avoid any slang or geographic references to my location.

Through virtual training, we can type our questions and answers in the chat window, which we often volunteer to do, perhaps recognizing the accent issue on our own. In other cases, I concluded that some students were what Elaine Biech called the "dominators": "Dominators take up too much airtime by talking, sometimes repeating themselves and sometimes speaking slowly and in great detail."[47] Again, it's my job to learn how to address these students respectfully and effectively instead of simply ignoring them.

Ms. Biech goes on to list numerous ways to address dominators, which included these: "Break into the middle of a lengthy statement when they take a breath and ask for other opinions and put out a question, asking learners to raise their hand so you can call on someone other than the dominator." While these methods may be effective, you must still collaborate with the

---

47   E. Biech, *Training for Dummies*, (Hoboken, NJ: Wiley Publishing, Inc.), pgs. 237-238.

dominator so they don't feel left out of the learning experience. Either way, I had to engage these folks more often.

How to do it

The keyword in this tip is "often," as in the tip title: "Engage students *often*." While lecturing, frequently check in with everyone by name. If you haven't heard from a student in fifteen minutes, you risk losing them.

Often, it's simply a matter of taking a portion of your break time (see tip 45 about giving frequent breaks) and using it to skim through your list of participants (see tip 1 for creating this list). You'll quickly get a sense of which students you may be neglecting. Make a mental note of it. Everyone should feel they're an essential contributor to the class. This is not just a nice sentiment; it's something you must put into practice. In other words, it isn't sufficient to engage students often; you must find ways to make each student's voice known and understood to play a positive and beneficial role for all attendees. Every student has something to contribute and it is often something you, the trainer, would not be privy to. If you fail to execute on this tip, you might as well record a video and let your learners passively watch it.

Challenges

- How often do you engage with each student in your class?
- What is your preferred method of engagement?

Solicit instant feedback.

Background

Feedback is great and disappointing and satisfying. It's necessary. It's all of these things and more.

Without feedback, at best, we'd miss some of the joy of training and, at worst, we wouldn't stand a chance of improving our craft.

In his book *Good to Great*, Jim Collins examines the Stockdale Paradox, which states, "you must retain faith that you will prevail in the end, and you must also confront the most brutal facts of your current reality."[48] Feedback is how we confront the brutal facts. Positive and negative feedback is equally helpful.

In his book *Setting the Table, The Transforming Power of Hospitality in Business*, restauranteur and CEO of Union Square Hospitality Group Danny Meyer addressed the need for timeliness when requesting feedback. "The time frame for addressing mistakes is crucial."[49] He suggests taking the initiative in several ways, including these from *Setting the Table*:

- "Respond graciously and do so at once."

- "Learn from the mistake. Use every new mistake as a teaching tool."

- "Make new mistakes every day. Don't waste time repeating the old ones."

How to do it

The feedback has to be honest and forthcoming to be practical and actionable. So how do we solicit this type of feedback?

As soon as you know you need input, such as after an exercise that you struggled to create or after a quiz you've never given before, it's best if you act quickly. Those honest feelings that you seek are freshest immediately after the event. The student is in the midst of the emotion, and that's when you want to solicit feedback.

The key is to avoid taking too much class time to get that feedback. Here are a few options:

48   J. Collins, *Good to Great*, (New York: Harper Business), p. 86.
49   D. Meyer, *Setting the Table*, (New York: HarperCollins Publishing), p. 225.

- Verbally ask students for feedback, striking while the iron is hot! Ask them to reply in the chat window (privately, if that's what they prefer).

- Ask feedback questions like the following:

- Was this an effective use of our time?

- How challenged were you on a scale of 1 to 10 during that lab exercise?

- Let them know that you'll allow only one to two minutes for this feedback so that you can resume class.

- Alternatively, consider adding one to two minutes to the next break so they can provide feedback.

- Either way, always let students know that they're welcome to email you at any time during class to discuss any issues. Be sure to check your email every day after class and every morning before class begins.

Sometimes learners' feedback is less than constructive. We can see they're unhappy but are unsure why or what we can do about it. Share the experience with your supervisor or, if you're an independent trainer, share it with another trainer for more constructive feedback.

Brainstorm ideas regarding what prompted a learner's dissatisfaction: "Professional trainers profess to build on the foundation of adult learning theory. If something is not working, step back, determine why, and fix it. You're not practicing good adult learning principles if you're not doing that. You may need another trainer to guide you."[50]

Resources

Once again, *Training for Dummies* offers an excellent suggestion: soliciting feedback from a fellow instructor. Have your colleague watch you teach while using the training feedback form provided in the book. The form prompts the trainer/coach to look for very specific feedback on your learners' sense of hearing and sight.

In the "What Do You Hear?" section, the trainer/coach observes speech style:

- Projection

50 E. Biech, *Training for Dummies*, (Hoboken, NJ: Wiley Publishing, Inc.), pgs. 2 p. 28.

- Pitch

- Pace

- Pauses

- Pronunciation

- Filler words

Note: Have your coach keep a click-timer to note how often you use your filler word. You can keep track of filler works with ummoapp (http://www.ummoapp.com/).

For software that monitors your rate of speed and other speech issues, try Orai (https://www.orai.com/).

In the "What Do You See?" the trainer/coach looks observes body language:

- Body stance

- Gestures

- Facial expressions

- Eye contact (tip 27)

- Nervousness

Challenges

- How do you solicit instant feedback from your students?

- What are some ideal times to solicit feedback from students?

- How do you solicit feedback from your clients or direct reports?

- Do you have a coach or mentor? If so, how do they provide feedback?

Begin every topic by creating a need.

Background

Perhaps the most honest feedback I've received from a learner happened during the student introductions, where an attendee boldly proclaimed, "I don't even know why I'm here." Talk about challenging! I, of course, respected his feelings and never suggested that he'd figure it out. I made an extra effort to get to know him better. Fortunately, I'd done an extensive needs analysis with the group's management and felt confident that we had discovered the correct needs of the group and the training that would fill that need.

This student's feelings were genuine, and as the course unfolded, he did indeed become aware of why he was selected to attend the training. The more I thought about it, the more I realized the notion of "Why am I here?" probably arises more often than we think. I began to see this learner's voiced opinion as more of a macro-thought and wondered about all of the micro-thoughts along this line like, "Why is he teaching this?" and "How will this help me?" Engaged students are motivated students, and it's our job as technical trainers to motivate them.

How to do it

We can effectively motivate students by creating a need before each topic we present. There are a number of ways to create a need both explicitly and implicitly. The following sections describe these six methods:

1. Describe a problem
2. Use a relevant example from recent news
3. Use an analogy.
4. Cite a fact or statistic that relates to the topic.
5. Use a short quotation from a recognized source.
6. Ask learners, "What is the benefit of knowing this technique?"

Describe a problem

Present a scenario that introduces a problem experienced by workers, followed by a discussion of how to solve the problem. Here are two examples:

1. "Have you ever arrived at a meeting at the wrong time or missed a critical meeting completely? Were you convinced that your email software had plugged the meeting into your calendar? What did you

do wrong? Let's talk about invitations to meetings and automation so you can fix this problem once and for all!"

2. "How many of you have been involved in a project that failed because a critical path was missed? Doesn't your project management software prevent that? Isn't that why you chose this software? Let's take a look at why this happens and how you can prevent it from happening again."

Use a relevant example from recent news

The *Wall Street Journal*, published an article on demand for Flash engineers (https://tinyurl.com/yckjdd7p). I was teaching a tremendous number of both private and public Adobe Flash and Adobe Flex classes at the time. The following quote from the article was perfect for grabbing attendees' interest:

> Top full-time Flash engineers can now command more than $150,000 a year in salary, says Stuart Liroff, a headhunter at Greene-Search recruiting firm. That compares with $50,000 to $80,000 a year, three years ago, several entrepreneurs say.[51]

In a class I taught on web application development, we started with a discussion of Webvan, the, failed online grocery store. We discussed strategic and operational failures and, more specifically, consumer testing, A/B testing, web design, and user experience.

> Webvan's site did not work well with WebTV or American Online, or with the smaller screens and Netscape browsers that are more common with older computers. HomeGrocer users encountered bugs and JavaScript errors. These bugs were not uncovered until Webvan expanded beyond Silicon Valley into places like San Diego.[52]

It didn't take long for these discussions to resonate with attendees on many fronts, including setting the stage for the course content and its relevance. It also helped build anticipation and motivation before the class started.

Use an analogy

Ask your learners to compare and contrast two scenarios, for example, scrum versus kanban, level logging versus comments, test-driven development versus behavior-driven development, and so on. Be sure to dig deep and don't let superficial answers suffice.

---

51 P. Tam, "Demand Up in Engineering Specialty", Wall Street Journal, August 26, 2010.
52 San Jose Mercury News

Always let the worker's job dictate the content of the analogy; if content doesn't relate directly to workers' jobs and the company's business goals, a productive discussion can become an academic debate that holds little real-world meaning for learners.

Cite a fact or statistic that relates to the topic

Try beginning your lesson with a compelling or surprising statistic. Avoid statistics that are common knowledge or controversial. For example, "Cybercriminals can penetrate 93 percent of company networks.[53]"

Here are more examples from a *Forbes* article[54] on the sectors most targeted by hackers in 2021: Most Targeted Sectors Worldwide by Hackers in 2021

- Education/research sector (up by 75 percent)
- Healthcare sector (up by 71 percent)
- ISP/MSP (up by 67 percent)
- Communications (up by 51 percent)
- Government/military sector (up by 47 percent)

Use a short quotation from a recognized source

Introducing a quote from a known expert in the field or even a relatively obscure individual with a pertinent opinion is the basis for a great discussion. For example, offer the quote: "One line of working code is worth 500 of specification." Then ask the class: "What do you think Allison Randal had in mind when she made this statement?" A lively discussion will likely follow, perhaps with thoughts on the role of the software architect and input from developers who encounter problems.

Ask learners about benefits and uses

I love to brainstorm with my students, and introducing a lesson is an excellent time for everyone to generate ideas about the topic. This act, by itself, creates interest in the lesson and eagerness to begin. The key is to allow this free-wheeling discussion to take place without judgment. As trainer, you should limit the time devoted to evaluating a quote or topic and gently guide any responses toward the subject at hand.

---

53   I. Barker, "Cybercriminals can penetrate 93 percent of company networks," Beta News, Dec. 11, 2021, https://betanews.com/2021/12/20/cybercriminals-penetrate-93-percent-of-company-networks/

54   C. Brooks, "Cybersecurity in 2022—A Fresh Look at Some Very Alarming Stats, Forbes, Jan. 21, 2022, https://www.forbes.com/sites/chuckbrooks/2022/01/21/cybersecurity-in-2022--a-fresh-look-at-some-very-alarming-stats

In short, be sure your topic introductions (whether written or verbal) include answers to the following questions:

- Do learners need this information?
- Do they need it right now?
- How will learners benefit from this information?
- How will they use this information when they're back on the job?

More ways to create a need

Perhaps one of my favorite techniques is to open the class by shouting out the lesson's topic as briefly as possible (brevity is critical here). Then I reverse the Q and A by asking learners to generate questions they have about the subject and would like the class to cover.

For example, I could say, "inversion of control" and ask learners to generate questions in the chat window. Good examples would be "What is inversion of control?" "Is inversion of control the same thing as dependency injection?" and so on.

Finally, throughout the lesson, it can be helpful to instill in learners a sense of responsibility. You might ask them directly, for example, "As a software tester, is it your responsibility to both conduct the test and analyze the results? Is the testing responsibility divided between unit tests and regression tests?"

I've witnessed amazing displays of personal responsibility. Frequently my classes consist of attendees all working for the same company but from various parts of the world. It's inspiring to see conversation break out among attendees, all seeking to understand how to help their colleagues do their jobs better.

On one occasion, this kind of socializing was becoming time-consuming. The department leader saw the concern on my face and quickly came over to let me know the value he saw in these personal connections. "This is great," he said, "I couldn't ask for a better outcome." He thanked me for prompting the discussion, but I couldn't help but think it was his excellent staff that took the initiative. I did learn the significance of motivation through personal responsibility that day.

Challenges

- How do you typically start a new topic?
- How do you ensure your learners are not already experts in the topic?
- How do you sense the need for a topic to be addressed?

Tell stories.

Background

Wouldn't you like to command your learner's attention like you were their favorite actor (better still, their favorite actor in their most influential movie role)?

Even though I'm often mistaken for Brad Pitt[55], I could still use some help getting and holding my students' attention as quickly as their favorite movies would. Fortunately, most trainers are natural speakers and storytellers. And aren't movies really just stories?

What if you told a story about an experiment you once tried that failed miserably or a colleague (certainly not you!) who wrote code that derailed the company website and resulted in millions in lost sales? Sure we could lecture about a known software bug or a process gone wrong, but that wouldn't be nearly as compelling.

During a discussion on user experience and user interfaces, I introduce one of my favorite stories: the $300 million button. The story centers around the annoying practice of ecommerce websites that force a user to register with the site before completing a purchase; a practice that causes many potential buyers to forgo their purchase and leave the site. The designers fixed the problem simply. They took away the Register button and replaced it with a Continue button with a simple message: "You do not need to create an account to make purchases on our site. Simply click Continue to proceed to checkout. To make your future purchases even faster, you can create an account during checkout." The results: The number of customers purchasing went up by 45%. The extra purchases resulted in an extra $15 million the first month. For the first year, the site saw an additional $300,000,000."[56] That's a very compelling way to introduce designing and implementing buttons for ecommerce websites!

Most of us know what an impact storytelling can have. Technical training materials of all kinds, including those on safety training, manufacturing processes, and more, often contain important topics that have a significant impact. For example, the consequences of learners misunderstanding the content can be deadly.

---

55 This never happened.!
56 J. M. Spool, "The $300 Million Button", Center Centre–UIE, Jan. 4, 2009, https://articles.uie.com/three_hund_million_button/

Storytelling can enhance the significance of a lesson, and the emotional component of the story can help the learning to stick. One of the best classes I ever took was a driver's education class. Let's categorize it as "compliance training" (I was sort of required to take the class!). It was not one of the driver's education classes taught by a comedian. The teacher was a woman who knew how to drive a point home engagingly and compellingly—not an easy task. I had dreaded the day of the class because I knew how difficult it would be for me to sit for eight hours, yet the time flew by. Why?

For her first exercise, the trainer asked us to write down what we were doing when we received our violation ticket. She did not ask what type of ticket we'd gotten, just what we were doing that day. We had to confess what we'd written to the person seated next to us who then described to the group what we'd been doing when we got our ticket. Needless to say, after participants told their classmates' stories, we realized that trying to save five minutes to fetch a quart of milk was hardly worth the risk we took and the eight hours we were now spending together. She continued to engage us with compelling stories of driver safety and provided helpful tips that we could implement in less two minutes. These tips made considerable differences in the way we drove or thought about driving. I don't doubt that the instructor saved a lot of lives that day. It was indeed her calling.

The ability to tell or create short stories on the fly can add a bit of drama to a topic—just enough to make the lesson have more impact. As Barbara Oakley put it, "The best lectures in math and science are often framed like thrillers, opening with an intriguing problem that you just have to figure out."[57]

Typically, there's often more material to cover than time in my training, and I'm sure you can relate. So, how can we benefit from storytelling without the time expense of telling stories?

Dr. Ray Jimenez agrees, saying, "I'd love to add stories and storytelling in my lessons, but they are long, tedious, and hard to do, not counting the fact that it's costly."[58]

How to do it

Dr. Ray Jimenez is chief Learning architect and founder of Vignettes Learning. com. He suggests something he calls *hyperstories.* These are stories that have immediate meaning and context; they heighten involvement. Dr. Jimenez looks first at the components of a story: the theme, characters, conflicts, emo-

---

57 B. Oakley, *A Mind For Numbers,* (New York: The Penguin Group), p. 177.

58. https://vimeo.com/512573206

tions, and resolutions, and the discovery of the moral of the story. Adding all these features can make storytelling too time-consuming for most training classes. So, focus on the parts of the story that will be most helpful when you want to move and engage learners: conflict, emotions, and resolutions.

To make a hyper story, try to abbreviate it. Make it brief, simple, and concise. Focus on the most exciting parts of the story. In short, hit the highlights.

The act of abbreviating the story results in some pieces going missing. Happily, learners will interpret the story and fill in the gaps. In fact, an incomplete story heightens curiosity. Provocative stories engage listeners. A hyper story should bring out the learner's version of the story and allow learners to think (and learn). The hyper story gets learners thinking and makes a perfect starting point.

Here is a hyper story from my Introduction to Computer Graphics class. A student created a CD cover for a band. His mom got him the job and he was very excited. The rest of the class was busy listening to my lecture on file formats and related concepts. At the first break, the student pulled me over to his computer and beaming with pride, showed me the artwork he created. "I'm sorry I couldn't pay attention this morning but I have to put this on a CD and FedEx it to the client at lunchtime so he can have it printed tonight" he said. "This can't be printed tonight" I said. He was crushed. What did he do wrong?

The learners now guess what could be wrong with the file. I show them the file in Photoshop. They guess more. They think. They recall. They have been challenged with that "desirable difficulty" that is so helpful. The story took less than two minutes to tell but it creates a sea of knowledge recall from the learners. After allowing the class to shout out answers, we commenced a lengthy discussion on RGB vs CMYK and screen resolution. The learners were hooked. "Was he able to fix it?" "Could he recreate the art correctly?" He could not I said and asked them why not? Again a lot of discussion around Photoshop layers, saved selections and filters ensued along with a great deal of empathy for that student.

Challenges

- Do you have a favorite story you tell?

- Can you turn it into a hyper story (as described by Dr. Jimenez)?

- How often can you tell stories before it becomes tedious for your learners?

Make your lessons memorable.

Background

Think about a favorite class you took. Was it yesterday or several years ago? Maybe it was in college or high school. No matter how long ago it was, it's memorable and something made it that way. Spend some time thinking about what you remember about the class, and then try to trace the qualities that made it memorable.

How to do it

Do you remember tip 7 about being yourself? This is the time to tap into what makes you unique as a trainer. What is it about your delivery style in general that's uniquely you? This is the kind of thing that will make your lessons memorable.

There are as many techniques for being memorable as there are trainers. Here are a few supplemental ideas:

- Show a cartoon (ideally modified or chosen for the subject matter).
- Read or show a slide that contains a memorable and relevant poem or quote.
- Show a short movie clip and then tie it into the lesson.
- Tell a compelling and personal anecdote, one they couldn't hear from anyone but you!

Challenges

- What have you done in past classes to make a lesson memorable?

Switch between ideas while teaching.

Background

In the Chapter 3, you learned about the significance of interleaving, which comes into play when you're learning two or more related concepts. You begin interleaving after focusing exclusively on one idea or skill followed by a related but different skill. Interleaving lends itself to technical training very easily because technology often involves more than one solution to a problem. The solutions are related because they solve the same problem. The approaches, however, may be radically different. To interleave, you alternate between solutions.

The traditional form of teaching a new skill, whether learning to play the saxophone, improving your shooting in basketball or mastering trigonometry, is called *blocking*. Blocking is essentially practicing one skill at a time. For example, when learning an instrument, you'd practice scales; when learning how to shoot a basketball, you'd practice free throws, and so on. Interleaving has been the subject of numerous studies in sports, and it has also been proven very effective in subjects like algebra and geometry.[59] The best part of interleaving is the long-term effect. The theory is that interleaving helps strengthen those memory associations between the hippocampus and the neocortex. It's these connections that allow workers to return to the job, be confronted with a problem, and recall what they've learned in class.

How to do it

The first step is identifying what parts of your course would benefit from interleaving. Locate areas of your course where you are blocking and consider how you might interleave those topics. The process shouldn't require additional class time.

Also consider adding exercises that require the learner to jump from topic to topic. It should become evident that interleaving has achieved two beneficial side effects: practiced retrieval and desirable difficulty. Interleaving is an order of magnitude greater than blocking because it incorporates multiple techniques proven to increase understanding and retention.

---

59 S.C. Pan, "The interleaving effect: Mixing it up boosts learning," Scientific American, Aug. 2015, https://www.researchgate.net/publication/281454770_The_interleaving_effect_Mixing_it_up_boosts_learning

Challenges

- Do you practice blocking in your course?
- Do you think there are opportunities for interleaving?
- What areas of your course would benefit from interleaving?

Grab your learner's attention at the start of each and every lesson.

Background

Trainers love to talk, and most of us are naturally gifted in this area. Perhaps that's what draws us to this profession. I've met more than one trainer who was also a professional actor. The suggestion that trainers are performers is not to imply that we're acting or even putting on a persona when teaching. Our learners would see right through that. But it makes me think that we have the same bag of tricks used by professional performers at our disposal. We all want engaged learners and know that involved students stand the best chance of success after class. Engagement doesn't just happen; you have to plan for it! One constructive tip and one that I advise before each lesson is to grab the learner's attention from the very beginning of each lesson.

How to do it

There are as many ways to introduce lessons as there are technical trainers. Below are some methods designed to grab the learner's attention.

Start your lesson with the consequences

Example: describe an unstable system, show a statistic that represents how developers are spending their time for the last six months (e.g., primarily system maintenance and making quick bug fixes), describe missing documentation and testing, scrum standups where the choice is "do it right" or "do it quickly." Ask your learners what is happening and solicit comments until you get the answer you are looking for (e.g., technical debt).

Example: describe a scenario where an application manages a weeks' worth of data successfully but falls apart after six months. Ask your learners what went wrong? When did it go wrong? Answers might include additional hardware needs, poor data access choices, and so on. You can solicit these answers via the chat windows, where you can read them aloud and focus on the "correct" answers.

Begin your lesson with a provocative statement

Edward Tufte (author of *The Cognitive Style of PowerPoint*) blames the space shuttle Columbia disaster in January 2003 on the use of PowerPoint."[60]

---

60 E. Tufte, "PowerPoint Does Rocket Science---and Better Techniques for Technical Reports," https://

For an opposing or at least additional point of view, see http://newsalespresentation.com/nasa-powerpoint-2003.

Tufte's argument remains a controversial topic, but it's nevertheless one that grabs your learners' attention. Arguably, a subject so emotional and controversial might be better left out of your training course. There are still numerous other provocative statements that can arouse interest without stirring up a heated but unconstructive debate. Here are some pretty dramatic quotes about XML taken from http://quotes.cat-v.org/programming/.

- "The essence of XML is this: the problem it solves is not hard, and it does not solve the problem well."
  — Phil Wadler, POPL 2003

- "XML is like violence. Sure, it seems like a quick and easy solution at first, but then it spirals out of control into utter chaos."
  — Sarkos in Reddit

- "If we'd asked the customers what they wanted, they would have said "faster horses."
  — Henry Ford

- "The whole HTML validation exercise is questionable but validating as XHTML is flat-out masochism. Only recommended for those that enjoy pain. Or programmers. I can't always tell the difference."
  — Jeff Atwood

Cite an unusual or dramatic statistic

Here are a few examples:

- "In the third quarter of 2020, DDoS (distributed denial-of-service) attacks averaged 106 per day."[61]

- "An application that spends 1% of its execution time on garbage collection will lose more than 20% throughput on a 32-processor system. If we increase the GC time to 2%, the overall throughput will drop by another 20%. Such is the impact of suspending 32 executing threads simultaneously!"[62]

A dramatic slide that represents the statistic is even more impactful.

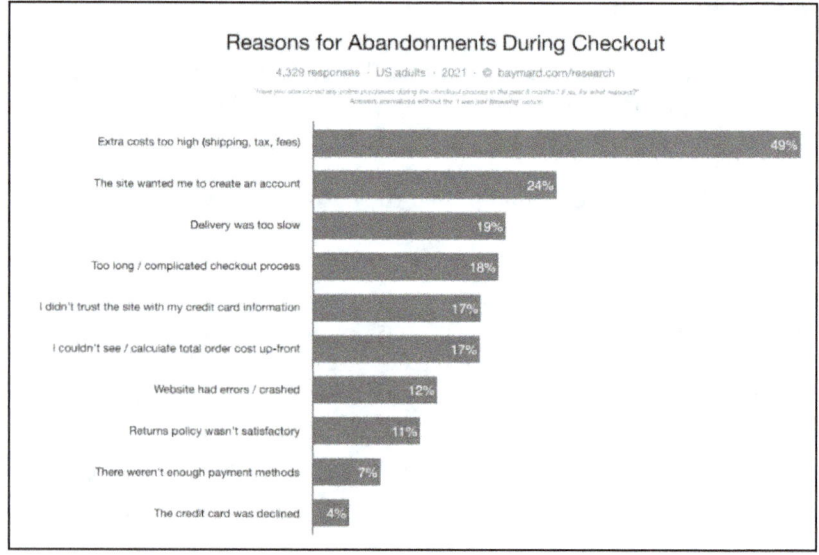

Figure 40: Baymard Institute article on cart abandonment.

61   I. Kidd, "The Shocking DDoS Attack Statistics That Prove You Need Protection," Sept. 30, 2021, https://www.infosecurity-magazine.com/blogs/ddos-attacks-stats-protection/

62   "The Impact of Garbage Collection on Application Performance," dynatrace, https://www.dyna-trace.com/resources/ebooks/javabook/impact-of-garbage-collection-on-performance/

Teaching a JavaScript class? Why not start with the following survey?

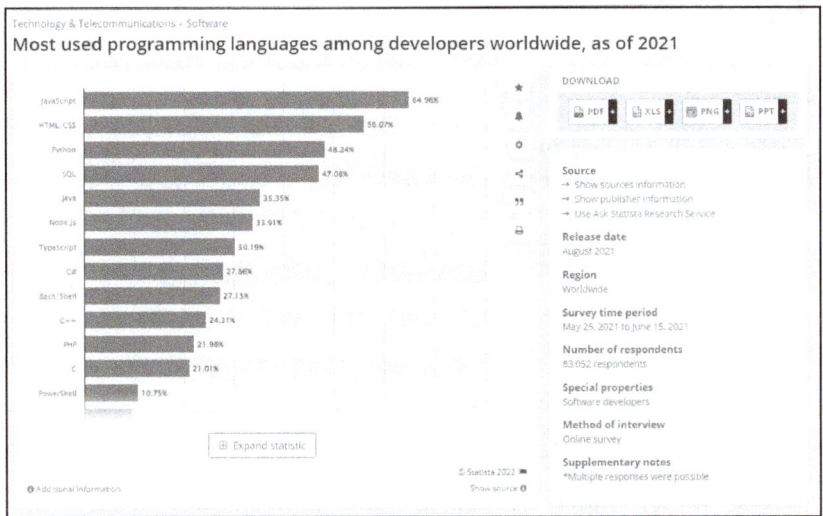

Figure 41: *statista article on the most used programming languages as of 2021 https://www.statista. com/statistics/793628/worldwide-developer-survey-most-used-languages/.*

Display a dramatic visual

In his superbly written book *Confessions of a Public Speaker*, author and speaker Scott Berkun suggest we "Take an interesting angle from the beginning. If you choose your topic and opinion, pick something interesting. Take a stand. Force a point of view into the title, and let it grow into the points you make. Even if your topic is only interesting to you, if you express your passion well, the audience will want to follow simply because of your enthusiasm."[63]

Challenges

- How do you typically introduce a new topic?
- How do you introduce a group of topics that make up a single lesson?

---

63   S. Berkun, *Confessions of a Public Speaker*, (Sebastopol: O'Reilly), p. 163.

Cut out your filler words.

Background

At some time or another, most of us use filler words: "ah," "um," "well," and so on. My filler words have changed over time, proving how persistent the habit can be. Like roaches in a New York apartment, just when I think I've gotten rid of the last one, another one takes its place! My latest is "so." The problem with filler words is two-fold: (1) It can simply be annoying to some people attuned to hear them (myself included); and (2) They can make you sound unsure of yourself or even flustered.

Even if you think you have no filler word, you may be guilty of the nearly constant "okay." The key is to train yourself to pause, breathe, and don't utter a sound while you're collecting your thoughts; that's when the dreaded filler word presents itself. Simply replace your "ums" with breaths.

How to do it

My first recommendation is to record yourself and play back the audio recording to find your filler word. (This is easier if you stick to an audio-only recording.)

Another technique I've used during mentoring (via Zoom) is to have the trainer simply lecture for about fifteen minutes. For the first three to five minutes, I do nothing, but after that, I make a small hand gesture every time I hear the filler word. The filler word will slowly go away, replaced by another filler word or a slight pause. I repeat this exercise weekly, and eventually, the filler word goes away.

Technology

Orai (https://tinyurl.com/4wkbarn9) has an excellent product that can analyze your speech, including your pronunciation, rate of speed, and more.

Rehearsal (https://www.rehearsal.com/details/features/)provides virtual practice and coaching through both human mentors and artificial intelligence.

Challenges

- Do you know what your filler word is?
- Do you know how to figure out what your filler word is?
- What tips do you have for eliminating your filler word?

62 Use videos that break up the monotony of the single lecturer.

Background

I love Massive Open Online Courses, also known as MOOCS. MOOCs are often but not always free, and anyone can enroll. Some are regular classes in the catalogue of your favorite university or your alma mater. I've taken courses at Tulane, Stanford, Duke, and more—and all without paying a penny! See "Resources" below for finding MOOCs and other online learning opportunities.

As soon as the class begins, I immediately judge whether or not I'll enjoy the course. Almost instantly, I decide if I'll learn anything or—as I often do,—wonder if I'll remember any of the subject matter for any length of time. The courses are often very passive and almost always involve listening to long lectures. I've discovered that the most compelling talks use small but impactful techniques that keep me engaged.

One of the techniques that has worked well for me as a student and teacher is the subject of this tip: play videos (of someone other than yourself).

Videos break up the monotony of having a single lecturer, but I was reluctant to use them in my corporate training sessions. I couldn't escape the feeling that I was playing the part of the dreaded substitute high school teacher, who, arriving unprepared, quickly pops in a movie for the students to watch. The use of an explanatory video, even one that I had vetted as an excellent resource, seemed like cheating.

Once I bit the bullet and tried this idea, the feedback was unanimous. Everyone loved it. (Of course, never pick a video just for the sake of playing a video; choose one that adds significant value to the topic at hand.)

How to do it

Acquire a video and make sure you have the legal right to play it for your learners. Some videos are behind a paywall, and it would be unfair to use them in class even if you've paid for the video. The license agreement typically prohibits spending once and playing for a larger audience.

Your colleagues can be an excellent resource for finding good videos. Perhaps they have skills that are part of your class but at which you aren't proficient. Ask a colleague or a subject-matter expert you know to either record a brief lecture (five minutes or so) or interview them by asking the questions your learners would ask. Videos available for educational purposes abound on sites like YouTube. I make it a practice to reach out to the author for permission, which I have never been denied.

Next, you must choose the best delivery method for these videos. You can select the best software on your machine and simply share your screen, but you must also account for the audio portion and how it's received on the learner's machine. See "Technology" below for information on dealing with audio in various classroom environments such as Zoom.

Finally, you can make your own video using a combination of screen capture software, other videos, and content you've made with fellow trainers.

Technology

The following resources will help you share video and audio directly to your students as opposed to having the sound broadcast from your speakers then back to your microphone.

- Zoom: https://tinyurl.com/33uc9nub
- Teams: https://tinyurl.com/4h4swa9x
- GoTo Meeting: https://tinyurl.com/ycynznu5
- Webex: https://tinyurl.com/2p87s7d5

Challenges

- What techniques do you use to give the users a different voice?
- How do you break up the monotony of a single presenter?

Ask one or more of your learners to deliver the end-of-lesson summary.

Background

I admit it: I'm guilty of a common beginning trainer mistake. It goes something like this:

> I have (or should have) all the answers. I am the most important person in the room. The client has asked me to travel from the other side of the world to speak and teach. I've conclude, therefore, that I should be doing all of the talking. That's what they're paying me for, I surmise.

Not so! Of course, you know that the client is paying you to empower learners to perform better when they return to work. Armed with new information, skills, techniques, and critical thinking skills, learners should become more confident and productive and have a greater capacity to deliver a higher quality product or service.

But I also knew that, at the time, I didn't understand how to teach in the most effective way. I also didn't get that that didn't involve me doing all of the talking.

Shouldn't this information inform us (trainers and course designers) of the proper lecture, discussion, and exercise ratios? I should think so, and many of us do. We keep talk to a minimum and devote a substantial portion of our classes to hands-on exercises.

What gets shorted is typically learners' participation in the form of comments and discussion. We tend to think (and to some extent, it's true) that if we allow learners time to speak, we'll quickly run out of time for course content; we may also lose control of the class. Given the statistics, we should find a compromise by factoring in time for our learners to speak. One way to do that is to take the time during which we typically talk and hand that time over to more students. This way, we're not taking any more time than we would typically have; the only difference is who is talking.

How to do it

When done correctly, handing issues directly over to students to address is no more time-consuming than when you lecture, but it's also far more effective at making the learning stick long after class ends. Any time a learner can arrive at the correct answer, conclusion, or technique on their own, the benefits far outweigh those when a trainer simply states the information. Yes, this takes some practice, but it's well worth the investment, and you'll get better and better at it the more you practice.

Now let's look at the technique that's the subject of this tip: ask one or more of your learners to deliver the end-of-lesson summary.

Sharon L. Bowman describes a *learner-led summary* as follows: "A learner-led summary is a discussion or series of statements, led by the training partici-pants, which summarizes what they've learned. **Remember:** You're not doing the summary; the learners are.

Besides being an effective way for learners to review content and for you to assess their learning, a learner-led summary also gives you—the trainer—an opportunity to evaluate what learners know. For example, during a learner's summary statements, if you hear erroneous information, make a mental note to meet with that learner after the training (or at another time) to address the misconceptions. You wouldn't even know there was a misunderstanding if you did the summarizing for the participants."[64]

I've had success with running the learner-led summary as follows:

1. I ask one learner, by name, to summarize how they'd use the lesson. Typically, you'll need to supply a scenario for this to work.

2. After I provide positive feedback to the learner, I ask a different learn-er to expand on the first step.

3. I repeat this process until I've called upon all participants (if possible).

The trainer's job is to keep the conversation in the context of a summary and not let it veer off too much. This helps with time management as you try to make the summary as concise as it would have been had you delivered it yourself.

Challenges

- Who does most of the talking in your classes?
- How can you incorporate more learner-centered discussion?
- During what parts of the class might you be able to solicit learner feedback?

---

64 S.L. Bowman, *Training from the BACK of the Room*, (San Francisco: John Wiley & Sons), p. 213.

Tips for dealing with questions

"The art and science of asking questions is the source of all knowledge."

— Thomas Berger

Keep a record of student questions that have gone unanswered.

Background

Like tips 23, 31, and 32 this tip serves as one of the many small gestures that help establish trust. I do a postmortem after all my classes where I use different techniques to help me determine class successes and failures, both large and small. Confirming that I've answered all student questions is very time-consuming. I make the effort because at the beginning of class, I promise to answer all questions, and nothing erodes trust as much as a broken promise.

Answering on-the-fly questions is what live instructor-led training is about! My clients have repeatedly told me that the main reason they chose live instructor-led training is so that workers can ask questions. Interacting with a trainer makes live instructor-led training far more effective than "canned" video training. If the attendees can't ask questions and get answers, they might as well be using eLearning or video training where they're far removed from a live human being.

How to do it

Sometimes a learner poses a question, and I may not have the answer but know who to ask for a much better response than I might be able to supply. Other times, questions require a bit of research on my part. I promise my learners I'll do that research and get back to the question first thing in the morning.

To facilitate this, I have a document open for the duration of the class; it serves as the proverbial "parking lot" for unanswered questions (modify the tip 2 template by adding a new section to capture these questions). This document sits on my dedicated ancillary monitor where I have utility software. I use Microsoft Word because I type much faster than I write. I type up their questions as they ask them, letting them know I've made a written note.

My students typically ask great questions. Sometimes they're beyond the scope of the class or too complex to answer quickly, but they're almost always good enough for the whole class to benefit from the response.

After researching, I write a brief and cogent answer, often including resources (books, websites, our courseware, etc.). I begin each class by sharing this document with the class and confirming with the learner who asked the question, "Steve, does this answer your question, or do you need more information?"

The result is twofold: (1) I'm slowly building a job aid for this and future classes with the ever-popular "Frequently Asked Questions" (FAQ) document. (2) I'm developing a library of questions for a class that doesn't exist yet but will undoubtedly be a part of future courses. The students walk away with this FAQ containing answers to their questions and additional resources.

And sometimes students send me other resources via the chat window. I add those to the document right then and there—a win-win!

As a last step, save the chat log at the end of every class. You can read it after class and make sure you haven't missed any questions.

Challenges

- How do you keep track of unanswered questions?
- How do you confirm with learners that their questions have been addressed before class ends?
- What do you do when you need more time to answer a question?

Ask specific questions and ask them often.

Background

I believe students come to a class with the hope of success and expectations that a trainer will facilitate that success. They want to score well on quizzes, complete lab exercises successfully, answer questions correctly, and be better at their job than before class.

To help learners succeed with that last item, we have to avoid asking them ambiguous questions. These can lead to awkward pauses as the learner tries to decipher our inquiry and the class waits patiently (or not so patiently).

According to the *Handbook for College Teaching*, "To be an effective instructor, one must be an effective questioner."[65] Unfortunately, far too many technical trainers teach by lecturing uninterruptedly for fifteen minutes or more. In his book *Confessions of a Public Speaker,* Scott Berkun puts it very well, saying: "No one says regretfully on his deathbed, 'If only I'd gone to more lectures!' We know that the best way to learn something is by doing it, and in a lecture, you never do much of anything except sit and stare (two things few of us need to practice)."[66]

I have the luxury of attending many conferences and webinars throughout the year. These meetings are always about a topic for which I have a tremendous passion (often science, coding, and training). I've attended too many conferences about coding, highly motivated to participate, only to sit and watch someone code for close to one hour straight, and I love to code! I've had many questions, too, but have never been given a chance to ask them.

Webinars are notorious for this, and even the better ones where questions are encouraged can be challenging. Without clarification from the trainer, students are sometimes confused about whether or not they're supposed to ask or answer questions. Absent physical cues (as in live, on-site, instructor-led training), students may also be reluctant to speak over others or interrupt the current speaker. In short, you need to "facilitate more than you lecture."[67]

---

65 W.R. Miller and M.F. Miller, *Handbook for College Teaching,* PineCrest Publications, p. 131.

66 S. Berkun, *Confessions of a Public Speaker,* (Sepbastopol, CA: O'Reilly), p. 81.

67 E. Biech, *Training for Dummies,* (Hoboken, NJ: Wiley Publishing, Inc.), p. 36.

How to do it

The first step is to avoid confusing your students about whether they should answer questions. You can do that by setting some ground rules. The first is to enforce (with some exceptions) *prioritizing all questions over the topic at hand.*

Immediately after I pose a question, I remind students of the method they should use to answer. For example, for a thought-provoking or opinionated question, I may say, "Okay everyone, this is one for the chat window. Let's see ten answers as quickly as you can!" (assuming, for this example, that there are ten attendees). I'll then read and elaborate on the individual answers, always calling out and rewarding the learner by name. I may say, "Linda says we should…. I like that, Linda—especially how you elaborated on part two." Other times I might say, "Okay, everyone unmute!" and let learners know that I expect answers to be shouted out. I'll follow up with something like, "Wow, almost everyone said XYZ, but I thought I heard a dissenting voice; Chris, was that you? Why do you feel that way?" After doing this a few times, I've noticed I get more and more participants. It breaks the monotony of previous response methods and gets everyone's vocal cords warmed up.

At the start of class, I often tell students that if they have a question but don't feel like it's an appropriate time to interrupt, the can simply type a question mark in the chat window, and I promise to keep my eye on the chat window and address their question. Keep that promise, and the system works very well indeed.

You need to check in with learners and ask for their questions frequently in a virtual classroom. Even with webcams, we can no longer rely on facial expressions or body language to determine if a learner is confused.

Coming back to the first part of this tip—"Ask a specific question"—let's look at some examples of good and better ways to ask specific questions.

Good	Better
Does this make sense?	Do you know why we wrote this line of code?
	Do you know why we chose this query?
	Do you know how we resolved this discrepancy?
	Do you know why this part X was chosen over this part Y?
	What are the consequences of omitting this step?
How's my pace?	Am I moving too fast, too slow, or just right?
Does this answer your questions?	Does this last step answer your earlier question about why we do [insert task here]?
Is everyone good?	Have you entered the code I gave you (or completed the last task? Use the chat window to say "No"; if I don't hear from you, I'll move on.
Is everyone with me?	Does everyone understand this last concept [insert concept here]? Give me a quick yes or no in the chat window, please.
How are you all doing?	This is an acceptable question if you ask your learners to answer with emoji (like those for confused, bored, tired, great, etc.). Request emotional feedback directly. You can't get the feedback you need if you don't ask for it! "Send me some love or send me some hate.... or maybe you're lost and confused. Let me know how you're feeling!"

General tips

- Open each question you ask with the action a learner needs to take to answer the question (e.g., "How did you…?" "Describe this task…," "Define this term…." "Justify this action…," and so on).

- Speaking deliberately and slowly can benefit both you and your learners.

- Encourage the conversation between learners by asking one learner to comment on the question or comment of another learner.

- When in doubt about your questioning strategy (or any of your training strategies), ask your learners to contact you privately to give you feedback. You'll get a more significant response if you let them communicate with you privately, but be sure to ask all attendees). Don't be afraid to ask your learners for their advice. Each cohort is unique, and what works for some may not work for others. When you ask your adult learners how best to teach them, you're being respectful of their experience and skillsets, and they'll appreciate it.

- Ask or define what something is not. Provide a question with false answers to truly test understanding and note rote memorization.

Technology

I have several favorite questions, including some that help me understand the prevailing mood of the room. I keep these questions in a text document that I leave open so that I'm ready to copy and paste into the chat window.

Using third-party software, you can broadcast a single question to everyone in the group. (See tip 80 for broadcasting messages in Zoom). I use the Power-Point slide shown below to indicate that I'll be randomly engaging students. That typically gets a quick laugh. A simple mouse click causes the wheel to spin; another click brings it to a stop. For some reason, after I show that slide, everyone screams "Big money" and wants to play *Wheel of Fortune*!

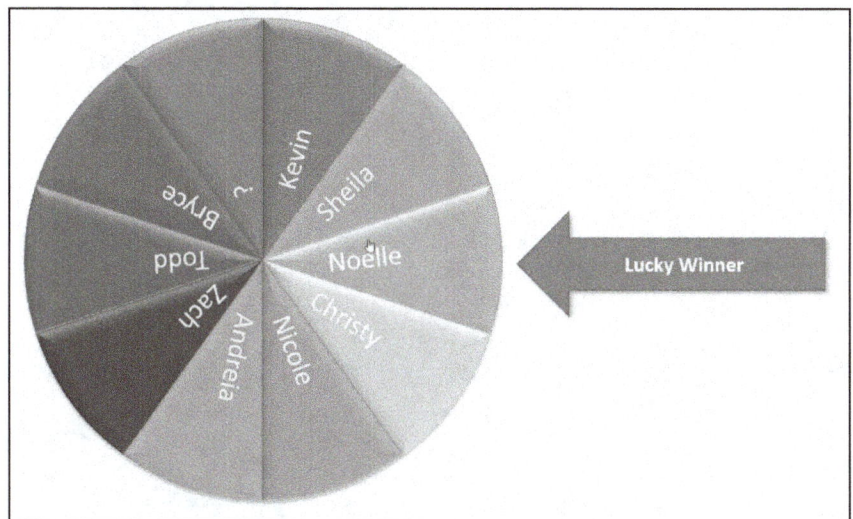

Figure 42: PowerPoint name picker built from YouTube tutorial at https://www.youtube.com/watch?v=ANP6ZYrWZ3U.

You can find additional pointers from Kinetic Slides at https://www.youtube.com/watch?v=Bn6u9N8EWOA.

Challenges

- How do you ensure your questions are specific enough?
.

Give learners a second chance when they're having difficulty answering a question.

Background

I love to watch the game show *Jeopardy!* I answer approximately 50 percent of the questions correctly…about ten seconds *after* the timer goes off (or shortly after the contestant beats me to it)!

It can be frustrating when you know you know something, but the pressure gets to you and you can't summon the answer in time. I bet this happens to my students, and I probably frustrate them when they can't answer a question and I move on to someone else. I've even had a few students tell me, "Oh yeah! I was just going to say that" I've decided to stop frustrating my students in this way.

How to do it

Because my training consists of a great deal of questioning, it's common to periodically hear the following response: "I don't know." Instead of asking other students to jump in and help, I now respond to the learner by saying, "Okay, can you tell me what problem we're trying to solve here?" Nine times out of ten, the learner is halfway through describing the problem when it comes to them: "Wait, can we just…?" and they solve the problem and answer the original question.

Remind the learner that they just went from not knowing what to do or where to begin to solving the problem within minutes. Confidence builder? You bet!

Challenges

- How do you respond to a learner who has answered a question incorrectly?

- What can you say to provide a second chance?

Tips for Training Materials

*"It seems that perfection is attained not when
there is nothing more to add, but when
there is nothing more to remove."*

— Antoine de Saint-Exupery

Consider using a slide deck.

Background

Ah, the great Microsoft PowerPoint debate is back! Is PowerPoint an awesome learning aid or an evil and unnecessary distraction? As you've learned by now, my response comes down to this: Does it help learners?

I've given talks that included four slides to highlight an impactful image, chart, or statistic. I've also taught classes with 400+ slides. Some slides move quickly, more quickly than the five minutes of a lecture needed to explain the point absent a slide. replace the slide. Other slides are shown briefly for dramatic purposes—for example, a crazy graphic designed to be unforgettable. Case in point: A learner may have trouble recalling Eben Hewitt's thoughts on ambiguous software requirements and the notion that "software architecture requires a continual refinement of thought, a repeated straining of ideas until we have determined the essence of each requirement in the system."[68] Still, they're not likely to forget staring at a huge image of consommé.

How to do it

Ultimately, I've decided that learners benefit from slide decks. I let the content determine the number of slides.

I have some boilerplate slides that I use for every training. Given how many sessions are recorded for later use, these slides add to the overall professionalism of the presentation:

- The "Welcome to class" slide lets learners know they're in the right place.

- A reminder slide lets students know what to focus on while introducing themselves.

- Class setup slides confirm that learners have everything they need to participate in class.

- Introductory slides provide information relevant to the current activity. These are very helpful given that students often miss what's going on in class because they've walked away from their computers. When

---

68   E. Hewitt, *97 Things Every Software Architect Should Know*, (Sebastopol, CA: O'Reilly Media Inc.), p. 190.

they return, slides like the following tell them what's going on with the following:

- o   Classroom breaks

- o   Classroom materials.

- o   Learning style of the class (e.g., how we'll complete exercises)

- o   Introduction to objectives

- o   Introduction to quizzes

Note: Some of the slides above are created in presentation software, others by using Open Broadcast Software (OBS) tools.

Here are some best practices when using slides to deliver content:

- Don't read slides to your learners. When presented with text, people typically begin reading independently (and at their own reading pace). If you read to them, you're adding to their brain clutter. Allow your participants a minute or two to read the slide and reflect on it at their own pace if you absolutely must include text. But consider removing the slide text and replacing it with a simple graphic to be presented while you lecture.

- Don't reveal more information per slide than necessary. Sometimes a slide full of text seems unavoidable. Perhaps you have a list of significant checkpoints that you would like to discuss one at a time that results in an eight-item list. Animate the slide so that learners see only one item at a time. The more content you show, the more your learners will read ahead and miss the discussion entirely. By revealing one thing at a time, you can have a distraction-free debate on each point.

- Don't use complex and cluttered charts and diagrams. Charts and graphs can be constructive when digesting new material, but reduce the visual complexity by animating only those parts of the diagram that are needed to conclude one piece of the content. Once that piece is understood, you can reveal the next part of the diagram. When carefully coordinated with the lecture, these diagrams become easy-to-follow concepts.

- Most slide decks benefit from the following edits:

  - o   Remove any logos (training company, trainer, and so on)

  - o   Remove titles

o   Remove most of the words

o   Remove the background

The argument for not using a slide deck

There are significant studies indicating that students prefer hand-drawn lectures over PowerPoint-type slides. Students have rated whiteboard drawing high in all measured metrics including course enjoyment, learning of key concepts and course outlines. In addition students score higher on exams and instructors score higher on areas like instructor involvement and enthusiasm and student instructor interaction.[69] So called "chalk talks" where the lecturer relies on live in-class drawing to accompany lectures have numerous advantages. A cursory look at this technique in light of what has been discovered regarding the neuroscience of learning makes complete sense: learners remain engaged as the drawing and subsequent concepts begin to unfold. Virtual training eliminates the blackboard but we can make use of whiteboard software. You can continue to use your whiteboard if you provide a camera that captures both you and your drawing. Drawing live in front of your students can be time-consuming and without practice, unpredictable. I argue that a well-animated slide will closely mimic a live drawing and ultimately advocate a mixture of both techniques.

Technology

Here is a list of software used to create presentations.

- **Google Slides** (https://www.google.com/slides/about/)

- **PowerPoint** (https://tinyurl.com/2cj747u6)

- **Home-made online slide deck** with HTML using reveal.js (https://revealjs.com/)

Many years ago, I had a system in which I wrote with Markdown (https://www.markdownguide.org/) and generated both workbooks and presentations with a document converter called Pandoc (https://pandoc.org/). The system not only created HTML5 slides with the markdown language, but also output to PDF. If you need an efficient system to simultaneously create workbooks, presentations and course outlines you should consider a system like this one. Pandoc can output many formats, so you can customize the system to your liking.

---

69   C.M. Waters, "Rock the Chalk: A five-year comparative analysis of a large microbiology lecture course reveals improved outcomes of chalk-talk compared to PowerPoint," May 27, 2019, https://www.biorxiv.org/content/biorxiv/early/2019/05/27/644567.full.pdf,

Below are some additional automation tools (I haven't personally used these tools and would love to hear about your experiences):

- **Hacker Slides** (https://github.com/jacksingleton/hacker-slides)
- **Landslide** (https://github.com/adamzap/landslide)

Challenges

- Do you use a slide deck?
- How many slides do you present per hour and per day?
- What is the typical duration of a single slide?
- Do you ever skip slides? (**Hint:** Hide them instead!)

Don't rush past slides.

Background

It's simple. If you're consistently rushing past slides, it's probably time to re-move them. If you are uncertain or feel you may use them in the future or you simply want to preserve them as a reminder to update them later, just hide them instead of deleting. Technical subject matter, in particular, is often best described using a real-world context (e.g., showing code in a code editor rather than in a slide, especially if you're going to be editing that code). That's the end of this tip.

Challenges

- What's the shortest amount of time you've ever displayed a single slide?

Consider eliminating summary slides.

Background

The time to summarize a lesson is the ideal time to practice retrieval. Don't step on one of your best tools for making your lessons stick! Get rid of the summary slide and involve the students in the review.

How to do it

See tip 63 on student-led summaries and tip 70 on turning bullet points into conversations.

Challenges

- Do your summary slides contain only text?
- How do you summarize your lessons?
- How do you involve students when you're summarizing lessons?

Consider turning bullet points into conversation.

Background

The last words I want to see in my end of class evaluations are "Death by PowerPoint." I'd much rather hear, "What a great presentation. It really held my interest."

Is PowerPoint the problem? PowerPoint slides are props, and "props get students' attention and help with recall; they make the lesson memorable, and they provide an anchor for knowledge recall. They can be used to spice up a boring lesson or to add drama and suspense,"[70] according to the Institute of Teacher Aide Courses.

Given this context, slides, even those with bullet points (arguably what PowerPoint is best known for), can help students when they're back on the job by supporting recall of information from class. But these slides are merely *anchors* for recall. An instructor must do the heavy lifting, engaging students and effectively utilizing what we know about learning. Use those PowerPoint bullet points as jumping-off points for spaced learning, practiced retrieval, and desirable difficulty.

How to do it

In tip 70, I discussed slowly revealing slides to allow for point-by-point discussion. In tip 67, I discussed not reading slides to participants. In tip 22, I discuss asking students to introduce themselves by answering questions that have been supplied in a slide deck. In these and similar situations, slides with text should be conversation starters. Unfortunately, too many trainers simply read slides to their learners.

Bullet points don't have to be solutions or even thoroughly analyzed thoughts. They're a perfect starting point for analysis and interpretation.

A particularly effective technique is to turn your bullet points into questions. But because bullet points can be broadly interpreted or ambiguously worded, your questions must follow specific rules to be effective:

- **Make questions concise:** The notes you've written to accompany a given slide can include the specific question that will lead the learner

70   A. Green, "Teaching aids and props: the basics for teachers and teacher aides," Institute of Teacher Aide Courses, https://www.itac.edu.au/blog/teaching-strategies/teaching-aids

from a mere bullet point to a relevant and precise concept, task, or technique.

- **Limit a question to one idea.** Here we defer to our understanding of working memory. Keep new ideas short and they will be easier to consolidate later into long-term memory.

- **State questions in familiar language:** Don't be tricky with terminology. The idea is to relate prior knowledge with new information.

- **Focus on material critical to the worker.** The end of the lesson is the perfect time to turn the worker's attention back to their job and ask questions that directly relate to their work.

This question and answer quickly becomes a conversation when the trainer poses the question to another learner rather than answering it him- or herself. Try the following questions in response to the learner's initial answer:

- How would you have answered that?

- What do you think of that answer? Do you agree?

- Are there any other plausible solutions to that question?

As learners respond, be sure to maximize your position as the facilitator. If a learner misses a critical point, ask questions to draw out the correct response. In short, don't "tell" what you can "ask."

The majority of conversations that take place in class should be preplanned. You, as the instructor, know what material can and should spark discussion. Dialogue must have a purpose, such as providing the benefits of a particular skill or defining pros and cons. Shining a light on the limitations of technology can be very effective.

Challenges

- How many of your slides contain only text?

- Do your slides contain sentences and/or short bullet points?

- Have you ever read your slides aloud to your learners?

- Find a slide you want your learners to read and see if you can turn it into a conversation instead?

Implement quizzes that are effective at practiced retrieval.

Background

If you've read the introductory section entitled "A Brief Overview of What Happens to Your Learners While You Teach," you understand how practiced retrieval works and how it's proved to be one of the most effective ways to make learning stick. There are numerous ways to implement practiced retrieval, and frequent quizzing can be a particularly effective method.

How to do it

Properly written quizzes are challenging to create. Fortunately, scientific studies lead the way. There are countless resources on the web regarding writing effective quizzes; most are aimed at quizzes that test for knowledge or assessment.

Quizzes designed for practiced retrieval are slightly different, but we can learn a lot from following the science of writing effective quizzes of the other sort. Ground rules and best practices are essential because you must ask the right questions in the right way:

- Refer to your performance objectives for each topic as the blueprint for creating questions.

- Give three-answer choices for multiple-choice questions[71]. Research shows that these typically perform better than those with more than three choices.

- Make your answers to multiple-choice questions plausible; do this even for incorrect answers. The answer choices you provide shouldn't give any clues that would immediately rule out one option.

- Avoid "None of the above" because it doesn't confirm the learners' knowledge on the topic.

- Avoid "All of the above" because it makes your question much harder; each option requires too much analysis, so it takes too long for the typical virtual class.

71   Afsaneh Dehnad, Hayedeh Nasser, Agha Fatemeh Hosseini, A Comparison between Three-and Four-Option Multiple Choice Questions, Procedia - Social and Behavioral Sciences, Volume 98, 2014, Pages 398-403, ISSN 1877-0428, https://doi.org/10.1016/j.sbspro.2014.03.432.

- Reread each question and answer to ensure that the correct answer is unambiguously correct, precise, and easy to understand.

- Don't write trick questions!

- Generally, avoid writing true-or-false questions. They can be helpful only when there are two answer options.

- Consider drag-and-drop functionality in place of multiple-choice as it's more interactive.

Challenges

- What types of questions do you ask your learners? Do you ask memorization-type questions?

- Do your testing methodologies implement best practices regarding the questions asked?

 **Turn your favorite, most effective analogies into movies, animations, or compelling graphics to make learning stick!**

Background

Trainers are inherently great at analogies. Some of the best teachers I've had excelled at tying together an idea I was very familiar with to a new idea I was trying to learn. I've seen some excellent trainers seemingly pull these analogies out at will during Q and A sessions. It's truly amazing, and I bet you're a natural at it too.

Now take it a step further: add an image to that analogy and leave your learners with, not only a better grasp on the concept, but also a compelling memory they can recall at will long after your class ends.

How to do it

A constant area of debate is whether or not to use a slide deck. For this tip, I'll avoid that topic (see tip 67 for more information about using a slide deck). Instead, I'll focus on images that may or may not appear in your slide deck. ☺

While many people believe the notion of visual learners has been debunked, there's little debate about the effectiveness of images for a substantial number of learners. In *A Mind for Numbers*, the author explains: "Part of the reason an image is so important to memory is that images connect directly to your right brain's visuospatial centers. The image helps you encapsulate a seemingly humdrum and hard-to-remember concept by tapping into visual areas with enhanced memory abilities."[72]

I also like the short but compelling explanation from the book *make it stick*: "Humans remember pictures more easily than words. (For example, the image of an elephant is easier to recall than the word "elephant.") So it stands to reason that associating vivid mental images with verbal or abstract material makes that material easier to retrieve from memory. A strong mental image can prove as secure and bountiful as a loaded stringer of fish. Tug on it, and a whole day's catch comes to the surface."[73]

Do you see what they did there? They added imagery in the form of a stringer of fish to the phrasing. What if I added the image below?

72 B. Oakley, *A Mind for Numbers*, (New York: The Penguin Group), p. 159.
73 P. Brown, H.L. Roediger III, M.A. McDaniel, *make it stick*, (Cambridge: The Belknap Press of Harvard University Press), p.243

Figure 43: Photo 93705558/Stringer Fish ©Daniel Thornberg|Dreamstime.com.

To remember the impact of one compelling image on your learner's memory, think of this loaded stringer of fish. Tug on one fish [photo] and recall a wealth of information.

I wonder why we keep showing our learners slides filled with words and redundant blocks of text. While that may sometimes be necessary, those blocks of text are ineffective in making concepts stick well beyond class.

Technical training is full of complex subject matter. Images, especially those that slowly reveal content, allow learners to digest smaller chunks of information at a time. Virtually all slide deck software enables an author to create images with animation. One huge color-coded graphic full of arrows and callouts can be confusing. But the same image slowly revealed during the lecture allows the learner to reflect on the content a little at a time.

Revisit some of your static graphics and consider "refactoring" them into multiple images that can be animated. The result is a seamless, fully prepared lesson that puts the learners' needs first.

Sometimes your learners need a little prompting to arrive at their ideas concerning the topic at hand. A great technique is to initiate a learner-led summary of a completed topic (see tip 63 for more on learner-led summaries). In this technique, one or more learners (I prefer more if it's a complex topic) recite what they've learned in summary. You can prompt users with a partially completed concept map like the one below.

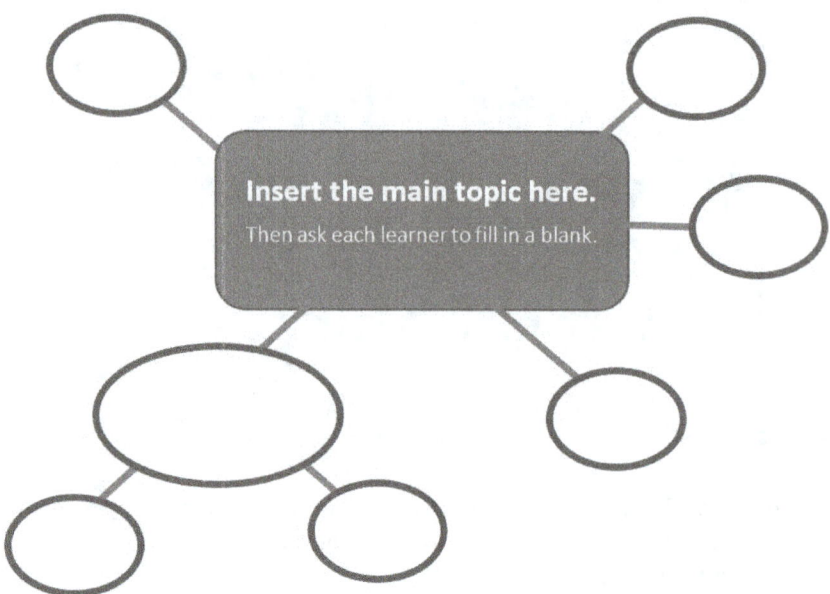

Figure 44: A partially completed concept map.

Ask your learners to fill in the blanks using the virtual classroom's annotation tools.

When dealing with a particularly tricky concept, the more bizarre the image, the more it sticks. Of course, you have to tie the image to the idea to help the learner make the mental connection.

One of my favorite techniques to show an image representing the topic: A problem, a scenario, a finished project, and ask the learners what this image means to you?

Challenges

- How do you add impact to your training?
- How do you signify the importance of a particular lesson?
- What types of visual aids do you use in class?
- Where do you get your images?
- How do you choose the most impactful image?

Consider using workbooks.

Background

I took bookkeeping classes in high school, and for as long as I can remember, I've had an interest in personal finance. As a result, I've attended countless financial and investing workshops, both in person and online. Being an instructor and a natural people-watcher, I often observed participants entering a workshop.

Each time an instructor invited students to take a workbook, I could see the delight on the attendees' faces. Smiling, they'd pick up the workbook and nod approvingly to their classmates. I would watch as participants flipped through the book and could see them sharing the exercises with those around them.

Viewing the workbook, they immediately knew that they'd be involved in the class in a hands-on way. The existence of the workbook added perceived value to the presentation.

Wouldn't you like your learners to see value in your class from the moment they first take their seats? As Robert Pike states in his book *Creative Training Techniques Handbook*, "As trainers, we need to constantly be selling the value of the training that we're delivering. When participants go back to the workplace with well-organized materials that they can show to supervisors and coworkers, those materials are saying, 'This seminar is worthwhile.'"[74]

From a technical training perspective, this tip should be viewed under the heading: "Does it help the learner?" Not all learning environments lend themselves to printed learning materials. In some cases, learning materials might be cumbersome and of little value to the learner. In such cases, job aids and handouts might be more appropriate. Each trainer will need to give this careful consideration. As usual, getting feedback from your learners is essential.

How to do it

The contents of a workbook will vary tremendously depending on the course topic. Typically workbooks provide in-class exercises that reinforce the course content. They may include job aids such as cheat sheets, workflow diagrams

---

74   R.W. Pike, *Creative Training Techniques Handbook*, (Amherst, MA: HRD Press Inc.), p. 100. (Rosenshine, 1988) (Reynolds, 1992, p. 145)

and so on. They can range from complete and comprehensive textbooks to a few pages with instructor-led exercises.

In addition to workbooks, consider providing your learners with helpful job aids such as cheat sheets for everyday tasks, programming commands, software tips, and anything else you can think of that will help workers on the job. Cheat sheets can also include flow charts and diagrams of especially complex processes, and handouts with charts and graphs are often enough to trigger recall of an entire lesson.

Reading lists and online resources are also helpful, and PDFs are an excellent format to deliver this content. Be sure to enable Acrobat users to highlight and select content so they can quickly copy and paste relevant hypertext links and code if necessary. A popular PDF in my courses is a collection of frequently asked questions that I pull together from previous classes.

Challenges

- Do you use workbooks?
- Are they digital, printed, or both?
- What are the qualities of a good workbook?
- How do you know if your workbooks are practical?

Consider using a whiteboard.

Background

My handwriting is somewhat on the terrible side without a slow and concentrated effort, and my diagramming leaves a lot to be desired as well. I vividly remember one class where I was drawing away like Picasso in action. Remembering to never lecture to the whiteboard, I turned back periodically to speak to my students. I was intense and focused on delivering a complex concept with ease, all the while thinking what a genius I was at producing these lucid analogies and diagramming them with speed and precision. Finally, I turned around to complete the lesson by viewing my masterpiece while watching the learners enjoying a meaningful ah-ha moment. Unfortunately, upon viewing my artwork strewn with numerous arrows, callouts, and illegible text, I was severely underwhelmed. And based on the looks on my students' faces, they were too. I could barely read what I'd written.

Thankfully, in virtual classes, we have software that can help us draw perfect shapes and legible text and allow our learners to participate. I'm not referring to the annotation tools built into platforms like Zoom, although I find those tremendously helpful. I'm referring to a lecture that requires me to draw on the fly or at least one where I've determined that drawing on the fly is the best approach. Often, I need to draw a picture in response to a question that I wasn't expecting, so I can't just navigate to a prepared slide in my slide deck. This is when tools known as whiteboards, or digital whiteboards, can be super helpful.

How to do it

I like to use different whiteboards for different purposes. For example, here are a few apps I can use if I need to demonstrate a concept through artwork:

- If I want to use something I can launch from my desktop PC, I'll use Microsoft Whiteboard (available for download at https://tinyurl.com/2p84cps8).

- I also use a web app for the same needs. I prefer diagrams.net (formerly draw.io) for this.

- Both of these applications are free, but if you'd like a more robust application offering free and paid versions, I highly recommend Lucidchart (https://lucid.co/).

Sometimes, I'd like my students to contribute to the artwork. In that case, I have these options:

- I can try the annotation tools provided by the platform (but you must test these first). Not all whiteboards accept content in this way.

- Alternatively, you can use collaborative whiteboards like https://web-whiteboard.com/.

One drawback of whiteboards that support collaboration is that you have to share the board, which can be cumbersome for learners. Most collaborative whiteboards work like this:

- The trainer creates the whiteboard by visiting the site and making a diagram.

- The trainer shares the whiteboard by copying the URL into the classroom chat window.

- The students visit the URL and can participate immediately.

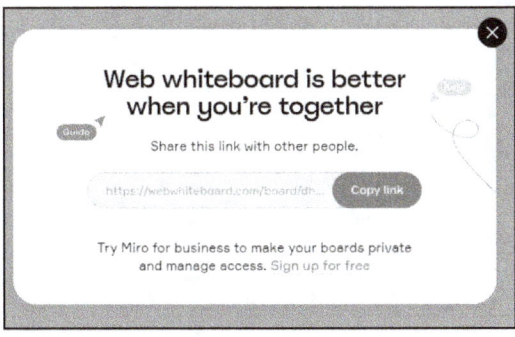

Figure 45: Sharing a whiteboard at webwhiteboard.com.

Finally, you can use a real live whiteboard! If you have a camera setup that supports viewing at a distance that's sufficient for learners to see the whiteboard in detail, you're all set. See tip 80 about switching cameras while you teach.

Resources

Online whiteboards

- Collaborative whiteboard (https://whiteboard.explaineverything. com/)
- For use by trainer only (https://draw.chat/)A diagramming tool I find incredibly helpful (https://app.diagrams.net/)

Challenges

- Do you have a favorite whiteboard?
- For what specific tasks do you turn to the whiteboard?

When it comes to course content, try to underpromise and overdeliver.

Background

Continuing reading for more tips! (See what I did there?)

Consider using breakout rooms.

Background

While mentoring new trainers, the most common question I receive concerns all trainers: How do I instruct a group of attendees who have varying levels of skills, background, and proficiency with the subject matter?

A disparate skillset is a common challenge for us technical trainers, and there are many helpful techniques we can implement to solve or at least mitigate this particular problem. No doubt, you have some solutions that you've acquired over the years and regularly implement in your live, on-site instructor-led classes. But what about the "virtual" class? Do those same techniques work, or are they impossible to replicate?

Before tackling that specifically, recall that disparate skill sets are not the only differentiating factor within our cohorts. Here are some examples:

- We often have attendees who must code after class and managers who won't be coding but need to level up their skillset and overall knowledge.

- We may have both junior- and senior-level developers.

- Regardless of the group they're in, each individual may be intimidated for a variety of reasons.

- They also present trainers with a range of issues to resolve. A case in point: a class attended by the "team lead" can often result in attendees following their team lead instead of the instructor.

- Other issues include junior developers or new hires intimidated by the presence of senior developers. In that case, a trainer might be able to improve the situation by indicating that junior developers are now in a unique position to learn from senior developers who have a vast project and technical experience. That's one way to turn a perceived negative into an exceptionally large positive!

Now, let's review one technique many trainers are familiar with and adapt it to the virtual environment: pairing students. For this discussion, *pairing* is defined as seating the students next to one another physically (at least in the live classroom environment) and encouraging them to work together and ask one another questions when the instructor is busy assisting other attendees.

The general premise behind the technique involves pairing experienced learners with less experienced learners. **Note:** This type of pairing is not the same as pairing fast learners with slow learners.

There are potential pitfalls to both scenarios. So, before we discuss implementing this technique, we should look at the positives and negatives.

Pairing learners with opposite learning styles

In the case of pairing fast and slow learners, the trainer must consider the feelings of both types of learners. The fast learners can feel "used" and conclude that the training session is not advancing their skills. At the same time, the slow learner may feel intimidated. In both instances, not being physically in front of students can be a handicap.

If you find yourself facing this situation, it can help to take the opposite approach: pair fast learners with fast learners and slow learners with slow learners. Pairing similar learning styles allows both learners to relate to one another, feel comfortable, and advance their skills at the same rate of speed.

Pairing more-experienced with less-experienced learners

The idea of pairing more experienced learners with less experienced learners is a favorite technique of many instructors. The reason may be somewhat selfish (albeit ultimately in the best interest of the attendees): it moves the class along faster than it might move without the pairing because you effectively now have a handful of teaching assistants. Such "assistants" can be highly efficient in large classes because as we help one student, we know that attendees are helping their coworkers. Be aware that some of the same downsides for pairing fast and slow learners may also present here. For example, you must make an extra effort to ensure the more experienced learner is also increasing their skills.

Pairing in the virtual classroom

The pairings above reveal how often we trainers rely on intuition or that gut feeling we get from seeing our students' faces and body language. Absent that, I rely heavily on chat, chat, and more chat (and specifically private chat).

Beyond chat, there's another way to bring this technique in the virtual classroom: *breakout rooms.*

Breakout rooms are available in Zoom, webex, Adobe Connect, and GoTo Meeting. They allow you to "seat" students next to one another virtually, and this can be ideal if you determine that, for a portion of the class, pairing students will provide benefits.

To illustrate, I'll share the experience of a trainer I've been coaching who at first implemented it with caution but came to use it with a confident delivery. What did he do right? As it turns out many things; he followed best practices with these basic steps:

- He made sure he got to know the students first so the pairings would be deliberate and deliver the highest rate of return.

- He did it only for one lab exercise to improve his comfort level for future endeavors. This approach allowed him to better scrutinize, thus providing a more direct feedback loop as well as the opportunity to focus on what he did right and what he could do to improve the experience.

- He clearly defined the objective of the task and the criteria for success criteria. He also provided some hints to get the students started on the right track.

- He briefly discussed the fundamentals of pair programming.

- He set the ground rules regarding his expectations for the two-member groups.

- He set an appropriate time limit for the task.

- He monitored the groups throughout the task while simultaneously honoring that one of the goals was for attendees to rely on one another instead of the trainer.

All in all, it was a success!

The only thing I'd add would be to ask for specific and immediate feedback in the chat window to determine if the effort was an effective use of class time. I'd ask this question of learners directly.

In this case, in addition to the technical task taught, there were numerous other benefits. The students also learned how to communicate effectively with a teammate, use nomenclature while adding new terminology to their vocabulary, and they got a sense of the pair programming experience.

How to do it

Breakout rooms provided by virtual environments are, for the most part, very similar in what they offer and how they function.

Here's a summary that may answer some of your questions about Zoom breakout rooms:

Hosts and cohosts have these "powers":

- Hop between rooms
- Broadcast messages to all rooms
- Enter rooms
- Monitor what's going on in rooms (e.g., watch activity and see screen shares)
- Close all rooms, which provides a default one-minute timer for participants
- Extend countdown time to closing)
- Reopen rooms as needed
- Set breakout room options

Room participants can chat and share screens.

At the end of the breakout session, be sure to thank both parties in each pair for their patience and understanding.

Challenges

- What part or parts of the class would benefit from a breakout room?
- What do you hope to accomplish in a breakout room that you can't accomplish with the group as a whole?

Consider replacing (or combining) a lecture with an animated graphic.

Background

Have you ever attempted to understand something that you'd initially de-scribe as incredibly complex and way outside your skillset? Maybe you started small and read short explanations online. Perhaps you purchased a book or two on the subject. You might even have taken a multiday course. But after all of this training, you still had little confidence in your subject-matter knowl-edge.

Then one day, out of the blue, you met someone with expertise in the topic. This expert showed you a simple graphic that described the subject and put all the complex pieces together in a clear demonstration. After a five-minute conversation, you suddenly felt that you truly understood the topic: what was once overwhelming now made complete sense!

Masterful training is a worthy goal. Expert training that's also time-efficient is even better.

Imagine that you're introducing a new concept (machine learning algo-rithms, cyclomatic complexity, dependency injection, call stack, shallow neu-ral networks, etc.), and your goal is to focus on this high-level concept. You begin to lecture on the topic, with or without live code or demonstrations. Then you move quickly through the overall idea and into the details. There's a problem with this approach.

Moving too soon into the inner workings of a high-level concept can confuse learners. They won't understand the concept and miss how they might apply the concept in various contexts. When the central idea is not understood, learners are challenged for the duration of the lesson as well as long after the class ends.

How to do it

One solution is to use a simple graphic to explain the concept from a high level. Follow up with concrete examples only after you're certain (by ques-tioning your learners) that they understand the concept. The challenge for most trainers is that they're pressed for time; some would argue that they don't have the time or skills to generate graphics.

Admittedly a "simple" drawing can be anything but simple to create. Images are time-consuming to design and build and are often revised and edited, much like text. The result—the practical (and quick) transfer of knowledge—is worth it.

Students often ask for a copy of my slide deck specifically because the images are compelling. I concluded this when I sent PDF copies of the presentation upon request of the students and they immediately asked for the slide deck, specifically for the animated graphics. The static image had much less impact than the animated one, and that impact resulted in more effective recall of the lecture.

Compelling graphics have the following characteristics:

- They're animated. By slowly revealing concepts one at a time, you decrease the cognitive load on your learners and can more quickly and easily confirm their understanding.

- The impact of animations on the learner increases the likelihood of concept retention. Avoid boring, canned concept maps, flow charts, and the like that consist of simple shapes that are quickly forgotten. Use memorable wild images! The images can be displayed at a swift pace because they are quickly understood, and just because they're animated doesn't mean they will render slowly on low-bandwidth internet connections but you should always test them first. Images allow the instructor to move through content quickly and let the pictures do the talking!

- They load fast. There's no fumbling back and forth between your software, browser, and any other screens you need to share. When you're moving too fast, you distract students and are challenging to follow. Simply load the graphic and begin. I use an animated GIF already loaded into my slide deck when demonstrating a common topic (for example, finding my code repository and cloning it).

- In short, graphics should do one or more of the following: clarify, simplify, or amplify.

Learning sticks if you ask your students how a concept can be implemented in their projects. Using graphics also provides a beneficial side effect. They load quickly and communicate professionalism far more than jumping from screen to screen with the lag time inherent in virtual training. Use of graphics tells the learners you're well-prepared and have considered the material from their point of view.

Technology

- **Canva and, specifically, their infographics** (https://www.canva. com/; https://www.canva.com/infographics/templates/)

- **Lucidchart** (https://www.lucidchart.com/)

- **ScreenToGif** (https://www.screentogif.com/)

- **Gliffy** (https://www.gliffy.com/)

Challenges

- How many of your slides contain graphics?

- Could any text-heavy slides be replaced with graphics?

- Where do you find your graphics?

Miscellaneous Tips

Take care of yourself physically and emotionally.

Background

How would you respond to a worker who approached you with the following commentary?

"I'm so tired. I'm really trying to pay attention in class, but I've been working on a project with an unrealistic deadline. I haven't slept more than four hours at a time in the last two weeks. I keep plowing on, but I know my work is suffering. I'm hoping this training will help. I think I'll work through lunch this week so that I can make more progress."

Odds are you know that "plowing through" under these conditions won't get these workers where they need to be. And then participating in training while the worker is exhausted is an exercise in futility and working through lunch only exacerbates the situation. The worker would be well-advised to resist their current reaction and instead take a break, relax, get some rest, and resume proper hydration and diet.

Yet, many trainers are guilty of the same overdemanding routine.

Keeping up with the technology we teach can be a full-time job, leaving trainers with little time for the teaching itself. Yet, that's how we make a living. It can be very demanding.

While the temptation to overwork can be very compelling, if we want to remain effective and energetic trainers, we must manage our overall workload. Far too many trainers I mentor are self-branded "overachievers" or "workaholics."

It requires a candid evaluation of our work habits to solve the problem. Time management is a crucial and necessary skill for those who task themselves with learning new material, real-world execution of that material, implementing the practice, creating learning materials, and, ultimately, teaching. If you overcommit, something in that pipeline will give: at worst, your work will fail entirely and, at best, it will be of diminished quality. I've pulled all too many overnighters to prove this notion. If we're honest with ourselves, we might conclude that the result is often teaching when you don't want to. Put another way, the spirit is willing, but the flesh is weak.

Let's look at some solutions to this problem.

How to do it

In short, take the time to realistically calculate how much time these preclass tasks will take and don't overcommit. It can be helpful to hash this out slowly and in writing. This extra time may result in a monetary loss to some extent; however, that's in the short run; in the long run, you'll earn more and have more fun doing it.

The Pareto Principle can be a helpful guide. The Pareto Principle states that 80 percent of our output comes from 20 percent of our input. Put another way: 80 percent of consequences come from 20 percent of causes. Step one is to determine where your outputs come to fruition, what the consequences, both good and bad, come from at each step in the process of delivering training. Rebudget your attention on the 20 percent of effective causes.

Finally, when faced with teaching a class while dealing with exhaustion, re-energize yourself and find your motivation. Reenergizing means different things to different people. Some techniques that I like include listening to my favorite music, reminding myself what it felt like to teach my first class, and most significantly, reminding myself that this training opportunity is one my learners may never receive (at least from me) ever again. They've committed to me, and I must, in turn, deliver the best possible class that I can!

Challenges

- What methods do you use to determine how long it will take to complete preclass tasks?
- How do you put preclass tasks on your schedule?
- What do you do to re-energize when you are feeling physically lethargic or emotionally exhausted

79 Make an effort to know your stakeholders and their motivation for purchasing the class.

Background

Technology training is typically motivated by a business need. Ultimately, when done correctly, our job adds to the bottom line of the business in some way. It could be by increasing production that can be verified with statistical analysis. It could be by contributing to a happier, more satisfied workforce or delivering a perk that allows workers to learn new skills.

For a class to be truly successful, trainers must understand the motivation for the company to purchase your course. The more we know about motivation, the better we know the actual success criteria and the better the outcome will be.

I conducted an interesting class where the participants did not readily accept the technology I demonstrated. The group intended to use new software that didn't fill the requirements established by the workers. The company hired me to teach this software, and as the students challenged its efficiency for the job, I became concerned. They were right, and the company's choice of software, which was the course's subject matter, was wrong. The team's management was in attendance. At my earliest opportunity, I pulled them aside to discuss my concerns. Lo and behold, the manager quickly agreed and said he knew this all along but needed his staff to come to the same conclusion independently.

In this tip, I reference stakeholders who are not your participants. Corporate technical training is often motivated by front-line workers who desperately need to learn modern technology. Sometimes corporate training is encouraged by management for reasons uniquely their own (such as, confirming a decision made by the company to choose a specific technology). In such a case, the instructor is expected to extoll the virtues of the chosen technology and pay little to no attention to alternatives. Likewise, you may be teaching in an all-Microsoft shop where it won't be taken well should you decide to deride Microsoft products in favor of a competing technology. Whatever the motivation, it behooves the instructor to know as much as possible before the class begins.

How to do it

This tip may be more about staying out of trouble than about adding value. Here are some examples:

- Questions that seem innocent might have a political aspect that's sure to set the class on fire.

- Political questions can cause the subsequent discussion to veer way off-topic.

- Questions that require extreme answers are always best deflected at first. For example, the question "What do you think is the best project management software?" while teaching a Microsoft Project class can be a loaded question. In such instances, I often tell participants that it would be somewhat arrogant of me to answer questions requiring a deep and thorough understanding of their company's environment, processes, clients, and so on. I make it clear that they're in a better position than me to judge and have or will have the answers to those types of questions when the training is complete. Simply tabling the discussion for later typically strikes attendees as a fair compromise.

- Sometimes it helps to ask learners a probing question such as, "What is the problem you're trying to solve, and is it unique to your organization?" or "Why do you ask that?" An additional question like this can provide extra time for you to formulate your answer and also may suggest the questioner's motivation.

Challenges

- What type of questions make you think the answer would be a volatile trigger?

- How do you handle corporate political questions?

Make a classroom.

Background

Trainers are now responsible for their classrooms. Gone for many are the days of traveling to our classrooms and delivering training in a room set up for us by others. If you're primarily conducting virtual training, then you must supply the classroom. This is by no means a complete how-to. That's beyond the scope of this book. It is, instead, a simple checklist of what is absolutely necessary to have, some nice-to-haves, and some setup ideas to think about.

How to do it

Plan your classroom before you build it. It will help you make the decisions that are right for you and to avoid unnecessary expenses.

What do you absolutely need to "make a classroom"?

Necessities

1. **Workstation:** If possible, use a reasonably sized workstation. Some trainers are capable of teaching on a small desk or podium with a laptop; others require large desks that accommodate multiple pieces of equipment.

    If you're just beginning to create your classroom, you might wait to purchase a desk until after you've determined what type of equipment the desk needs to house.

    Consider using a sit/stand desk and be sure to have enough wire to accommodate both the sit and stand positions. If you stand often, consider purchasing an anti-fatigue mat which can help relieve the fatigue associated with standing all day.

2. **Chair:** Locate a comfortable, ergonomically correct chair and a place to put it when you choose to stand up.

3. **Keyboard:** Use an ergonomically placed keyboard. For more information, visit https://tinyurl.com/yxzvw3ex.

4. **Monitor(s) and stand(s):** Use one or more monitors and ergonomically correct monitor mounts. Again, this decision is subjective. The more equipment you add to your classroom, the more you have to worry

about loose connections, missing drivers, power requirements, and so on. The number of monitors you use may be a direct result of the other equipment you choose.

5. **Microphone:** Microphones are discussed in detail in tip 11.Consider where you place the microphone:

   - Directly on your desk

   - In a movable desk mount

   - On a floor mount or tripod

   - On the ceiling
   Determine if you need a shock mount.

6. **Audio out or speakers:** Determine if you prefer to use speakers or a headset.

   Figure out where you'll place the speakers. Consider a configuration for audio that includes a backup system. For example, use a microphone and speakers but have one or more headsets as a backup. Consider having both a wired and a wireless headset.

7. **Clock:** If you teach in across time zones, consider using multiple desktop clocks that have enough room for a label to mark the time zone.

8. **Refreshments:** Have a dedicated area for bottled water, coffee, cell phone, mints, gum, and so on, preferably not near any electronics.

9. **Backup computer(s):** Have a desktop or laptop that's ready to use without additional hardware requirements. A Keyboard Video and Mouse switch (KVM) allows you to use the same keyboard, monitor, and mouse for multiple computers. A variety of top-rated KVM switches can be found at https://tinyurl.com/2p895psu.

   Also have a computer that's dedicated to logging into your class as a student.

10. **Uninterrupted power supply:** Locate power supplies with surge protection for easy access. You can find UPS Battery backups like this one (https://tinyurl.com/ye27m3z2) at Amazon.com.

11. **Peripherals:** Have multiport hubs for peripherals. You can find top-rated USB hubs at https://tinyurl.com/5944e3b7.

Optional nice-to-haves

1. **Green screen:** Green screens vary in price and setup. You can find portable green screens for less than $20 and room-sized ones in excess of $250. I use a ceiling-mounted, retractable green screen similar to Koah Ceiling Mount Green Screen from Focus Camera (currently $28.99). Some teaching environments like Microsoft Teams include built-in backgrounds so you don't need a green screen.

2. **Drawing Tablet:** Drawing tablets are often used by digital artists who prefer the comfort and familiarity of drawing with a pencil. While these effective devices have been around for many years, the will require some practice. Wacom makes a popular line of drawing tablets; you can learn more at https://www.wacom.com/en-us

3. **Camera switcher:** Camera switchers allow you to control multiple HDMI devices such as HDMI-enabled DSLR cameras and computers. Other devices like an iPad can be attached to the switcher using cables like USB-C to HDMI. You can also use USB-C to HDMI adapters such as those made by Belkin and Apple. The switcher becomes the camera source for your classroom. For example, if you're teaching with Zoom, the switcher appears as a camera choice. Once connected, the switcher allows you to present different views to your learners. One view might be a different computer setup for running demonstrations, while another view might be a camera focused on you as you lecture.

   ATEM Mini Pro: I use an ATEM Mini Pro from Blackmagic. For more information, visit https://tinyurl.com/2p854bdc. This switcher has features such as customized picture-in-picture, which allows me to show my face in the lower corner of the main screen, which might be showing my slide deck or the software I'm using in class. It also includes professional-looking transitions during screen changes. This feature needs to be tested because low band-width connections make them render slowly and herky-jerky.

   The ATEM Mini Pro also includes jacks for wiring up one or more microphones that can be controlled via the ATEM. The ATEM requires a headphone jack for plugging in your mic. The Yeti Blue mic, for example, includes a jack for a headphone mic. If you're using an XLR mic, you'll need an audio interface and proper adapters to go from the Main Out port of the interface to the headphone jack port of the ATEM Mini.

YoloLiv YoloBox: This camera switcher retails for approximately $299 to $1,298, depending on the model. The YoloLiv YoloBox Portable Live Steam Studio is a popular model that retails for roughly $798. It includes an HDMI video input, a USB video input, an HDMI video outport, ethernet, audio that connects with a lavalier microphone or mixer, and a USB Type-C power connector. It also has an audio output to connect to a headset, a SIM card slot to connect to the internet, and an SD card slot to use as a video source for recording. The YoloBox has a power button that the ATEM Mini does not.

4. **Stream Deck:** Stream Deck gives you one-click control over a variety of common tasks, including launching a website, starting up an application, and much more. Consider placing the Stream Deck close to your mouse and keyboard so that pressing buttons doesn't create an on-camera distraction. For seamless camera switching via Stream Deck, consider their new Stream Deck foot pedal.

   Stream Deck's buttons are lit from the back and contain custom graphics so your buttons can be customized; one glance and you'll recognize the button and what you have programmed it to do.

   Stream Deck supports built-in and third-party plug-ins that make it easier to use and customize. For example, you can program a button to play sound effects. (See tip 28 for more information about using sound effects in class.)

   Here are some of the things you can control with Stream Deck:

   - Play sound effects.
   - Open software.
   - Open a website.
   - Mute and unmute a microphone.
   - Control Zoom settings.
   - Control any software with hotkeys.
   - Control the scenes in your Open Broadcaster software.
   - Control which camera you want to stream.
   - Generate text (add a common chat message like the ones in tips 13, 16, and 24).
   - Play multimedia.
   - Move and resize windows.

- Run a speed test to check internet speed.

Combine your stream deck with software called Companion to automate multiple steps into one button. See "Optional Software" next to learn more about Companion.

Figure 46: Stream Deck by Elgato.

Optional software

Cursor highlighters: Cursor highlighters allow your students to follow your mouse more easily. This can be done with a setting in your operating system or with separate software.

To highlight your mouse in Windows 10:

1. In the Windows Start menu, type "mouse settings." This will open the windows shown below.

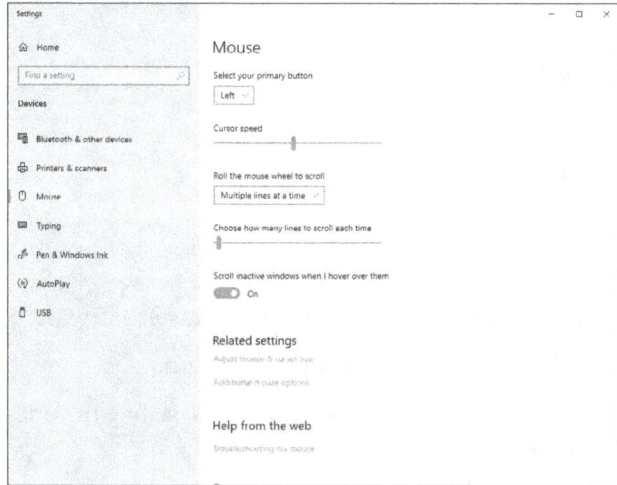

Figure 47: Windows 10 mouse settings.

2. Click Additional Mouse Options (circled in red above).

3. Cllick the Pointer Options tab and look for the visibility section.

4. Check the box "Show location of pointer when I press the CTRL key.

5. Press the CTRL key to confirm it works as you expect.

One mouse for multiple screens and computers: If you use more than one computer and more than one monitor for each computer, it can be challenging to move between screens. To help alleviate some of the frustration of using two or more machines, I use software to move my mouse seamlessly between them. It's called Mouse without Borders (https://tinyurl.com/2p9a9w2e). All machines will need to be on the same network.

Equipment control software:

The more software and hardware you have, the more you will have to integrate. While integrating your system can be time-consuming, it will result in an efficient and effective classroom. **Warning**: If you were to purchase all the software and hardware mentioned in this tip, you would have a lot of equipment to maintain. The drawback of using this much equipment is there is more to breakdown; more software and hardware issues, more setup and maintenance, and you have to make sure everything is compatible

Companion software: When combined with Stream Deck, Companion allows you to control all kinds of software and hardware by simply pressing buttons on Stream Deck. Companion is open source and free, and you can download it from https://bitfocus.io/companion. It works on Macs, Windows, Linux, and even the Raspberry Pi.

Once downloaded, you can begin to connect devices that you'd like Companion to control. There's a button configuration tool where you can configure the buttons on your Stream Deck to Companion, as well as a configuration tool to connect Stream Deck to Companion. Once your Stream Deck is connected, you can start programming buttons. For example, using Companion, you can set a button on your Stream Deck to display a particular camera on your camera switcher. I can click a button that automatically switches my desktop computer screen to my DSLR camera, and now I'm ready to lecture. I can press another button that activates the screen with my coding software plus a small image of me as I lecture. Another button places my face in the lower-right corner of the screen while my slide deck occupies the remaining space. Companion software comes with some preset buttons that make the process easier.

Companion buttons can do much more than activate your camera switcher. They can also execute multiple tasks like switching cameras, zooming in or out, and setting backgrounds. Without having to remember anything, you can stack tasks and add pauses in the right order and at the right time. Think of Companion as akin to a macro runner if you need to open software, load a file, and more.

You don't need Stream Deck to use Companion. The software includes simulation software that you run on a tablet and that will serve as your stream deck.

Note: Sticky buttons are one troubling aspect of Stream Deck. Sometimes I click a button and nothing happens. Several attempts later, it works, and I'm not the only one reporting this issue.

Zoom automation tool: ZoomOSC gives you more control over Zoom. This software acts as middleware between your Zoom client and your Zoom meeting. It exposes Zoom meeting features, which it can then interact with on your behalf. ZoomOSC uses the Open Sound Control software to receive its commands allowing you to control the Zoom client. Think of it as intercepting instructions sent to the Zoom meeting so they can be enhanced and controlled by you.

Basically, "ZoomOSC allows you to send commands from one application to another (Zoom). Think of it like a telephone line. You send a command with one piece of software, and ZoomOSC relays that command to Zoom. ZoomOSC is the middleman." [75]

You have to acquaint yourself with the ZoomOSC command syntax to write your own commands for Zoom. (Learn more about these commands at https://tinyurl.com/28r9jb7b.) These commands can do all kinds of things like control the gallery view, pin participants, target a specific group of users for a macro command, control video and mic settings, allow hand raising, and much more. One of my favorite features to use is pushing out a single chat message to multiple attendees. I use this feature when implementing tips 13, 16, and 24.

---

75   https://www.liminalet.com/zoomosc

Have an ace in the hole.

Background

In the game of stud poker, each player is dealt one card facedown, known as the hole card; the rest of the cards are dealt faceup. Even the savviest of poker players can only hope the hole card is an ace, which gives the player a hidden advantage. In the 1800s, a cowboy with a gun concealed in a shoulder holster had an "ace in the hole." Today, we use the phrase to describe a hidden advantage we can pull out as needed. While having an ace in the hole in stud poker is beyond our control, we can and should have an arsenal of aces in the hole for training.

How to do it

When do we need an "ace in the hole? How about when we lose our audience, going off on a tangent with no learners along for the ride. Perhaps you see the fatigue on their faces. What's your ace in the hole—the usual "time for a break?"

Humor works wonders here. Times like these might be ideal for switching gears and using one of those ice breakers I warned against in tip 25 or one of the reset techniques introduced in tip 28.

Challenges

What are some of your aces in the hole?

How do you remember them?

Keep your ear to the ground.

Background

Technology is constantly changing. You must remain well informed about whatever you teach, but you must also be on the watch for new trends and information. You want your learners to get the most up-to-date information, but it's challenging to stay current in such an ever-changing environment.

Whatever the industry, the technology always delivers a new invention, technique, tool, or methodology. What was golden yesterday has been disproven today. Many JavaScript programmers know the idiom 'today's pattern is tomorrow's anti-pattern,' which means what was once a best practice is now frowned upon.

How to do it

Don't be caught off guard. A day before class, look up new theories and the latest critiques against what you are about to teach. Specifically, look for emerging techniques and best practices. Be sure to take notes and add them to your checklist. Remember this new information will not be on your course outline.

Challenges

How do you keep up with the latest developments in your area of expertise?

How do you anticipate your learner's most up-to-date type questions?

Discern when to facilitate and when to teach.

Background

To teach is to cause to know something, impart knowledge or give instruction. We teach when we lecture or demonstrate through various techniques. Sometimes our approach is heuristic, sometimes in a content-focused method, and sometimes we're more interactive. Nevertheless, we are teaching. Ironically, there are times we should be aware of the importance of not teaching. Perhaps more than occasionally, we should merely facilitate.

How to do it

To facilitate is to make it easier, to assist a person's progress. A facilitator is responsible for leading or coordinating the work of a group, which is not the same as teaching. Remember those desirable difficulties that help the learner? To facilitate, you must be reluctant to provide answers. Lead your learners down the path to discovery. Be quiet while the learner and her coworkers find the best approach. Don't be in a rush to correct them.

Challenges

In the last class you taught, give an example of when you faciliated rather than taught?

Always go one better.

Background

The phrase "go one better' originated with gamblers who offer a higher bet than their opponent. In going one better, the stakes for trainers are not merely a satisfied customer but an ecstatic one.

There are a lot of mediocre trainers out there, and I mean a lot! How do I know? My learners tell me both in person and during their end-of-course evaluations. As a result, many workers arrive in class on day one ready to be bored or disappointed. If you really want to knock them out—exceed their expectations. It's amazing how different your class will be if, on day one, just before your students arrive you say to yourself, "I'm going to wow them today!" This may seem trite but it is important to practice especially for those successful trainers who teach back to back sessions and often succumb to burnout.

How to do it

If a student wants to know the difference between product A and B? After class, write them a quick white paper and deliver it first thing in the morning. Are they peppering you with questions? Give them a frequently asked questions (FAQ) document on the last day with their questions followed by complete answers, including resources.

Do they want to know how to apply what they've learned to their current project? Open up the project together, look at it, and have them explain the inner workings.

Whatever they need, find new and creative ways to go one better!

Challenges

How do you go one better?

85 Know what not to say.

Background

We've all done it at one point in our training career: we said the wrong thing. Sometimes a beginning instructor doesn't know it's a bad thing to say, and they learn the hard way. As you gain experience, you recognize when you've said something wrong. The key is to start a "what never to say" list. Here are a few to get you started.

How to do it

1. Never say, "this is easy."

   Picture this: we are about to start an exercise after a bit of introductory lecture. "OK, everyone, you'll love this; it's super easy," I said. We got started, and I repeated how easy it was. Lots of head nods; everyone agrees. Except, not everyone agreed; specifically, not the student in the first seat of the first row. Every time I said, "See? Isn't it easy," I could hear him…ouch—right in the ego. It was *not* easy for him, and now he was embarrassed, and it was my fault.

2. Never say "this goes without saying" for obvious reasons.

3. Keep a careful watch on the use of acronyms. Students are often hesitant to ask you, "what does ABC mean"?

Challenges

What's on your "never say" list?

Consider using picture-in-picture.

Background

Remember when big screen TV's came out and you could watch your favorite show while a smaller screen showed a different channel with the ball game on? The feature was called picture-in-picture and we can use it while training. Picture in picture superimposes a second source over your broadcast video source in a small box you can position and customize. It's use as a teaching tool has mixed reviews. Some trainers believe it distracts the student and at times, I agree. For example, when the students are working on a lab exercise, they don't need to see me, but it may be helpful to see my webcam when I'm going through my slide deck or lecturing on an important topic. This additional content (my video) might help make the lesson more impactful and memorable. In addition, I feel that if learners have their webcams on it only seems fair that I should have my camera on as well.

How to do it

Depending on the hardware and software you use, there are several ways to implement picture-in-picture. In this tip, you will learn how to use picture-in-picture using OBS, Atem Mini Pro, and mmhmm software while showing a slide deck.

Picture-in-picture with OBS.

1. Launch your slide deck.

2. Launch OBS.

3. Click the + button from the scenes tab in the lower left corner of the interface, then create a new scene.

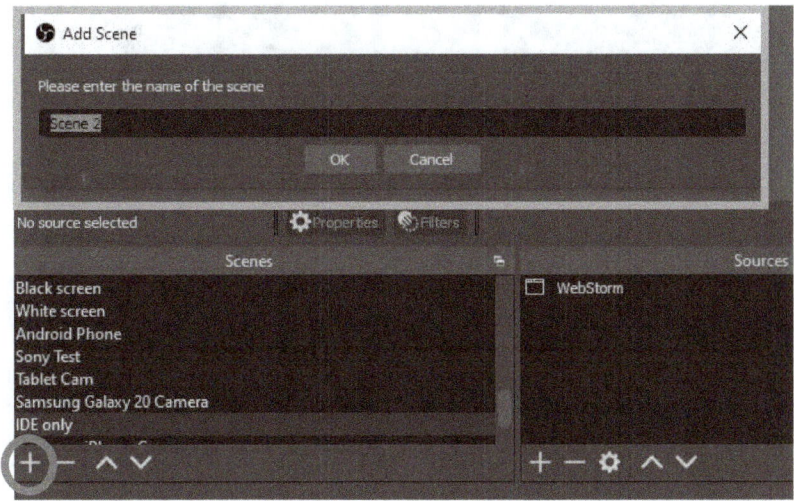

Figure 48: The Scenes tab with the "Add scene" + button circled in red. Above is the Add Scene
dialog box shown with a blue rectangle.

4. Name the scene anything you want. I chose picture-in-picture.
    Click OK.

5. From the Sources tab, add a new source by clicking the + button.

6. Choose Video Capture Device and select your camera.

7. Move your camera wherever you want the smaller picture-in-picture
    to appear.

8. From the Sources tab, add a second source by clicking the + button.

9. Choose Window Capture and click the Create New radio button.

10. Click OK and navigate to the Window that is displaying your slide
    deck.

11. Be sure that your camera appears above the PPT window in the
    Sources tab as shown in Figure 49.

Figure 49: The sources tab showing the webcam source (Sony Test Cam) on top of the slide deck source (PPT).

12. Start a meeting and choose OBS as your camera and select the picture-in-picture scene.

13. Start your virtual camera with the button shown in Figure 50.

Figure 50: The OBS Controls. The virtual camera has been started from here and is showing the lable "Stop Virtual Camera."

14. In your conferencing software, choose OBS Virtual Camera as your webcam.

15. If you have a green screen, you should make a chroma key in OBS.

16. Click Filters as shown in Figure 51.

Figure 51: The filters tab.

17. Choose Chroma Key and adjust the settings until you see only yourself on the webcam.

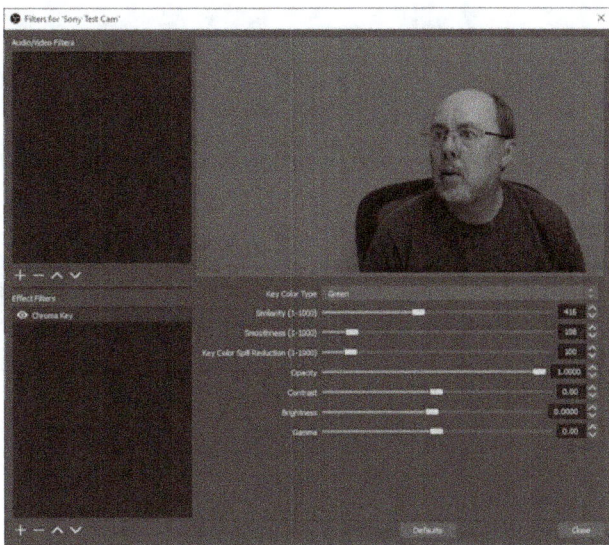

Figure 52: Filter settings for the Chroma key filter. The goal is to adjust the settings to remove the background, leaving only yourself visible without any artifacts.

18. Return to your meeting and confirm you have picture in picture working.

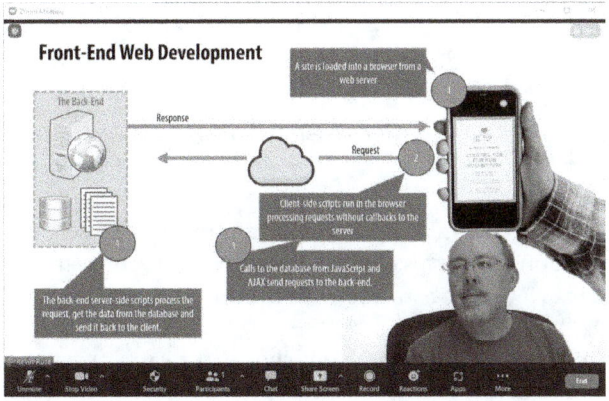

Figure 53: A Zoom meeting with picture-in-picture.

Picture in Picture mmhmm

Getting Started

1. Go to https://mmhmm.en.softonic.com/ and click the "Free Download" button.

2. Follow the instructions to install mmhmm on your computer.

3. Launch mmhmm.

4. Backgrounds in mmhmm are called Rooms. Select a room from the menu as shown below. You can also add your own graphic to use as a background.

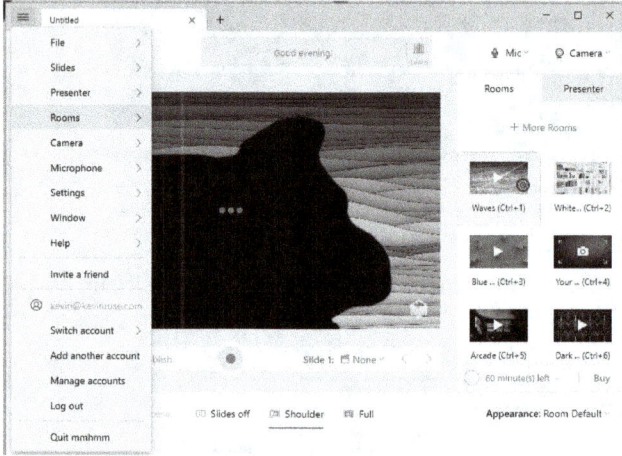

Figure 54: The Rooms option accessed via the hamburger menu.

5. You can add slide decks and other content in mmhmm as well. For more information visit https://help.mmhmm.app/hc/en-us/articles/360050985073-Getting-started-with-mmhmm.

6. From the Camera menu shown below, choose the camera you would like mmhmm to use.

Figure 55: The Camera picker where you choose your webcam.

7. Connect to your conferencing software (Zoom, etc.)

Start a meeting

1. Choose mmhmm as your camera and confirm that you can see yourself in the zoom meeting.

Set up Picture in Picture

1. Click New Slide ❧ Import presentation to import an existing slide deck (e.g. PowerPoint, Keynote, PDF)

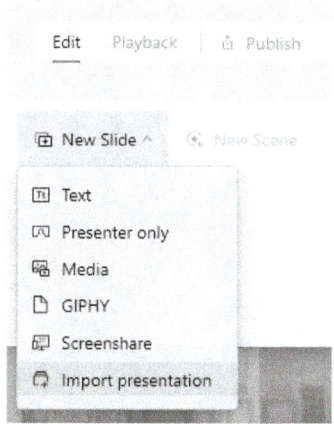

2. If you don't have a presentation to import, you can choose a content type (text, videos, images, GIPHY, screen share on your device, or a

second camera) and add.

- Click Shoulder to see your slides appear on screen over your shoulder.

- Click Full and the slide will take up the entire background while your camera is actively showing you.

5. Note: I've played with the green screen and room settings but found some difficulty getting a crisp image. I expect steady improvement as I refine the settings.

Picture-in-picture with Atem Mini Pro

The HDMI input 1 is the default picture in picture source, so if you'rebroadcasting your screen and want to superimpose your webcam, plug your camera into input 1 and it will appear in picture in picture.

Enable picture-in-picture

1. Make sure your video to be inside the small picture in picture box is plugged into HDMI input 1.

2. Plug your main video into HDMI input 2, 3, or 4.

3. In the picture in picture buttons on control panel, press 'on'.

4. You will now see the picture in picture box appear on the screen. To select a different position, press any of the position buttons.

Figure 56: Top right of the ATEM Mini Pro showing the Picture In Picture buttons.

87 **End class early.**

Background

Some students could stay in class forever. You know the ones; they arrive early, stay late, and we love them. But even those hardcore students can get fatigued by day five. Training can be challenging and staying focused throughout the class is even more challenging.

Technical careers are often isolating. When an opportunity to participate in a class comes along, our learners find themselves thrust into an environment with a large group and feel they have to always be "on." It can be fatiguing to remain always ready to answer questions, take quizzes, participate in discussions, and so on.

Many of my classes last from the moment the students arrive to work to the moment they leave: 9 a.m. to 5 p.m., for example. Before they begin work for the day, many employees need to check email, tend to office protocols, button up their office equipment, check in with managers or colleagues, and so on. They look forward to ending class early so that they can attend to pressing work matters and get back home on time. Essentially, the idea of ending class before its official ending time is another way to show respect for your learners' time.

When participating as an adult student, I was always comforted by the instructor who ended class by announcing she'd stay as long as necessary to assist in any way possible. It says so much about the instructor's enthusiasm and genuine desire to help students perform better at work. At some point in our lives, most of us can relate to this experience. Back in high school, geometry was complicated for me, but as long as I showed a willingness to make an effort, my geometry teacher would stay after class and help me. Whenever I walked past him in the hallways, he'd always stop and find a way to challenge and praise me simultaneously.

This is a skill worth mastering. You never know how much impact a simple gesture will make. In adult learning, it could be a factor in a pay raise, a layoff avoided, or a promotion. I'm not suggesting all of that happens because we stayed an extra fifteen minutes after class, but I'm suggesting that it motivated a learner to continue on the path to success.

How to do it

I've found that by announcing on day one that I'll end class approximately fifteen minutes early, students feel less distracted at the end of the day. They know they'll have time to take care of any work issues that arise during class, and they're less likely to "check out" early.

So no one feels cheated out of valuable training time, I let them know that I'll remain in the classroom until the class's official end time and longer if needed. It can be tempting to wait in the virtual classroom until no one engages and then sign off. The safest approach is to wait until there are no longer any participants online before you end the session. Some students want to speak privately and wait until all others have left the classroom before engaging with you.

If there are only one or two participants, be sure to check in with them before signing off. Equally important is to avoid, at all costs, ending late. There's a significant difference between offering to stay late to cover additional material and requiring everyone to stay late to ensure you meet the course objectives.

Challenges

- What time do you end class?

- What is an appropriate time to end? Is it five minutes, fifteen minutes, or longer before the official ending?

- Do you communicate your early dismissal plan with the relevant stakeholders?

Summary

The following summarizes the principles of neuroscience that drive the majority of the tips in this book.

Learning is not deeply understood by learners or trainers

Learners are poor judges of when they are and aren't learning. They're equally poor judges of how long they may retain what they've learned.

Learners sometimes believe if they reread material, they'll better retain it. This isn't true; the best method for retaining knowledge is retrieval practice—that is, recalling what has been learned from memory. Flash cards are much better for this than rereading workbooks.

Learners believe that if they ignore newly learned material for a few days, it will be lost. In fact, periodic practice, even separated by a few days, helps learners retain knowledge. Spacing out retrieval practice on a regular basis is the most effective way to retain new information. The delay before practiced retrieval is essential. A little forgetting between practice sessions is a good thing, because recollection becomes more effortful; think desirable difficulty.

Trainers believe that they should introduce a solution before asking learners to solve a problem. Even if your learners first attempt is incorrect, it's still better for trainers to ask learners to solve a problem before they teach about it. Learners believe tests are used by trainers to test their knowledge and memory when, in fact, tests are used to help learners understand, store, and retain knowledge.

Trainers believe they should always supply solutions for their learners. Studies show the more effort made by the learner to retrieve information, the stronger the learning connection will be.

Reflection is one of the most effective forms of cognition. Trainers should encourage reflection through critical-thinking types of questions.

Training principles

Start complex topics at a high level and work your way to the details slowly. Basic elements come first, and those are used to introduce conceptual knowledge.

Use flash cards in your slide deck to quiz learners.

Interleave two or more subjects as your class progresses. Demonstrate a problem and multiple solutions. Ask your learners to discern the best solution. The multiple solutions you provide allow for interleaving related concepts.

Don't solve every problem you introduce. Allow learners to move between topics, problems, and solutions.

Use learners' prior knowledge when introducing new topics and help them make the connection between past experiences and what they're currently learning.

Allow learners time to forget what they've learned before you initiate some of your retrieval practice sessions.

Make learning a little difficult. If it's too easy, it doesn't stick.

Help your learners generate answers independently.

Add repetition to your lessons.

Further Reading

How to Be a Successful Technical Trainer
Terrance Keys and Andrew R. Zeff, McGraw Hill
https://www.amazon.com/How-Successful-Technical-Trainer-Certification/
dp/0072130334

The Art of Learning
Josh Waitzkin, Free Press, A Division of Simon & Schuster
https://www.amazon.com/Art-Learning-Journey-Optimal-Performance/
dp/0743277465/

Training from the Back of the Room!
Sharon L. Bowman, John Wiley & Sons, Inc. Published by Pfeiffer, An Imprint of Wiley
https://www.amazon.com/Training-Back-Room-Sharon-Bowman/dp/0787996629/

Learning to Listen, Learning to Teach
Jane Vella, John Wiley & Sons, Inc. Published by Jossey-Bass,
A Wiley Company.
https://www.amazon.com/Learning-Listen-Teach-Dialogue-Educating/
dp/0787959677/

A Mind for Numbers
Barbara Oakley, Ph.D., Jeremy P. Tarcher/Penguin, Published by the Penguin Group
https://www.amazon.com/Mind-Numbers-Science-Flunked-Algebra/
dp/039916524X/

Confessions of a Public Speaker
Scott Berkun, O'Reilly, Published by O'Reilly Media, Inc.
https://www.amazon.com/Confessions-Public-Speaker-Scott-Berkun/
dp/1449301959/.

Virtual Training
Jeb Blount, Published by John Wiley & Sons, Inc.
https://www.amazon.com/Virtual-Training-Bible-Conducting-Knowledge/
dp/1119755832/.

Training for Dummies
Elaine Biech, Wiley Publishing, Inc.
https://www.amazon.com/Training-Dummies-Elaine-Biech/dp/0764559850/.

make it stick
Peter C. Brown, Henry L. Roediger III, Mark A. McDaniel, The Belknap Press of Harvard University Press.
https://www.amazon.com/Make-Stick-Science-Successful-Learning/dp/0674729013/.

Talk Like Ted
Carmine Gallo, St. Martins Griffin.
https://www.amazon.com/Talk-Like-TED-Public-Speaking-Secrets/dp/1250061539/.

Presentation Zen: Simple Ideas on Presentation Design and Delivery
Garr Reynolds, New Riders.
https://www.amazon.com/Presentation-Zen-Simple-Design-Delivery/dp/0135800919/.

The Naked Presenter
Garr Reynolds, New Riders
https://www.amazon.com/Naked-Presenter-Delivering-Powerful-Presentations/dp/0321704452/.

Presenting Secrets.
Martin Manser, Collins, A division of HarperCollinsPublishers.
https://www.kobo.com/us/en/ebook/presenting-collins-business-secrets

Presentations.
Daria Price Bowman, F+W Publications, Published by Adams Media, an F+W Publications Company. https://www.amazon.com/Presentations-Techniques-Creating-Critical-Business/dp/B001QCX7GA/

How to Communicate.
Martha Davis, Patrick Fanning, Matthew McKay, MJF Books, Published by New Harbinger Publications. Inc. https://www.amazon.com/How-Communicate-Improving-Professional-Relationships/dp/1567310311/

Handbook of College Teaching.
W.R. Miller, editor; D. and Marie F. Miller, Ph.D., PineCrest Publications.

https://www.amazon.com/Handbook-College-Teaching-Marie-Miller/dp/0962888710

Creative Training Techniques Handbook.
Robert W. Pike, CSP, CPAE Speaker Hall of Fame®, HRD Press, Inc.
https://www.amazon.com/Handbook-College-Teaching-Marie-Miller/dp/0962888710/dp/0962888710

Index